Coloring in the White Spaces

Studies in Criticality

Shirley R. Steinberg
General Editor

Vol. 513

The Counterpoints series is part of the Peter Lang Education list.
Every volume is peer reviewed and meets
the highest quality standards for content and production.

PETER LANG
New York • Bern • Frankfurt • Berlin
Brussels • Vienna • Oxford • Warsaw

Ann Milne

Coloring in the White Spaces

Reclaiming Cultural Identity in Whitestream Schools

PETER LANG
New York • Bern • Frankfurt • Berlin
Brussels • Vienna • Oxford • Warsaw

Library of Congress Cataloging-in-Publication Data
Names: Milne, Ann (Educator)
Title: Coloring in the white spaces: reclaiming cultural identity
in whitestream schools / Ann Milne.
Description: New York: Peter Lang, 2016.
Series: Counterpoints: Studies in the postmodern theory
of education; vol. 513 | ISSN 1058-1634
Includes bibliographical references and index.
Identifiers: LCCN 2016032919 | ISBN 978-1-4331-3484-5 (hardcover: alk. paper)
ISBN 978-1-4331-3483-8 (paperback: alk. paper) | ISBN 978-1-4331-3739-6 (ebook pdf)
ISBN 978-1-4331-3740-2 (epub) | ISBN 978-1-4331-3741-9 (mobi)
Subjects: LCSH: Critical pedagogy—New Zealand.
Māori (New Zealand people)—Education.
Classification: LCC LC196.5.N45 M55 2017 | DDC 370.11/50993—dc23
DOI 10.3726/b10459
LC record available at https://lccn.loc.gov/2016032919

Bibliographic information published by **Die Deutsche Nationalbibliothek**.
Die Deutsche Nationalbibliothek lists this publication in the "Deutsche
Nationalbibliografie"; detailed bibliographic data are available
on the Internet at http://dnb.d-nb.de/.

Cover art: "Tupuranga" (future generations). Original Artwork by the author's granddaughter,
Kairangi Ihimaera. The red, white, and black, partly-colored pattern is taken from the design of
Kia Aroha College's Māori Performing Arts costumes. It represents the need to "color in"
Māori and indigenous spaces in our education systems.

The paper in this book meets the guidelines for permanence and durability
of the Committee on Production Guidelines for Book Longevity
of the Council of Library Resources.

© 2017 Peter Lang Publishing, Inc., New York
29 Broadway, 18th floor, New York, NY 10006
www.peterlang.com

All rights reserved.
Reprint or reproduction, even partially, in all forms such as microfilm,
xerography, microfiche, microcard, and offset strictly prohibited.

Printed in the United States of America

Cover Art: *Tupuranga* (future generations)
By the author's granddaughter, Kairangi Ihimaera
The red, white and black, partly colored pattern is taken from the design of Kia Aroha College's Māori Performing Arts costumes. It represents the need to "color in" Māori and indigenous spaces in our education systems.

For the Warrior-Scholars:
My Grandchildren and Great Grandchildren
and
The young people of
Kia Aroha College

CONTENTS

List of Figures — xi
List of Tables — xiii
Papahueke — xv
Foreword — xvii
Acknowledgements — xxi

Part One: Identifying White Spaces

Chapter 1. The Whitestream — 3
  Introduction — 3
  The Girl at the Principal's Door — 7
  Schooling in New Zealand — 8
  School Reform in White Spaces — 10
  Māori Spaces in the Whitestream—"as Māori" — 14
  Pasifika Spaces in the Whitestream—"as Tongan," "as Samoan" — 17
  "Academic" Achievement — 18
  Overview of Book Chapters — 19
  Notes — 22
  References — 23

Chapter 2.	Naming the White Spaces	27
	Whiteness	28
	Privilege and Supremacy	30
	The Curriculum as a White Space: The Politics of Knowledge	31
	Note	42
	References	42
Chapter 3.	Cultural Identity	47
	Cultural Identity	48
	Essentialist Frameworks	49
	Postmodern Frameworks	51
	Critical Frameworks in Education	54
	Indigenous Perspectives	56
	Shape-Shifting: Identity Changing, Identity as Resistance	59
	Identity Lost: Social Toxins	61
	Schools and Cultural Identity	63
	References	64

Part Two: Coloring in the White Spaces

Chapter 4.	Kia Aroha College	71
	Born Out of Struggle	72
	The Schools	72
	Winning the War	76
	Through Aroha	78
	Note	79
	References	79
Chapter 5.	Changing the Lens	81
	Truth-Telling: Auditing Schools' White Spaces	82
	Designing a School	83
	Changing the Lens	87
	The Power Lenses Learning Model	89
	References	93
Chapter 6.	Coloring in the School-Learning Space	95
	The School-Learning Lens	95
	The Concept of Whānau	98
	A Critical Pedagogy of Whānau: Whanaungatanga in Practice	101

School Spaces as Whānau Spaces	102
Authentic Critical Caring	104
Students' Experience of Whanaungatanga	106
Student-Driven Learning	108
Notes	124
References	124
Chapter 7. Coloring in the Self-Learning Space	129
The Self-Learning Lens	129
What Is Success?	130
Assessment as a White Space	131
How Do We Know?	133
Cultural Standards	134
Using the Indicators	144
Key Competencies	146
Self-Learning Lens: Progress Over Time	147
Putting Self and School Lenses Together	148
The Purpose of the Self-Lens	152
Learning in the Self-Lens	153
The Place of Kapa Haka/Performing Arts in Self-Lens Learning	153
Determining Success: Whose Knowledge Is of Most Worth?	157
Notes	158
References	159
Chapter 8. Coloring in the Wider Learning Spaces	161
The Global-Learning Lens	161
Solidarity in the White Space	162
Challenged Spaces	167
Youth Spaces	172
Note	174
References	174
Chapter 9. Powerful Spaces	177
Self-Determining Spaces	178
Te Ara Tino Rangatiratanga: The Pathway to Self-Determination	179
Identity Found: Colored Spaces	185
Breaking Free	188
Warrior-Scholars	197

Graduate Profile: Redefining Success and Achievement	198
What Did We Learn?	202
Notes	205
References	205
Glossary	209
About the Author	215
Index	217

LIST OF FIGURES

Figure 5.1:	The Power Lenses Learning Model	90
Figure 7.1:	Suggested Self-Learning Lens Diagram	145
Figure 7.2:	One Student's Self-Lens Assessment over Six Years 2010–2015	148
Figure 7.3:	Self and School Lens Results: One Māori Student, 2007–2009	149
Figure 7.4:	Self and School Lens Results: One Cook Islands Māori Student, 2012–2015	150

LIST OF TABLES

Table 7.1:	Alaska Cultural Standards Indicators	135
Table 7.2:	Māori Identity Indicators	137
Table 7.3:	Samoan Identity Indicators	138
Table 7.4:	Tongan Identity Indicators	138
Table 7.5:	Cook Islands Māori Indicators	139
Table 7.6:	Generic Identity Indicators	140
Table 7.7:	Relationship with Learning Indicators	141
Table 7.8:	Peer Relationship Indicators	142
Table 7.9:	General Cultural Identity Indicators	144
Table 7.10:	Alignment of Self-learning Lens Indicators with New Zealand Curriculum Key Competencies	146
Table 9.1:	Kia Aroha College TEN Priority Surveys Results, 2015	196
Table 9.2:	Graduate Profiles for Māori Learners	199

Source: Te Rito, Blaine. (2013). *Papahueke*. Original Artwork. Reprinted with permission of the artist.

PAPAHUEKE

The design was initially inspired by the black and white image of a classroom scene in which the faces of two pupils were colored in brown shade. It reminds me of how over time we as tangata whenua (indigenous people) have had to fit in and conform to the structure and values of foreign interests. This design reflects the cultural diversity of the students within Kia Aroha College. I focused on artistic symbols from throughout Aotearoa (New Zealand) and the Pacific region from which many of the students descend. These symbols also refer to their proud and noble ancestors through whose authority we were successful in developing thriving and effective societies throughout these regions—until the arrogant establishment of foreign interests within these borders, which is still perpetuated today. This situation is not unique to Aotearoa.

    The circle represents the importance of these pre-colonial societal structures viz.; education, language, culture, theology, and environmental resources. The break in the circle represents the disruption and the white spaces incurred, and the difficulty of re-completing the circle with pieces or structures that just don't fit. The name, Papahueke (to be relentless or unyielding), represents our resistance. (Blaine Te Rito, 2013)

FOREWORD

Jeff Duncan-Andrade, PhD

Associate Professor
Raza Studies & Education
San Francisco State University
Founder and Board Chair, Roses in Concrete Community School

I first met Ann Milne in 2006 at the annual meeting of the American Educational Research Association (AERA). She had come with staff and community advisors from Kia Aroha College (then known as Te Whanau o Tupuranga) and they attended a session where I presented with some of our staff and students from East Oakland, California (USA). In our conversation after the session, it was immediately clear that we were aligned in our commitment to creating culturally and community responsive educational environments for the children in our communities. However, I had no idea the depth of the impact that Ann and her community would have on me personally and the ways I approach the work.

A little over a year later, myself and two of my closest colleagues flew to Aotearoa New Zealand and spent two weeks at Kia Aroha College. In my 24 years of teaching, no single event has had a more significant impact on my work in education. At the time of my first visit, I had a reputation as a highly skilled classroom teacher and researcher whose work focused heavily on culturally and community responsive curriculum and pedagogy. As part of this work, I had studied the work of incredible teachers and programs across the United States. But, I had never seen a school that was delivering on cultural and community responsivity in the ways that I witnessed at Kia Aroha College. What I saw during my time there convinced me that something fundamentally different was possible in my own community. Since then, I have visited Ann's school every other year, and Ann and her team have visited our school in East Oakland on the alternate years.

Eight years after my first visit to Kia Aroha College, we opened the Roses in Concrete Community School (RiC). We modeled the school cultural practices at RiC, in large part, after those that I experienced at Kia Aroha College. Although our school functions as a lab school and has influenced school planning and practices all over the United States, we have named only one school as an official partner school—Kia Aroha College. We describe this relationship as "ukukura", a Māori word created by Māori language keepers to describe two community schools in solidarity with one another in the struggle for educational autonomy. Our community is very cautious about partnerships, particularly around the education of our most vulnerable children. We do not enter lightly into the decision to publicly name Kia Aroha College as our ukukura. From our cultural frame of reference, this public acknowledgement of our partnership is the highest form of respect for another set of educators.

When I recommend readings for educators that are thinking about how to develop school cultures that are community and culturally responsive, this is the first book I will tell them to read. While I certainly have not been to every school in the United States, I can say that none of the schools I have visited (and that's quite a few) have accomplished what Ann Milne and the staff at Kia Aroha College have achieved. This book provides profound critiques of existing colonial models of education and viable alternatives that value the language and culture of those young people and families that have largely been demonized and pathologized in "white"stream models of schooling. It does not need to be this way. If we are ever to achieve the levels of cultural pluralism necessary to achieve pluralistic, multi-racial democracies we must reconsider the ways in which we school our children. For my money, this book is the primer for schools and systems of education in post-genocidal colonial societies like the United States and New Zealand to finally come to grips with the harm it has been doing to children from outside the dominant culture. Nothing is more important in this next generation than a fundamental rethink about how we educate our children, and no book that I have seen should be more influential than this one in those efforts.

ACKNOWLEDGEMENTS

My grateful acknowledgement to the Board of Trustees of Kia Aroha College for your permission to write this story and for your trust that I would tell it with the deepest respect for our collective journey.

This book would not have been possible without the support of the staff, and Boards of Trustees of the three schools involved in this journey; Clover Park Middle School and Te Whānau o Tupuranga, which merged to become Kia Aroha College in 2011. This story belongs to you and the whānau (families) and community, whose courage over nearly three decades inspired, and continues to drive, the dream that it is possible to make education fit our children, in spite of the opposition we faced at every step. That experience taught me about respect, integrity, responsibility, reciprocity, truth, and real accountability to our future generations.

The story also belongs to the students, past, present, and future, of these three schools, who inspired me every day to be a better learner, a better teacher, a better school leader, a better researcher, and a better advocate against the injustice and inequity that education has delivered for Māori and Pasifika learners. You show us the meaning of critical hope and a strong secure identity as Māori, Samoan, Tongan, Cook Islands Māori—as who you are. That powerful understanding will change our educational landscape for the better, so that education has to work much harder for you than it has done in the past. Thank you for keeping me focused on what really matters.

To my family who have all shared so closely, both personally and professionally, in this journey, there are not enough words to say thank you. My grandchildren and great-grandchildren are the epitome of the dream to reclaim educational sovereignty for our children, and I celebrate the strength of your Māori language and identity. My children and grandchildren are woven into the fabric of all three schools where they have been students, teachers, and staff members themselves. That's what whānau is about.

PART ONE

IDENTIFYING WHITE SPACES

· 1 ·
THE WHITESTREAM

Introduction

It is an honor and a privilege to be standing here today to offer some reflective thoughts and speak on behalf of those who are leaving today for the big wide world.

I came to Kia Aroha College, wearing a red shirt like the teina (junior students) sitting in front of me. I was a little intimidated by the journey ahead of me. I'd like to think that in the seven years I have been a student at Kia Aroha College, I have learnt what it means to be Māori and how to question the dominant discourse. I have learnt that the marginalization of Māori and Pasifika people is more about our dominant society being unwilling to share power and authority than it is about us not deserving better. My challenge to all the younger students at Kia Aroha College is to open your minds to the teachings of the school that will make you understand that you deserve a life that honors your cultural heritage.

To those students who will be returning in 2016, Whāia te iti kahurangi. Ki te tuohu koe, me he maunga teitei.[1] Continue to work hard to meet the goals you, your families, and the school have set for you. Be proud of your cultural knowledge and understand that it has value beyond measure.

My final acknowledgement is to my brothers and sisters who will be leaving with me. As our last days at Kia Aroha College roll toward zero, know that my heart goes out to you all. We have had the honor and privilege of being part of something only a few young people get to experience. And that is to be a senior[2] at Kia Aroha College. Take some time to reflect on what you have given to this school and what this school has given to you.

Ka ruia te kākano kei ngā rangatahi, kia tipu ai ngā hua, whāngaia ki ngā tupuranga.[3]
(Wiremu Waru-Waahi, 2015. Reprinted by permission of the author/speaker)

This excerpt from the valedictory speech of a graduating Māori student of Kia Aroha College in 2015 embodies all the elements of the school's graduate profile and its mission to develop "Warrior-Scholars"—which the school defines as young people, secure in their own identity, competent and confident in all aspects of their cultural world, critical agents for justice, equity and social change, with all the academic qualifications and cultural knowledge they need to go out and change the world.

Kia Aroha College is a "designated-character" Years 7–13 (Grades 6–12) secondary school located in the community of Otara, in South Auckland, New Zealand. The aims of the special character of the school include honoring the Treaty of Waitangi,[4] and providing a learning environment where Māori and Pasifika[5] cultural identities, custom, languages and knowledges, and the philosophy and practice of whānau (extended family), are the norm. Critical, culturally responsive pedagogy is at the heart of the school's approach. The school aims to involve whānau in the education of their children, in culturally familiar ways that are empowering.

Scorza, Mirra, and Morrell (2013) explored the role of critical pedagogy across three domains: critical literacy development, empowered identity development, and the promotion of civic engagement for social change. They observe that while there are some examples of critical pedagogy in practice in classrooms and non-school spaces (Darder, 1991; Duncan-Andrade, & Morrell, 2008; Stovall, 2006), the concept of a pedagogy for critical consciousness has been largely theoretical (p. 15). Sleeter (2012) attributes what she describes as the marginalization of culturally responsive pedagogy to three primary reasons: "(1) a persistence of faulty and simplistic conceptions of what culturally responsive pedagogy is, (2) too little research connecting its use with student achievement, and (3) elite and white fear of losing national and global hegemony" (p. 562). Sleeter discusses the problems associated with trivializing, simplifying, or essentializing culture and states that, "Oversimplified and distorted conceptions of culturally responsive pedagogy, which do not necessarily improve student learning, lend themselves to dismissal of the entire concept" (p. 572). Sleeter believes it is important to find "rich descriptions" as important counters to these simplistic models.

This book provides a detailed and "rich description" of a school where a critical, and culturally responsive pedagogy drives all practice and underpins curriculum and decision-making. This is the 25 year counter-story of a New Zealand school and the determination of its community to resist and reject alienating school environments in favor of a relevant culturally-located, bilingual learning model based in a secure cultural identity, stable positive relationships, and aroha (authentic caring and love). The counter-story chronicles the efforts of the school to step outside education's "White spaces" (Milne, 2013) to create new space, to reclaim educational sovereignty and the absolute right to "be Māori" or "be Pasifika" in school. This journey is juxtaposed against pervasive, deficit-driven whitestream explanations of "achievement gaps" and the offensively labeled "long tail of underachievement" (Snook, O'Neill, Birks, Church, & Rawlins, 2013) of indigenous Māori and Pasifika learners in New Zealand schools.

New Zealand's education system has been largely silent on the topic of Whiteness, White privilege and supremacy, and the Eurocentric nature of our schooling policy and practice. However, when I talk to senior Māori warrior-scholars in Kia Aroha College about the White spaces (Milne, 2013, 2014, 2016) they have encountered in their schooling experience they can identify them all too easily. White spaces, they explain, are anything you accept as normal for Māori—when it's really not, any situation that prevents, or works against you "being Māori" and that requires you to be someone else and leave your beliefs behind. White spaces are spaces that allow you to require less of yourself and that reinforce stereotypes and negative ideas about Māori. Most telling of all was the comment from a Māori student that goes straight to the root of the problem, "White spaces are everywhere," she said, "even in your head."

Those White spaces are certainly in our heads. If we are serious about change, and the achievement of our indigenous and the learners we marginalize and minoritize, we have to name the elephant in the classroom that drives our education policy, our school and classroom practice, at all age levels. In Kia Aroha College our thinking about the pervasive whitestream environment our students learn in, is underpinned by this very simple premise. If we look at a child's coloring book, before it has any color added to it, we think of the page as blank. It's actually not blank, it's white. That white background is just *there* and we don't think much about it. Not only is the background uniformly white, the lines are already in place and they dictate where the color is allowed to go. When children are young, they don't care where they put the colors, but as they get older we teach them to color in more and more carefully. They learn about the place of color and the importance of staying within those pre-determined boundaries and expectations.

This is the setting for our Whitestream schools—that white background, and its unspoken privilege, is the norm. When we talk about multiculturalism and diversity what we are really referring to is the color of the children, or their difference from that white norm. It's about how they don't fit perfectly inside our lines. If the color of the space doesn't change schools are still in the business of assimilation, relegating indigenous and minoritized[6] children to the margins, no matter how many school reform initiatives, new curricula, or mandated tests and standards we implement. What the school in this story has done is change the color of the space, so that the space fits the children and they don't have to constantly adjust to fit in (Milne, 2014, 2016). Tomlins-Jahnke (2008) describes "mainstream" schools in New Zealand:

> Most Māori children in Aotearoa New Zealand are located in state mainstream schools where for many there is a disjuncture between the culture of the home and that of the school, between the lived realities of family and the school habitus. The term mainstream is a euphemism or code word for schools that privilege a western/Euro-centric education tradition. Mainstream schools in Aotearoa/New Zealand are controlled by those who have political, economic and cultural power and where western values, knowledge, culture and the English language are the central focus of the school habitus. Schools incorporate aspects of Māori language and culture as additions rather than core components of the curriculum or school knowledge. (p. 6)

Denis (1997) defines "whitestream" as the idea that while American society is not "White" in sociodemographic terms it remains principally and fundamentally structured on the basis of the Anglo-European, "White" experience (p. 178). Grande (2000) points out that "mainstream" implies "White." She uses the term whitestream as opposed to mainstream to "decenter whiteness" (p. 469). Urrieta (2010) defines "whitestream schools" as all schools, "from kindergarten through graduate school and to the official and unofficial texts used in U.S. schools that are founded on the practices, principles, morals, and values of White supremacy and that highlight the history of White Anglo-American culture." He believes however, that the normalcy of whiteness and White supremacy in "mainstream" schools is not exclusively the work of Whites and that, "Any person, including people of color, actively promoting or upholding White models as the goal or standard is also involved in whitestreaming" (p. 181).

I find the term "mainstream" in New Zealand schools to be a euphemism for an education system which normalizes practice that damages Māori and Pasifika learners and has "consistently treated [Māori learners] paternalistically, watching them to see whether they were capable of being as good as Pākehā"[7] (Penetito, 2010, p. 51). Penetito puts the concept into its rightful perspective when he lists "mainstreaming" amongst deliberate policies designed to establish the education system's hegemony over Māori: "Europeanisation, civilization, amalgamation, assimilation, integration and, today, mainstreaming" (p. 245).

In direct contrast to "whitestreaming," eminent Māori psychiatrist and academic, Sir Mason Durie (2001, 2003) proposes a framework for considering Māori educational advancement and "Māori-centered" education. He identifies three broad goals for Māori in our education system: to live as Māori, to participate as citizens of the world, and to enjoy good health and a high standard of living.

The Girl at the Principal's Door

A few years ago I was waiting in my office with a group of visitors for word from the Samoan bilingual unit that they were ready for the visitors to attend an "ava" (Samoan welcome) ceremony. I was seated with my back to my open office door and, as we chatted, I noticed the visitors' attention drawn to something behind me. I turned to find a Samoan girl seated on the floor in the doorway. When I acknowledged her she quietly said, "Lumana'i[8] are ready for you, Miss." She then shuffled, still seated, out of our sight. One of the visitors commented that we should have noticed her earlier as she must have felt too shy to knock and interrupt us.

When I related this story to our Samoan staff later they were delighted. No one had told the student to do this. She simply had been sent to let the visitors know it was time to come. Mageo (1989) explains that because relative physical elevation is a Polynesian metaphor for relative social elevation, Samoan children are not allowed to address seated elders while standing, but must sit down themselves so that their head is beneath that of their perceived superior (p. 420). The decision to follow this appropriate Samoan cultural norm was the student's alone. To Samoan staff this was an achievement worthy of the highest recognition and a clear indicator that the student was well versed in fa'asamoa.[9]

I have told this story many times since. It raises questions that are fundamental to critical, culturally responsive classroom pedagogy and practice:

1. Can a school create the conditions that empower a student to follow their cultural norms throughout the school day?
2. Why is this important?
3. How can a school ensure all students have this strength in their own cultural identity?
4. What are the specific *cultural* ways of knowing that young people are developing these skills?
5. How can schools recognize, and address, barriers that exist in their practice to the development of a student's secure cultural identity?

Although these questions are focused on culture, they illustrate the need for critical consciousness and participation of the school's staff and community in the co-construction of knowledge. Dei (2011) places the struggle to retain one's identity within the struggle to wrestle control of knowledge production from the colonizer. He states, "Indigenous knowledge is about resistance, not in the romanticized sense, but resistance as struggle to navigate the tensions of today's modernized, globalized world while seeking to disrupt its universalizing, hegemonic norms" (p. 168). The development of one's cultural identity in a whitestream education system cannot be separated from this struggle.

Penetito (2010) explains that being Māori "goes all the way down" and that while there are many ways to be Māori, one constant is that the collective has priority over the individual. The individual "can only become truly well-developed by evolving a consciousness of self in relation to objects (people, things and events) outside or beyond the self" (p. 269). The experience and practice of Kia Aroha College suggests that the development of a cultural identity for indigenous and minoritized learners in our schools also has to go "all the way back" to develop a critical awareness of the role of schooling as a tool of colonization and assimilation, "all the way across" to understand events, policies and thinking that shape contemporary whitestream schooling in the present, and "all the way forward" to develop new knowledge and pedagogies to co-construct a different educational pathway for the future (Milne, 2013, 2014, 2016).

Schooling in New Zealand

Schooling is compulsory in New Zealand for all students between six and sixteen years of age however, in practice, most families choose the option to begin school at the age of five years. New Zealand state or public schools fall into four broad categories; primary (elementary), intermediate (middle—usually

Years 7–10/Grades 6–7), secondary, and composite, the last being the official classification for a range of different grade configurations allowed in legislation. A composite school is defined as one that has some grade levels from both the elementary and secondary sectors.

While most students in New Zealand attend state-funded, public schools, there is a range of other options. Kura Kaupapa Māori are state schools where the philosophy is total immersion in Māori language, culture and values. Integrated schools are schools that were originally private or independent schools and have now become part of the state system in order to access government funding. Independent (or private) schools are governed by their own independent boards but must meet certain standards in order to be registered. Special schools are state schools that provide education for students with special education needs. Designated-character schools are state schools that teach the New Zealand curriculum but have used the opportunity, embedded in legislation, to develop their own set of aims, purposes and objectives to reflect their own particular values. Kia Aroha College is a designated-character school.

New Zealand's education system experienced a major upheaval in 1989 with the advent of *Tomorrow's Schools* (Department of Education, 1988), a reform that devolved the responsibility for school governance to individual school communities through community-elected Boards of Trustees. These reforms with their neoliberal, market-driven approach created two rival agendas right from the start. While promising partnership and equity from an educational point of view, the model for the government, Treasury, and business interests was about competition and choice. The tension between "parents as partners" and "parents as customers" (Snook et al., 1999) was felt nowhere more keenly than in communities such as Otara which were ill-prepared for such responsibility. The plight of schools in low socio-economic communities was exacerbated by the change of government immediately following the reforms and the introduction of dezoning or open enrolment, causing an exodus of students from these areas seeking "better" schooling options.

Although each New Zealand school has the autonomy to develop its own charter within the boundaries of a mandated broad national curriculum, and each community has the power to shape a school in the way they want for their children, very few schools break away from the colonial model. The process is deliberately convoluted, requiring consensus and determination from a school's community to dismantle the barriers the bureaucratic system puts in the way.

In 2015, Māori children made up 23% of the total school population in New Zealand. Although 16% of Māori children participate in bilingual education, just 3.8% of these attend Kura Kaupapa Māori (Māori language immersion schools). The majority of Māori learners therefore are in whitestream public New Zealand schools (Ministry of Education, 2015a). The problem is that education officials continue to push the rhetoric of New Zealand's "world class" education system, while avoiding the fact that we have one of the lowest equity scores internationally. New Zealand's school drop-out rates are among the OECD's highest, with one in three Māori students, and one in four Pasifika students, leaving school without formal qualifications (OECD, 2013).

School Reform in White Spaces

As is the case for indigenous people the world over, the history of British colonization in New Zealand had a profound effect on Māori. It decimated their economic, political, cultural, and social structures, invaded and appropriated their land and resources, and all but extinguished their language, through deliberate policies of assimilation and integration that used schooling as one of their most powerful weapons. As Māori academic, Linda Tuhiwai Smith (1999) describes, "They came, they saw, they named, they claimed" (p. 80).

Our current neoliberal education reforms implemented ostensibly to "fix" the problem we have created, perpetuate the colonial project with a scarily similar agenda to the history that Linda Smith names. Tuck (2013) discusses similar reforms in the United States as "the relentless pursuit of accountability" (p. 324), and links this to "neoliberal ideology (the logic that prizes accountability)" (p. 325). The situation in New Zealand schools is no different. Māori scholar Maria Bargh (2007) describes neoliberalism as a "translation of many older colonial beliefs, once expressed explicitly, now expressed implicitly, into language and practices, which are far more covert about their civilizing mission" (p. 13). Bargh and Otter (2009) observe that neoliberalism is not new to Māori and these practices "are but the latest in a long history of colonial endeavors that have sought to inculcate Māori into Western forms of individualism" (p. 155).

Thrupp and White (2013) refer to the "official fixation with data" (p. v) in their investigation of New Zealand's mandated National Standards, introduced in primary and intermediate schools in 2009. Introduced with urgency and little consultation, National Standards have been described by opponents as neither national, nor standard. Thrupp and White describe the policy as "one of the most controversial school-level developments in New Zealand for decades" (p. 3). There is no mandated national testing, but teachers are expected to make judgments, using a wide range of evidence, on students' progress in reading, writing and mathematics achievement on a four point scale: "above," "at," "below," or "well below" the standard. Teachers are expected to moderate these judgments within schools and with other local schools informally. The overall teacher judgments (OTJs) are reported publicly on the Government's education website. Thrupp and White find that some schools and children, including low socio-economic schools with high numbers of Māori and Pasifika children, are more likely to experience the damaging effects of the National Standards policy then others (p. 31). In their analysis of the policy, four years after its introduction, they are clear that the New Zealand's version of high stakes testing is merely a variation on the international theme, which is not going to avoid the problems encountered with similar policies internationally. Overall, they believe:

> National Standards are having some favourable impacts in areas that include teacher understanding of curriculum levels, motivation of some teachers and children and some improved targeting of interventions. Nevertheless such gains are overshadowed by damage being done through the intensification of staff workloads, curriculum narrowing and the reinforcement of a two-tier curriculum, the positioning and labelling of children and unproductive new tensions amongst school staff. These problems are often occurring despite attempts by schools and teachers to minimise any damaging impact of the National Standards. (p. 1)

O'Connor (2011), commenting on the Government's introduction of charter schools in 2012 describes this as an "ideological war," with battle lines drawn between "a Government intent on the imposition of neo-liberal education policies that have been spectacularly unsuccessful around the world," and teachers and principals who are portrayed by this Government as unwilling to adapt and change. Citing, "narrow national standards, which have little to do with the production of critical, meaningful knowledge and problem-solving," the privatization of schools, funding cuts, and corporate control of the curriculum as components of the attack, he observes:

> The social experiment will be conducted in schools in South Auckland, where the popular myth is that schools are failing, and in Christchurch, where the earthquakes[10] have provided a convenient excuse to wreak more havoc on a troubled city. I work regularly in South Auckland schools and, since the earthquakes, I have worked in schools in Christchurch. Neither area has a record of poor and failing schools.

> In contrast, schools and teachers in South Auckland are often the glue that binds together communities ravaged by inequality and poverty. (O'Connor, 2011)

Kia Aroha College's location in one of the lowest socio-economic communities in the country, in the heart of South Auckland, places the school firmly in the midst of this ideological, political, battlefield. The parallels with the experience of other countries engaged in what Sahlberg (2011) calls the Global Education Reform Movement, or GERM, are clear. Sahlberg characterizes the six global features of these reforms as: standardization of and in education, an increased focus on literacy and numeracy, teaching for predetermined results in low-risk ways, the transfer of innovation from corporate to the educational world as a main source of change, the adoption of test-based accountability policies, and stronger measures of control over schools (pp. 178–179). All of these features are played out in New Zealand's education system and none are more affected by the relentless neoliberal march of the GERM than indigenous Māori and minoritized children and their families and communities. Kia Aroha College's counter-story is an antidote in this situation.

There are a number of national initiatives, which seek to change the education experience of Māori learners. Most of these aim to develop an understanding of culturally responsive and Māori responsive pedagogy in school leaders and teachers, and some have been very effective in changing practice. However, when I asked a senior director of one of these initiatives, if the project developed Māori knowledge and competency in Māori students, the answer was, it did not. The measure of the success of these initiatives is based predominantly on gains in the academic outcomes of Māori learners.

In order to discuss the effectiveness of these school reform and schooling improvement initiatives for Māori and Pasifika students in whitestream New Zealand schools, it is important to reiterate that the context that initiates, supports and determines the shape of these initiatives is still a White space. As Tomlins-Jahnke (2008) explains, "what counts as school knowledge, the way school knowledge is organized, resourced, taught and evaluated, the underlying codes that structure such knowledge, access to and legitimation of school knowledge is determined by the dominant culture" (p. 4).

This is rarely considered in the design of school improvement and reform, which most often comes from a mindset of getting better at doing the same things. Hence, we see the major focus on raising literacy and numeracy levels, improving national secondary school qualifications results, and reducing high levels of non-engagement. These initiatives largely persist in seeing White space as neutral and their goal is to raise Māori and Pasifika students' achievement to "national norms." Dyson (1999) names this fulfilment of the fantasy that the White norm is neutral and objective, "whitewishing" (p. 219).

Gutirrez, Asato, Santos, and Gotanda (2002) observe that the key tactic to getting the public to support these types of reforms is to use, "code words, phrases, and symbols which refer indirectly to racial themes, but do not directly challenge popular democratic or egalitarian ideas, such as justice and equal opportunity" (p. 340). They argue that "backlash" pedagogies, "products of ideological and institutional structures that legitimize and thus maintain privilege, access, and control of the socio-political and economic terrain," underpin this type of educational reform, which "accepts substantial inequality as a neutral baseline for educational practice and reform and, simultaneously, enshrines the status quo." Thus whiteness, or "the status quo camouflaged as color-blind, becomes the uncontested baseline of educational reform" (pp. 336–337).

Often this requirement to measure success in terms of these national norms goes hand in hand with the expectations of the source of funding, usually the Ministry of Education, to have the outcomes defined and evaluated on their terms. Not only is the focus of these reforms generally to improve or 'fix' the children's deficits, many also expand their focus to "fix" the deficits in families, so we have initiatives like family literacy programs, to teach parents how to better support their children's reading, and projects that provide incentives to help families create "quiet" spaces for homework and reading. We thus imply to parents and whānau that the natural, noisy, busy, environment of the large extended family, common in Māori and Pasifika households, is not conducive to learning and to parents that they lack the skills to support their children's learning. In a just and reciprocal partnership, schools would go to equal lengths to learn about Māori and Pasifika norms, in oracy for example in cultures that have strong oral traditions, and incorporate these into "schooling improvement" initiatives. This is rarely the case. Not only does this practice reinforce to Māori and Pasifika families that the problem is of their own making, it robs children of exposure to their own cultural norms in their daily lives at school. Corson (1995) describes the impact of this:

> When people in majority culture education systems ignore minority culture discourse norms, for that moment the cycle of cultural reproduction reinforced by those norms is disrupted. More than just miscommunication results. Over time, culturally different children are deprived of the everyday reinforcers of values that are central to their culture's world view; and children deprived in this way of a developing and shared world view have less understanding of who they are, where they are going, and where in the world they might have a value as individuals and as group members. (p. 195)

Māori Spaces in the Whitestream—"as Māori"

Durie (2003) asks, "what is the benchmark against which Māori should gauge progress?" He suggests that comparison of Māori with non-Māori, "presupposes that Māori are aiming to be as good as Pākehā when they might well aspire to be better, or different, or even markedly superior" (p. 202). Durie believes it is misleading to assume that these types of comparisons provide useful information about Māori progress. There is no justification, he states, for educational disparities, which should not be tolerated. He advocates zero tolerance for education failure but points out present trends where Māori youth "are trapped in lifestyles that are essentially incompatible with healthy growth and development and will struggle to participate in either te ao Māori (the Māori world) or the wider global community" (p. 203).

Durie (2003) asserts that education should enable Māori to "live as Māori" (p. 199). This goal subsequently became the vision for the New Zealand Ministry of Education's strategy for Māori education, *Ka Hikitia: Accelerating Success 2013–2017* (Ministry of Education, 2013a). However, in the vision of *Ka Hikitia*; "Māori children enjoying and achieving education success, as Māori," the two key words, "as Māori" are the words most ignored by whitestream schools who have no understanding of what "as Māori" might be. Inevitably, "as Māori" becomes another White space, in that it is reinvented, and seen as no different from, "as Pākehā." This is not necessarily a deliberate action or intent on the part of principals and school leadership, but is indicative of the lack of understanding that is endemic throughout our education system. The default position is to ignore the words, "as Māori," and work towards the completely different goal of "Māori children enjoying and achieving education success"—with no attempt to explore notions of "success" from a Māori worldview. "Success" and "achievement" then become interpreted as the academic outcomes *of* Māori learners.

Durie (2003) is specific about the words. "As Māori" he states means, to have access to te ao Māori (the Māori world)—access to language, culture, marae (traditional gathering places), tikanga (customs) and resources (p. 199). He adds:

> If after twelve or so years of formal education Māori youth were totally unprepared to interact within te ao Māori, then, no matter what else had been learned, education would have been incomplete. Being Māori is a Māori reality. Education should be as much about that reality as it is about literacy and numeracy. In short, being able to

live as Māori imposes some responsibilities upon the education system to contribute towards the realisation of that goal. (pp. 199–200)

Durie (2006) makes a further important distinction about "as Māori" in a paper written for the New Zealand Treasury about measuring Māori wellbeing, when he clarifies that, "participation *of* a Māori is different from participation *as* a Māori" (p. 8) and that these two terms do not have the same meaning. He aligns "as Māori" with a secure cultural identity. This important difference has escaped New Zealand's Ministry of Education, which monitors the achievement *of* Māori students exclusively through quantitative data, based on literacy, numeracy, and senior school qualifications results. The hypocrisy of the rhetoric in *Ka Hikitia* however, did not escape the attention of the research conducted by a group of Māori student "warrior-researchers" at Kia Aroha College in 2015, and presented by them at the New Zealand Association for Research in Education (NZARE) national conference:

> The paradox that disrupts the *Ka Hikitia* strategy is that we have created an education system covertly designed to fail Māori and marginalize indigenous knowledge. Actually, as I read more about our education history I've decided I need to change that word to 'overtly' because I don't think it has been hidden at all. The system's failure for us as Māori learners is blatantly in our faces, over generations. Māori achievement outcomes and our participation in education are consistently, systemically, and historically below that of non-Māori. There is a fundamental fault in our education system that allows this situation to continue in our mainstream schools. Let's face it, if these results were for generations of Pākehā learners, people would lose their jobs and there would be marching in the streets!
>
> One of our survey participants told us that *Ka Hikitia* is hypocritical. I strongly agree with this. Although *Ka Hikitia's* fourth principle (and why this isn't the first?) is that identity, [Māori] language, and culture count, if you look for the actual goals for primary and secondary education in *Ka Hikitia* there are only two:
>
> 1. All Māori students have strong literacy, numeracy and language skills; and
> 2. All Māori students achieve at least NCEA[11] Level 2 or an equivalent qualification.
>
> There is no identity, language, culture, or "as Māori" in those goals. (Ebony, in Pirini-Edwards et al., 2015)

Dr. Paul Goren, who spent six months in New Zealand in 2009, on an Ian Axford (New Zealand) Fellowship in Public Policy,[12] chose the first version of *Ka Hikitia* (Ministry of Education, 2009) as the focus of his research (Goren, 2009). His report echoes the concern about the difficulty in changing both the rhetoric and teacher practice. Underlying both these official strategies for Māori and Pasifika learners is the issue Goren calls "the unspoken" (p. 53). Goren cites both the long-standing racism that has caused Māori to lag behind others for so long, and the reluctance of many "to enter the conversation about race and racism, and (who) need safe places to explore issues and build confidence related to Māori student achievement" (p. 54). These attitudes and reluctance to engage in the deeper conversations about race are endemic in our education system's White spaces. Penetito (2010) observes, "New Zealanders are not comfortable talking about race or racism and nowhere is this more obvious that in official educational discourses" (p. 63).

We Will Continue to Fight Forever

This gulf between the Whitestream perspective and Māori aspirations was highlighted in Te Whānau o Tupuranga in 2008 when we hosted a visit from two North American critical educators, Dr. Jeff Duncan-Andrade and Dr. K. Wayne Yang. Just before their visit, they advised me they wanted to bring a gift, in the form of a scholarship, to donate to two graduating students. The scholarship was designed to recognize that, "for indigenous youth, the pursuit of education under oppression is a revolutionary undertaking" and to acknowledge two "young revolutionaries who embody the historical struggle of oppressed peoples to liberate their minds and their communities" (J. Duncan-Andrade, personal communication, September 10, 2008). They asked staff to name the award so it reflected the values of the school.

I put that question to our Māori staff, who named the award, *Te Poho o Kia Aroha*,[13] with the subtitle, *Ka whawhai tonu mātou mō ake tonu atu* (we will continue to fight forever). The name of the school, *Kia Aroha*, is also the name of our school marae (a traditional Māori meeting place). In their written explanation of why the marae was central to the name of the award, Māori staff described the role of the marae as where a child is:

> Sustained with ancestral traditions, ancestral knowledge, unfailing love, nurturing, belief, a striving spirit, righteousness, kindness, and skills, where they develop an openness of mind, and become alert, alive, eager, and brave, where a child learns to treat kindly their world, and the surroundings that shelter them, and to become

aware of those that can harm them. From here, growth is seen as reaching the uppermost heights of the realisation of their aspirations, and dreams.

This statement captures Durie's (2003, p. 199) assertion that the purpose of education is as much about preparation for participation in Māori society as it is about participation in society generally. There was no suggestion from the critical educators that these prestigious scholarships, should be for specific academic achievement. Explicit in the award's intent is "liberating minds and communities," an expectation of reciprocity, clearly understood in Kia Aroha College, to give back to the school and the whānau. This award continues to be the school's most esteemed and highest achievement.

Pasifika Spaces in the Whitestream—"as Tongan," "as Samoan"

The use of the term *Pasifika* has both positive and negative connotations. The term is currently preferred by the New Zealand Ministry of Education, which has, in the past, used labels such as "Pacific Islanders" and "Pacific Nations." Samu (2006) explains that *Pasifika* is a good choice because it translates from the word, "Pacific" in several of the Pacific languages in New Zealand. She favours its use also because, "The fact that as a term, it 'originated' from us, is of no small consequence because being able to define ourselves is an issue of control" (p. 36). On the other hand, Kepa and Manu'atu (2006) argue that this mainstream construct of *Pasifika* simply reinforces assimilation by dismissing and devaluing different languages and cultures. They use the example of, "the tendency among the Samoan people, in particular those representatives from the Ministry of Education," to reinforce the numerical dominance of Samoan, "thus relegating to a marginal and devalued status the beliefs and practices of the numerically weaker Pasifika peoples" (p. 53). Samu (2006) believes there is value, however, in a "collectivising" term such as *Pasifika* in that its unifying effect can counter oppositional forces such as neo-colonialism and, for Pasifika groups in New Zealand, the oppositional forces of, "assimilation and social/economic/cultural marginalization" (p. 40).

The term *Pasifika* has been chosen as a collective descriptor in this book because it is the preferred term of Samoan, Tongan, and Cook Islands Māori staff at Kia Aroha College. Where possible, and where it is relevant, the different Pasifika cultures are referred to using their respective specific names.

Cook Islands Māori is used in all references to people from the Cook Islands, again following the advice of Cook Islands Māori staff.

The vision of the New Zealand Ministry of Education's strategy for Pasifika education, *The Pasifika Education Plan 2013–2017* (Ministry of Education, 2013b) is, "Five out of five Pasifika learners participating, engaging and achieving in education, secure in their identities, languages and cultures and contributing fully to Aotearoa New Zealand's social, cultural and economic wellbeing" (p. 3). This too, came under the scrutiny of the Kia Aroha College student researchers. Tongan student, 'Aisea, exposed the rhetoric in his research:

> The *Pasifika Education Plan* spells out what Pasifika success will look like which is, "demanding, vibrant, dynamic, successful Pasifika learners, secure and confident in their identities, languages and cultures." However, when you get to Page 7 of the Plan and the section on Schooling, the language changes. Now, it states that, "The focus is on accelerating literacy and numeracy achievement and gaining NCEA Level 2 qualifications as a stepping stone to further education and/or employment."
>
> What happened to our identities, languages and cultures? Apparently, if we look at the Ministry of Education's "Progress against Pasifika Education Plan targets" on the Education Counts website (Ministry of Education, 2015b), they must be hiding under some of these headings: literacy, numeracy, NCEA, suspensions, expulsions, exclusions, and whether our parents are on Boards of Trustees. This sounds like the Pālangi[14] Education Plan to me. ('Aisea, in Pirini-Edwards et al., 2015)

"Academic" Achievement

The acknowledgement of alternative perspectives however, does not mean that learning success is not an important goal, or that Māori and Pasifika learners should have some alternative achievement goals. Durie (2003) describes the three goals he proposes as relevant to Māori as "concurrent goals". They are "a parcel of goals—all of which should be pursued together," and he makes the point that "educational failure significantly reduces chances of success in any of the three areas" (p. 203).

For Kia Aroha College, it means that academic achievement alone, as defined by hegemonic White norms, is not enough. At the heart of the school's learning model is an emphatic belief that being able to put a reading, writing, mathematics, or an NCEA secondary school qualifications result alongside a Māori child's name, or analyzing these data to make comparisons with other ethnic groups, does not make it "Māori achievement." It is simply reading, writing, mathematics or NCEA achievement, with nothing specifically Māori about it. Similarly, reducing Māori students' truancy, or suspensions, or any other interventions which start from a position of deficit, may signal a school's achievement in changing its practice, but are not any measure of our children's success.

If achievement "as Māori" is exactly the same as achievement "as Pākehā," what's the point of the Ministry of Education's vision of, "Māori children enjoying education success as Māori" (Ministry of Education, 2013a)? If we use no indicators of Māori knowledge whatsoever and we define Māori achievement in White terms, which we determine for our Māori learners, how can that possibly be achievement as Māori? We need to authentically value other knowledges and broaden our narrow, limited, technical definition of "achievement." "Academic" achievement is not the sole prerogative of the Western academic tradition. Indigenous people the world over have knowledge systems, formal and informal, which developed complex learning, philosophy, and scholarship.

In his critique of New Zealand schools and schooling in the 21st century, experienced educator, David Hood (2015) comments:

> We have to ask ourselves why it is that we still measure the success of individuals, the success of schools, and the success of the system only on the basis of academic learning, and not on the full range of attributes we all see as so important? (p. 61)

He believes that treating secondary schools as "the supply chain" for universities constrains schools' ability to be innovative and to respond to the wide range of different student needs. He concludes, "In New Zealand the assessment tail wags the curriculum dog" (p. 54).

Overview of Book Chapters

This book is divided into two parts: the first section (Chapters 1–3) introduces and identifies the concept of White spaces in our education systems. It sets the story against the context of education for Māori and minoritized Pasifika learners in New Zealand, and discusses the importance of the loss of cultural identity. The second section (Chapters 4–9) "colors in" the White spaces, describing the philosophy and practice of Kia Aroha College in three domains of learning.

Chapter 1 has introduced the story of Kia Aroha College and posed five questions that are fundamental to critical, culturally responsive classroom pedagogy and practice. The chapter identifies education policy and practice that marginalize and minoritize Māori and Pasifika youth, and examines the failure of neoliberal school reform movements to address these barriers. The importance of cultural identity is discussed in this chapter and the central concept of White spaces in our Whitestream education system was introduced.

Chapter 2 takes this idea of White spaces further by naming them as spaces of privilege and supremacy, spaces that are embedded in curriculum, in pedagogy and in teachers' thinking, and aligns these spaces with school alienation for students of color. It raises the issue of information technology as a significant factor in the continued erosion of indigenous language and culture. This issue is further explored in Chapter 8.

Chapter 3 further discusses cultural identity. It explores how cultural identity develops and provides an overview of essentialist, postmodern, and critical identity frameworks. The concept of identity from indigenous perspectives, and the ways identities change and adapt in contemporary settings are discussed. The idea of "identity lost" through social toxins is explained and the renaissance of Māori culture in New Zealand is positioned as resistance to this loss of identity.

Chapter 4 leads into the second section of the book by introducing Kia Aroha College. It provides the context of the school community and describes the school and community's history of struggle with education bureaucracy, through three changes of name and three changes of official school status. This chapter provides the background for the school's determined and prolonged stand to challenge and resist a colonial model of education.

Chapter 5 asks us to change the lens we use to view education. It challenges schools to tell the truth about their White spaces, and to audit them honestly. Typical questions are provided to use for such an exercise, as are questions that ask us to see our spaces through other eyes and viewpoints. It also discusses the importance of school design to create ownership and a sense of belonging. The final section of this chapter describes the *Power Lenses Learning Model* (Milne, 2004) which is the school's response to "coloring in the white spaces" to empower Māori and Pasifika students to learn "as" Māori, Samoan, Tongan, Cook Islands Māori. The three lenses in this model are used as the contexts for Chapters 6–8, which examine the school's practice in each lens separately.

Chapter 6 describes Kia Aroha College's practice through the school-learning lens. The school's structure and organization, the learning programme in practice, the supports in place for this way of learning, and learning outcomes are all discussed. The chapter describes the pedagogical practices within the school that intentionally "color in" the school-learning white space and specifically introduces the concept of whānau, and a critical pedagogy of whānau. Five specific contexts for learning using youth participatory action research are provided as examples of a critical pedagogy of whānau in practice.

Chapter 7 looks specifically at the self-learning lens. It further explores Māori and Pasifika identities as these underpin the action research by school staff to develop an assessment tool to determine students' growth in their cultural identity and self-knowledge. This tool and the process to develop it are explained in detail. The purpose of this assessment tool is explained in terms of its use within the school. The tool does not intend to be aligned with standard psychological tests of identity or identity one would expect adults to have developed. Its intended use is as a tool to describe the learning and development that Kia Aroha College views as valid achievement in its own right for our students. The chapter also discusses the concept of "Māori children enjoying education success as Māori," and explores the use of the self-learning tool and the school's practice to examine this concept of "as Māori" or "as Pasifika." The learning seen through the self-lens is not intended to be a stepping stone to improve learning in other lenses, although the data provided in this chapter show that this certainly is the case. The chapter also asks questions about achievement and success, the White space of assessment, and answers these through the data provided by the self-lens research. The development of the self-lens tool, and the knowledge it gives the school about these previously undervalued, but crucially important skills, is knowledge that cannot be determined by assessments of literacy, numeracy, national standards or senior school qualifications. However, it is information which, coupled with the critical practice in the school learning lens, changes both the learning and the assessment White spaces to make them relevant and authentic places for Māori and Pasifika learners.

Chapter 8 examines two aspects of the global learning, lens: social justice, and new skills and knowledge for the 21st century. The global lens is concerned with all the identities and spaces our students navigate beyond school. These might be local spaces, such as youth or church groups, or youth gangs, or interaction with the wider Māori community, or international spaces, for example. The first section of the chapter describes social justice initiatives outside New Zealand and focuses specifically on four programs in the United States that I have personally visited and with whom Kia Aroha College has an ongoing association. The connection with these programs show our youth that they are not alone in the struggle for social justice and educational sovereignty, and that injustice, colonization, assimilation, racism and White spaces transcend borders to marginalize and pathologize young people the world over. This section identifies seven key principles that these initiatives and the philosophy and practice of Kia Aroha College have in common. The second section of this chapter looks at the new skills and knowledges needed for 21st century learners and describes the development of the High Tech Youth Network on the school's campus.

Chapter 9 takes its structure from a set of twelve guiding principles towards a pathway of self-determination, which were developed by senior students in 2010, and aligns these with the three lenses through which the school views learning, and which formed the basis of the three previous chapters. This chapter brings these powerful spaces together and uses the concept of "Breaking Free" to describe an initiative that develops hope and healing for our most troubled youth. The "Break Free" program traverses all three of the school's learning lenses and shows how they interact and overlap. The chapter answers the five questions posed in Chapter 1 as fundamental to critical, culturally responsive classroom pedagogy and practice. The answer to the last question; how can schools recognize, and address, barriers that exist in their practice to the development of a secure cultural identity, is linked to the school's expectations for students by the time they graduate as "Warrior-Scholars." The chapter discusses the restoration of genuine "audacious hope" (Duncan-Andrade, 2009), "radical hope" (Freire, 1998) and "radical healing" (Ginwright, 2009, 2010, 2015) as crucial elements in the reclamation of educational sovereignty and cultural identity of non-White learners in our schools. Finally, this chapter asks what did the schools learn from this journey and the changes that they have implemented. The lessons learned are made available to others who might explore the same issues and embark on a similar pathway, which they in turn can make relevant to their own communities and schools.

Notes

1. Māori proverb: Seek the treasure you value most dearly. If you bow your head, let it be to a lofty mountain.
2. "Senior" in the New Zealand context refers to a high school student in their final years at school (Grades 11 and 12).
3. Māori proverb: Plant the seed in the young, it will grow and bear fruit to nourish future generations.
4. With the signing of the Treaty of Waitangi in 1840 between the British Crown and more than 500 Māori tribal chiefs, New Zealand became a colony of Britain and Māori became

British subjects. The Treaty is generally considered the founding document of New Zealand as a nation. Despite this, the rights guaranteed to Māori have been ignored. New Zealand schools are expected to provide education to Māori that is "consistent with the principles of the Treaty of Waitangi."
5. The term Pasifika is the collective descriptor chosen by the Samoan, Tongan, and Cook Islands Māori staff at Kia Aroha College. Wherever possible, the different Pasifika cultures are referred to using their specific names.
6. Shields, Bishop, and Mazawi (2005) use this term to refer to those who are treated as if one's position and perspective is of less worth, who are silenced or marginalized, regardless of whether they are in the numerical minority or not.
7. The Māori word, Pākehā, means a New Zealander of European descent, a White person.
8. The name of the Samoan bilingual unit at Kia Aroha College, established in 1991—meaning 'future'.
9. The "Samoan way"—traditional Samoan practice.
10. On February 22, 2011, Christchurch, the largest city in the South Island of New Zealand, was badly damaged by a magnitude 6.3 earthquake, which killed 185 people and injured several thousand. Schools were significantly impacted and widespread restructuring through closures and mergers have been imposed by the Government as a result.
11. The National Certificate of Academic Achievement is New Zealand's senior secondary school qualification, studied for in Years 11–13 (Grades 10–12). There are three levels of NCEA certificate, depending on the difficulty of the standards achieved. At each level, students must achieve a certain number of credits to gain the qualification. Credits can be gained over more than one year and students may study a mix of standards at different levels. Depending on the standard, assessment can be internal (nationally moderated teacher assessment) or external (national formal examination).
12. Ian Axford (New Zealand) Fellowships in Public Policy were established by the New Zealand government in 1995 to facilitate public policy dialogue between New Zealand and the United States of America.
13. Te Poho means literally "the bosom." Te Poho was also the name of a taniwha (water spirit, powerful creature) who nurtured and fed the local, Ngai Tai, people. Kia Aroha means through love and compassion although aroha is a much wider concept than the English translation.
14. Pālangi is the Tongan word for a European/White person.

References

Bargh, M. (2007). *Resistance: An indigenous response to neoliberalism*. Wellington: Huia Publishers.

Bargh, M., & Otter, J. (2009). Progressive spaces of neoliberalism in Aotearoa: A genealogy and critique. *Asia Pacific Viewpoint*, 50(2), 154–165. http://doi.org/10.1111/j.1467-8373.2009.01390.x

Corson, D. (1995). World view, cultural values and discourse norms: The cycle of cultural reproduction. *International Journal of Intercultural Relations*, 19(2), 183–195.

Darder, A. (1991). *Culture and power: A critical foundation for bicultural education*. Westport, CT: Bergin and Garvey.

Dei, G. S. J. (2011). Indigenous knowledge and the question of development: Tensions of change, tradition and modernity. In G. S. J. Dei (Ed.), *Indigenous philosophies and critical education* (pp. 167–170). New York, NY: Peter Lang Publishing.

Denis, C. (1997). *We are not you: First Nations and Canadian modernity*. Peterborough: Broadview Press.

Department of Education. (1988). *Tomorrow's Schools: The reform of education administration in New Zealand*. Wellington: Department of Education.

Duncan-Andrade, J. (2009). Note to Educators: Hope required when growing roses in concrete. *Harvard Educational Review, 79*(2), 181–194.

Duncan-Andrade, J., & Morrell, E. (2008). *The art of critical pedagogy: Possibilities for moving from theory to practice in urban schools*. New York, NY: Peter Lang.

Durie, M. (2001). *A Framework for considering Maori educational advancement*. Paper presented at the Hui Taumata Matauranga II (Māori Education Summit). Turangi, Taupo, New Zealand.

Durie, M. (2003). *Nga Kahui Pou: Launching Maori Futures*. Wellington: Huia.

Durie, M. (2006). Measuring Māori wellbeing. In *New Zealand Treasury Guest Lecture Series*. Wellington, New Zealand: New Zealand Treasury.

Dyson, M. E. (1999). The Labor of Whiteness, the Whiteness of Labor, and the Perils of Whitewishing. In R. D. Torres, L. F. Miron, & J. X. Inda (Eds.), *Race, Identity, and Citizenship: A Reader*. Malden, MA: Blackwell.

Freire, P. (1998). *Pedagogy of Freedom*. Lanham, MD: Rowman & Littlefield Publishers.

Ginwright, S. (2009). *Black youth rising: Race, activism, and radical healing in urban America* (192pp.). New York, NY: Teachers College Press.

Ginwright, S. (2010). Addressing root causes of health disparities: Promoting positive health & academic achievement among youth. In *Strengthening our practice: Refining our aim*. San Francisco, CA: Keynote address. National Professional Development (NPD) Conference.

Ginwright, S. (2015). *Hope and healing in Urban education: How urban activists and teachers are reclaiming matters of the heart*. New York, NY: Routledge.

Goren, P. (2009). *How policy travels: Making sense of Ka Hikitia managing for success: The Māori Education Strategy 2008–2012*. Ian Axford Fellowship in Public Policy Report, Fulbright New Zealand.

Grande, S. (2000). American Indian geographies of identity and power: At the crossroads of Indígena and Mestizaje. *Harvard Educational Review, 70*(4), 467–499. http://doi.org/10.17763/haer.70.4.47717110136rvt53

Gutiérrez, K. D., Asato, J., Santos, M., & Gotanda, N. (2002). Backlash pedagogy: Language and culture and the politics of reform. *Review of Education, Pedagogy, and Cultural Studies, 24*(February 2015), 335–351. http://doi.org/10.1080/10714410214744

Hood, D. (2015). *The rhetoric and the reality: New Zealand schools and schooling in the 21st century*. Masterton: Fraser Books.

Mageo, J. (1989). "Ferocious is the centipede": A study of the significance of eating and speaking in Samoa. *Ethos, 17*(4), 387–427.

Manu'atu, L., & Kepa, M. (2006). "Fetuiakimalie, talking together": Pasifika in mainstream education. *Waikato Journal of Education, 12*. 51–56.

Milne, A. (2004). "They didn't care about normal kids like me." Restructuring a school to fit the kids. (Unpublished Master's thesis). Massey University, Palmerston North,

Milne, A. (2013). *Colouring in the White spaces: Reclaiming cultural identity in Whitestream schools* (Unpublished PhD thesis). University of Waikato. Retrieved from http://researchcommons.waikato.ac.nz/handle/10289/7868

Milne, A. (2014). Colouring in the White spaces. In V. Carpenter & S. Osborne (Eds.), *Twelve Thousand Hours: Education and Poverty in Aotearoa New Zealand* (pp. 223–230). Auckland: Dunmore.

Milne, A. (2016). Where am I in our schools' White spaces? Social justice for the learners we marginalise. *Middle Grades Review, 1*(3). Retrieved from http://scholarworks.uvm.edu/mgreview/vol1/iss3/2

Ministry of Education. (2009). *Ka Hikitia—Managing for success: The Māori education strategy 2008–2012 (Updated 2009)*. Wellington: Ministry of Education.

Ministry of Education. (2013a). *Ka Hikitia—Accelerating success 2013–2017*. Wellington: Ministry of Education. Retrieved from http://www.education.govt.nz/ministry-of-education/overall-strategies-and-policies/the-maori-education-strategy-ka-hikitia-accelerating-success-20132017/

Ministry of Education. (2013b). *Pasifika Education Plan 2013–2017*. Wellington: Ministry of Education. Retrieved from http://www.education.govt.nz/ministry-of-education/overall-strategies-and-policies/pasifika-education-plan-2013-2017/

Ministry of Education. (2015a). *Education Counts: School rolls*. Retrieved from https://www.educationcounts.govt.nz/statistics/schooling/student-numbers/6028

Ministry of Education. (2015b). *Progress against Pasifika Education Plan targets*. Retrieved November 7, 2015 from https://www.educationcounts.govt.nz/statistics/pasifika-education/progress_against_pasifika_education_plan_targets

O'Connor, P. (2011, December 14). Good public education is at risk. *The Dominion Post*. Retrieved from http://www.stuff.co.nz/dominion-post/comment/6134611/Good-public-education-is-at-risk

OECD. (2013). *OECD Economic Surveys: New Zealand 2013*. OECD Publishing. Retrieved from http://dx.doi.org/10.1787/eco_surveys-nzl-2013-en

Penetito, W. (2010). *What's Māori about Māori education?* Wellington: Victoria University Press.

Pirini-Edwards, E., Tukutau, A., Katipa, M., Ropitini-Fairburn, K., Harris-Kaaka, J., & Bellamy, J. (2015). *Speaking out "as" us: Māori and Tongan secondary students investigate our education system's vision for Māori and Pasifika learners*. Whakatane, New Zealand, Symposium presented at New Zealand Association for Research in Education (NZARE) Conference.

Sahlberg, P. (2011). The Fourth Way of Finland. *Journal of Educational Change, 12*(3), 173–185.

Samu, T. W. (2006). The "Pasifika Umbrella" and quality teaching: Understanding and responding to the diverse realities within. *Waikato Journal of Education, 12*, 35–49.

Scorza, D., Mirra, N., & Morrell, E. (2013, February 18). It should just be education: Critical pedagogy normalized as academic excellence. *The International Journal of Critical Pedagogy*. Retrieved from http://libjournal.uncg.edu/ijcp/article/view/337

Shields, C. M., Bishop, R., & Mazawi, A. E. (2005). *Pathologizing practices*. New York, NY: Peter Lang.

Sleeter, C. (2012). Confronting the marginalization of culturally responsive pedagogy. *Urban Education, 47*(3), 562–584. http://doi.org/10.1177/0042085911431472

Smith, L. (1999). *Decolonizing Methodologies: Research and Indigenous Peoples*. London: Zed Books.

Snook, I., Adams, P., Adams, R., Clark, J., Codd, J., Collins, G., ... Pearce, D. (1999). Educational reform in New Zealand 1989–1999: Is there any evidence of success? *Delta, 51*(1), 23–54.

Snook, I., O'Neill, J., Birks, S., Church, J., & Rawlins, P. (2013). *The assessment of teacher quality: An investigation into current issues in evaluating and rewarding teachers*. Retrieved from http://papers.ssrn.com/abstract=2326315

Stovall, D. (2006). We can relate: Hip-hop culture, critical pedagogy, and the secondary classroom. *Urban Education, 41*(6), 585–602.

Thrupp, M., & White, M. (2013). *Final report: National standards and the damage done*. Research, Analysis and Insight into National Standards (RAINS) Project. Report commissioned by The New Zealand Educational Institute Te Riu Roa (NZEI).

Tomlins-Jahnke, H. (2008). The place of Cultural Standards in Indigenous Education. *MAI Review*, (1). Retrieved from http://www.review.mai.ac.nz/

Tuck, E. (2013). Neoliberalism as nihilism? A commentary on educational accountability, teacher education, and school reform. *Journal For Critical Education Policy Studies (JCEPS), 11*(2), 324–347.

Urrieta, L. (2010). *Working from within: Chicana and Chicano activist educators in Whitestream schools* (Vol. 6). Arizona: University of Arizona Press.

Waru-Waahi, W. (2015) Valedictory Speech. Kia Aroha College Celebration Day, Auckland, New Zealand.

· 2 ·

NAMING THE WHITE SPACES

Naming the White spaces in our schools is important in progressing understanding of the realities for students of color. Fitzsimons and Smith (2000) explain the importance of naming from a Māori perspective:

> Since naming the world is an exercise in power relations, interpretation by Māori is an exercise of power. For Māori … partnership in terms of the Treaty of Waitangi implies power sharing and involvement at all levels of policy development, application and evaluation (that is, to also reserve the right to determine what counts as success). The control of the evaluation and assessment factors to evaluate services for Māori is critical; it is a means for Māori to name their world. Naming is employed in the sense of using language to control conditions of existence through cultural definitions of the world. (p. 39)

Gillborn (2005) uses this quote from bell hooks (1989) to illustrate his gradual realisation of the role of education policy in the active structuring of racial inequity:

> As I write, I try to remember when the word racism ceased to be the term which best expressed for me exploitation of black people and other people of color in this society and when I began to understand that the most useful term was white supremacy. (hooks, 1989, p. 112)

Gillborn (2005) points out that a critique of Whiteness is "not an assault on white people per se," rather it is an assault on the socially constructed power of White interests and the constant reinforcement of these. He believes that, "it is possible for white people to take a real and active role in deconstructing whiteness but such 'race traitors' are relatively uncommon" (p. 488).

However, while agreeing that "race treason" is a definite choice for many White people, Leonardo (2005, p. 37) explains that, without accompanying structural changes even those Whites who do reject and work against White privilege still benefit from that privilege. He uses the analogy of Scheurich (1998) that "being white is akin to walking down the street with money being put in your pant pocket without your knowledge." This is a difficult concept to grasp for those who have grown up without ever needing to question their own Whiteness. McIntosh (1988) powerfully explains this in her long list of ways in which, "I enjoy unearned skin privilege and have been conditioned into oblivion about its existence, unable to see that it put me 'ahead' in any way, or put my people ahead." Leonardo (2009) argues that while some White subgroups (White women, poor Whites, gay and lesbian Whites) do not benefit equally from social relations, *all Whites benefit equally from race and racism* (p. 242).

Akom (2006) observes that many of the leading theories of social capital are silent on the issue of race, and ignore the contribution by young people in poor communities to a wide range of social networks, which "often exist as a way for youth to learn how to resist and cope with persistent racial marginalization." He calls for a new model of social capital that pays careful attention to race, racism, and the processes of racialization, identity-based frameworks; context dependency; and the issues of power:

> We have to move to the point where the very act of naming and mapping processes of racial subordination is not particularly radical or activist, but rather, part of a collective, normalized goal of worldwide black emancipation. I am hopeful. (p. 90)

Whiteness

This hidden, and unacknowledged nature of Whiteness and power is a fundamental cause of our apparent inability to make change in our schools that will benefit children of color. Only by naming race, and placing it at the center of the debate can we begin to challenge structures and institutions, and our own individual positions to combat inequality and injustice, "inherited from the past and continually reproduced in the present" (Apple, 2006, p. 234).

Those who are members of the dominant and powerful group in any society have choices about how they, as individual members of that group, behave. Tatum (2003) likens these choices about racism to a moving walkway at an airport. Active, racist behavior is the same as walking fast in the same direction as the conveyor belt. This person has identified with the ideology of White supremacy and is actively moving with it. Passive racist behavior is the same as standing still. Through absolutely no deliberate effort of your own you are still moved along without resistance to the same destination as those who actively walk. Some might recognize racism and turn their backs, not prepared to go in the same direction as those supporting or passively accepting it and not wanting to end up in the same place—but unless you are prepared to actively walk in the opposite direction, at a pace faster than the conveyor belt—unless you are actively antiracist—you will still inevitably be carried along with the others (pp. 11–12).

The common threads running through these different perspectives are the issue of power, the ideology of cultural superiority and the politics of knowledge. A Māori perspective is strongly articulated by Smith (1999) who states, "The nexus between cultural ways of knowing, scientific discoveries, economic impulses, and imperial power enabled the West to make ideological claims to having a superior civilisation" (p. 1). She believes that the major agency for "imposing this positional superiority over knowledge, language and culture in New Zealand was colonial education" (p. 64).

One example of New Zealand's reluctance to discuss Whiteness as problematic in education is inherent in the Ministry of Education's report, *Quality Teaching for Diverse Students in Schooling: Best Evidence Synthesis* [BES] (Alton-Lee, 2003). This report is one of a series commissioned by the Ministry of Education, intended to inform education policy and practice in New Zealand. Dimensions of "diversity" in this synthesis of evidence and best practice include, "ethnicity, socio-economic background, home language, gender, special needs, disability, and giftedness." Also included in the definition is diversity within ethnic groups and, "the diversity within individual students influenced by intersections of gender, cultural heritage(s), socio-economic background, and talent" (p. v). This definition of diversity together with the overall focus of the BES on quality teaching certainly does not put culture at the center of best practice, or give it any primacy. Although there are many references to cultural identity and to research that make cultural norms explicit (Durie, 2001; Hohepa, Smith, & McNaughton, 1992) the *Best Evidence Synthesis* does little to specifically name the inherent Eurocentrism of our education system and does little to challenge Pākehā teachers, searching for best practice examples, to address power relations in their classrooms. One of the nine characteristics of quality teaching identified in the *Best Evidence Synthesis* is that "the teacher leads in representing 'us' as everyone in our class community." The BES points out that New Zealand teachers need a "we" that is inclusive of the ethnicities and ethnic heritages which are part of each particular class community (p. 26). However, as Sleeter (2008) points out, "White teachers are often unaware of their own positioning and Whiteness" (p. 82). Gillborn reinforces this reality:

> One of the most powerful and dangerous aspects of whiteness is that many (possibly the majority) of white people have no awareness of whiteness as a construction, let alone their own role in sustaining and playing out the inequities at the heart of whiteness. (p. 490)

Privilege and Supremacy

Studies of Whiteness (Fine, 2004; Leonardo, 2005, 2009; McIntosh, 1988; McLaren, 2003; Sleeter, 2008) generally describe White privilege as the benefits and rights those who are White accrue without any deliberate effort on their part. Leonardo (2005) supports McIntosh's assertion that coming to terms with this unearned White privilege is "not about blame, shame or guilt." He argues however, that although this White racial domination precedes us, it is daily recreated by Whites on both the individual and institutional level. Leonardo believes:

> White domination is constantly re-established and reconstructed by whites *from all walks of life* ... it is not solely the domain of white supremacist groups. It is rather the domain of average, tolerant people, of lovers of diversity, and of believers in justice. (p. 43)

Leonardo (2002) differentiates between "Whiteness," a racial discourse, and "White people, a socially constructed identity, usually based on skin color" (p. 31). He identifies some of some of the strategies characteristics of whiteness as: an unwillingness to name the contours of racism, the avoidance of identifying with a racial experience or group, and the minimization of racist legacy (p. 32). Steinberg and Kincheloe (2001) explain that the power of White supremacy lies in its ability to erase itself, resulting in what they describe as "white nothingness" that is "one of the most powerful nothings we can conjure" (p. 17). This invisible but all-powerful Whiteness creates White spaces in classrooms when teachers are reluctant to discuss or are oblivious to Whiteness and where, to change this situation, "the white power of nothingness must no longer be allowed to tacitly shape the knowledge production and the academic canon of White schooling" (p. 18). As bell hooks (1989) explains:

> When liberal whites fail to understand how they can and/or do embody white-supremacist values and beliefs even though they may not embrace racism as prejudice or domination (especially domination that involves coercive control), they cannot recognize the ways their actions support and affirm the very structure of racist domination and oppression that they profess to wish to see eradicated. (p. 113)

Bourdieu and Passeron (1977) use the term "symbolic violence" to describe the "subtle process whereby subordinate classes come to take as natural or "common sense" ideas and practices that are actually against their own best interests." Because schools reflect the knowledge and values of the economically and culturally dominant groups in society they validate and reproduce the "cultural capital" that students from those groups bring from home. Symbolic violence is perpetuated through the overt and covert curriculum and the practice in schools that represent the dominant group's value systems and norms (Macedo, 1995; McLaren, 2003; Nieto, 2002). Schools devalue the cultural capital of students who occupy the subordinate class and cultural positions. McLaren states that low academic performance of students in this position does not represent a lack of ability or competence but is, "the result of the school's depreciation of their cultural capital" (p. 94). Gillborn (2005) names education policy itself as an act of White supremacy:

> This critical perspective is based on the recognition that race inequity and racism are central features of the education system. These are not aberrant nor accidental phenomena that will be ironed out in time, they are fundamental characteristics of the system. *It is in this sense that education policy is an act of white supremacy.* (pp. 497–498)

The Curriculum as a White Space: The Politics of Knowledge

If the implementation of a mandated or national curriculum or standards in Whitestream schools is going to effectively support the development of indigenous and minoritized students' cultural identity, the challenge is not only about increasing the levels or numbers of language learning opportunities. The challenge is also about how to support teachers, not to just rethink their classroom practice in terms of curriculum delivery, but to examine fundamentally the White space ideology that drives the development of the curriculum and identify their own personal viewpoints within that paradigm (Helfand, 2009; Kincheloe & Hayes, 2007; Sleeter, 2001). As Apple (1993) explains, "One thing is perfectly clear. The national curriculum is a mechanism for the political control of knowledge" (p. 234):

> What *counts* as knowledge, the ways in which it is organized, who is empowered to teach it, what counts as an appropriate display of having learned it, and—just as critically—who is allowed to ask and answer all of these questions are part and parcel of how dominance and subordination are reproduced and altered in this society. There is, then, always a *politics* of official knowledge, a politics that embodies conflict over what some regard as simply neutral descriptions of the world and others regard as elite conceptions that empower some groups while disempowering others. (p. 222)

Apple (2004) urges us to be aware of the origins and the history of the curriculum field and to understand that "the knowledge that got into schools in the past and gets into schools now is not random" (p. 60). Rather, it is organized around a set of values and principles that represent particular views of normality and deviance and of what "good people act like." If you ask, "What if existing social and economic arrangements *require* that some people are relatively poor and unskilled and others are not," then, you can begin to understand how schools may help to maintain this set of arrangements. Schools typically preserve and distribute what is perceived to be "legitimate knowledge" and confer "cultural legitimacy on the knowledge of specific groups" (p. 61). This is an exercise in power. Apple believes that if we examine current curriculum, and what counts as knowledge now, through its historical context, the ideological and economic purpose schools have served in the past, we can comprehend why school reform now is often unsuccessful.

As well as combating the effects of this ideology in the overt curriculum, we have to be aware of the covert or hidden curriculum at work in daily school practice. Darder (1995) describes this as "curriculum that is informed by ideological views that silence students and structurally reproduce the dominant society's assumptions and practices" (p. 331). She speaks of the persistent failure of schools to recognize the importance of cultural identity and "to make explicit the power relations and elitist interests which shape institutional life (including schools)" (p. 335). These hegemonic "rules of the game" represent an overwhelming White space that Māori and Pasifika learners struggle with every day, resulting in what Darder describes as, "a subordination of identity, consciousness and voice, carried out in part by the best intentioned and well-meaning teachers and educational leaders of our time" (p. 335).

Literacy as a White Space

The domain of literacy provides a good example of the impact of schooling on cultural identity and cultural capital when seen through a critical lens. No one would dispute that children need to be able to read and write well. Competence in literacy and numeracy are the primary goals of our education systems and the specific focus of the plethora of schooling improvement solutions implemented in schools in low socio-economic communities in New Zealand and internationally. However, in our determination to remedy the reading and writing "deficits" of young people in these communities, in ways reminiscent of the historical practices of punishing Māori children for their use of Māori language at school, few schools consider there may be a counter-narrative to the literacy percentage increases they proudly celebrate and publish.

Linda Smith (1999) directly implicates schools in the redefinition of indigenous worlds, and discusses the dangers implicit in reading and writing. She cites esteemed Māori author, Patricia Grace's (1985) assertion that "books are dangerous" to indigenous readers when:

> (1) they do not reinforce our values, actions, customs, culture and identity; (2) when they tell us only about others they are saying that we do not exist; (3) they may be writing about us but they are writing things that are untrue; and (4) they are writing about us but saying negative and insensitive things which tell us we are not good. (Smith, 1999, p. 35)

Grace is specifically referring to school texts and journals. McLachlan's (1996) analysis of 12,526 illustrations used in New Zealand state-produced beginning reader publications over a span of 89 years showed that, "Māori presence has been largely relegated to the past and with few exceptions unacknowledged in the present" (p. 128). The tendency in later years was the use of color as the single determining ethnic characteristic. This use of "dubious brown" (p. 103) without any other distinguishing features failed to differentiate Māori from any other ethnic group, thus making Māori identity largely invisible in texts that were widely used in schools and sent home with young children.

Writing can be dangerous, according to Smith (1999), because "we reinforce and maintain a style of discourse that is never innocent." She refers to the misappropriation of texts and the legitimization of texts, in academic, journalistic and imaginative writing that reinforce "myths" that are hostile to indigenous peoples (p. 36). Macedo (1995) also discusses this danger. He analyses the role of literacy in cultural reproduction and critiques the instrumentalist approach to literacy that reduces it to a "competency-based skills banking approach" (p. 77). He asserts that this notion of literacy is a major and popular goal of the recurring "back to basics" drive in our education systems. In this model the rewards go to the "good student" who may be a functionally competent reader but who passively receives information, and is rarely taught the skills to critically analyze "the social and political order that generates the need for reading in the first place" (p. 80). Students can be functionally literate but never learn to question the "racist and discriminatory practices that they face in school and the community at large."

Critical and New Media Literacies

Critical literacy, particularly critical media literacy, challenges this instrumentalist approach to literacy (Blackburn & Clark, 2007; Duncan-Andrade & Morrell, 2008; Lea & Sims, 2008; Morrell, 2007). Duncan-Andrade (2006) explains the high use of electronic media by youth and the need for a critical media literacy pedagogy, "that empowers urban youth to deconstruct dominant media narratives, to develop much-needed academic and cultural literacies, and to create their own counternarratives to those of the media, which largely are negative depictions of urban youth and their communities" (p. 149).

This high use of digital media by youth in the United States is consistent with New Zealand findings. A report jointly commissioned by the Ministry for Culture and Heritage and Te Puni Kōkiri in 2009 (Fryer, Kalafatelis, & Palmer, 2009, p.24) sampled 1,827 people aged 15 years and older. The report found that young people and Māori are two population groups who are heavy and extensive users of electronic media devices.

"I" for Identity

However, how often do we question this extensive use? We live in the world of the intensely market-driven lower case "i". Since the launch in 1998 of the "iMac", Apple Inc. has spawned a plethora of lower-case "i" devices and programmes. Even "non-i" users, like me, cannot help but be surrounded by fervent disciples of the iPhone, iPad, iPod, IMovie and iTunes. And I am not altogether immune. The model of the car I drive is the i30. What do these mean?

According to Jobs (1998), the "i" signified "the marriage of the excitement of the internet, with the simplicity of Macintosh," so the "i" stands for internet then? Jobs suggests, in the same speech, that the "i" could also stand for individual, instruct, inform, and inspire. According to the vice president of Hyundai Europe (Stein, 2007), the "i" in my i30, and their other "i" models, stands for inspiration and innovation. That is a lot to ask of one small letter!

Whatever the "i" signifies, which it seems can be anything you want it to be, there is no denying that it is pervasive. The small "i" is also insidious. It crept into our vocabulary, into our homes, our pockets and our handbags, and spun off into other products. The small "i" typifies many other takeovers, which marginalize or replace what we valued before, and become our new way of thinking. The question is, as these devices, and this language have become ubiquitous in our schools as essential tools to equip our children for the future, what has happened to the upper case "I"? Where am "I"? Where is the crucially important "I" for Identity? Where is Indigeneity? (Milne, 2016).

A 2011 policy brief to the UNESCO Institute for Information Technologies in Education (IITE) (Resta, 2011) identifies this issue and critiques the "long legacy of educational policies in colonized countries that have been significant factors in the erosion of indigenous language and culture" (p. 3). The report describes information technology and digital learning as a "two-edged sword" with the potential to exacerbate the erosion of indigenous and cultural knowledge, or the potential to empower and support the creation of new culturally responsive learning resources and environments for indigenous children. The report implicates information and communications technology (ICT) and its "unforeseen and unwanted consequences" in the erosion of indigenous cultures. Specifically, it identifies the influence of ICTs to "reinforce and accelerate the dominance of Western-based modes of thought, culture, and learning strategies":

> Media such as television, radio, films, and computer games have resulted in massive and continuous exposure of many indigenous youth to non-indigenous cultural values and information with few opportunities for reinforcement of their own cultural heritage and language. As a result, "After hundreds or thousands of years of development and evolution, we are facing the disappearance of unique human cultures and their intellectual heritages." (p. 4)

On the other side of the "sword" is the potential for ICTs, "when appropriate and under control of indigenous peoples," can be used to revitalize language and cultural traditions. The Waikato Tainui's *Tikanga Ora Reo Ora* strategy, described later in this chapter is one such example. The crucial point is the issue of who has control.

Ess (2004) challenges the cultural neutrality of computer-mediated communication (CMC) that "carry and further a specific set of cultural values and communicative preferences—ones that, far from being universally shared, are indeed limited to specific cultural domains," and describes this embedding and fostering of specific cultural values and communicative preferences as powerfully aiding and abetting a form of "computer-mediated colonization," which threatens to override and replace indigenous values and preferences. The threat to indigenous identities is obvious.

Māori/Tongan researcher Wolfgramm (2014) observes that in Indigenous worldviews all technology is information technology. She calls for a reclaiming of "technological sovereignty," which she defines as, "having the freedom, resources, ability and capacity to create, generate, design, develop, produce, and distribute one's own technologies and tools that express and support one's values, culture, and language, worldview and knowledge systems" (p. 5). Wolfgramm makes the indigenous perspective clear, explaining that, "We do not own knowledge; we are knowledge holders. Knowledge transfer in Indigenous culture reflects ecologies of relationships, appropriate to the space and place" (p. 2). She too raises the issue of technology and language in a globalized and connected world:

> For millions of Indigenous people, loss of their languages has meant a continuing struggle to keep their sense, understanding and knowing of themselves as individuals, families, communities and cultures, alive. Many of these are the languages of Indigenous peoples, including Māori, who struggle to keep their culture alive. Even as the world has become increasingly "globalised" and "connected", a significant number of people have become more isolated and disconnected from their cultural and linguistic roots.

Wolfgramm was a participant at a gathering in New Mexico in 2007, which brought together Polynesian, Lakota, Navajo, Cherokee, Tuscarora, Japanese-American and Euro-American scholars, computer scientists, artists and educators, to specifically ask the question: "Is it possible to develop Information Technology that reflects Indigenous Consciousness?" The gathering raised the issues of the responsibility of knowledge holders, protocols for the passing and preservation of knowledge and the ethical space in which the knowledge, the knowledge holder, and the learner live. They concluded that there is a "serious challenge of the cultural disconnect between Native and Western learning processes, values and traditions and the critical need for equitable, productive, co-existence between the world views" (Native Science Academy, 2007). This challenge was also recognized at The World Summit on the Information Society in 2011:

> Article 15 of the WSIS Declaration of The World Summit on the Information Society states "In the evolution of the Information Society, particular attention must be given to the special situation of indigenous peoples, as well as to the preservation of their heritage and their cultural legacy." (Resta, 2011)

Kamira (2003) suggests a wider definition of technology, expanding it to any means of storing or analyzing and disseminating information, including Māori concepts such as "matauranga" (education and intuitive intelligence) and "hinengaro" (the mind) (p. 4). She warns that if the colonizer has control of information technology, and is in a position to validate, discard or modify knowledge, then information technology becomes a tool for further colonization. This is even more dangerous when the "face of the colonizer" is not as visible, as is the case with information technology. This makes the issue of indigenous control vitally important.

How well is this issue understood in schools' ICT White spaces? In their comprehensive report to the Ministry of Education on future-oriented learning and teaching in New Zealand, Bolstad et al. (2012) provide a definition of "equity" which, is no longer seen as "sameness" (p. 18). They observe that, although many people believe that new technologies are synonymous with future-oriented education, research in schools suggests new technologies only enable transformation when they are supported by ideas and social contexts that enable transformative practice (p. 55). Rather than simply focusing on connecting schools to technology they advocate that we need "to take much more account of who learners are, where they are and to what and to whom they are connected, at all levels from the local to the global" (p. 26). They put forward three key ideas: "diversity," "connectedness" and "coherence" to structure the thinking that will be needed to develop a response to the question of how we can rebuild our education system for the 21st century. They believe we need to "join up" the thinking of the disparate parts of our system, rather than focus on the parts themselves, to develop shared ideas about future learning (p. 6). These views show that it is not simply a matter of improved access, or more technology or devices. As Kucukaydin and Tisdell (2008) point out, increased access to technology cannot cure historically embedded social ills such as racism, classism, injustice, inequality, and discrimination.

An example of Māori taking control over technology for their own purposes and for the preservation of cultural resources is Waikato Tainui's *Tikanga Ora Reo Ora* strategy, launched in February, 2016. The iwi (tribe) is counting on technology to help "revitalize tribal reo and tikanga" (tribal dialect and custom) to realize its dream of having 80% of its 70,000 people fluent in te reo Māori (Māori language) by 2050 (Waikato Tainui, 2016). The strategy states that the language will be made more visible through websites, Facebook and Te Hookioi (the tribal magazine, available online), and will be made more accessible via the radio (p. 10). Online learning tools include a New Zealand Qualifications Authority accredited Te Reo Māori program, and a professional development program for reo Māori teachers. A target for this strategy is to reach Waikato Tainui members who live in Australia and abroad, so the online aspect of the program is crucial. The tribe is calling on all its stakeholder groups, including tribal members, central government, the Māori Language Commission, tertiary providers and schools to support this direction. The strategy is seen as an investment into the economic and educational future of the iwi's youth (Radio Waatea, 2016).

Otara: Where Ancient and New Technologies Meet

Kia Aroha College's response to the colonizing influence of information technology has been the joint development of an after-school program as a partner in the High Tech Youth Network (HTYN). One of the core goals of HTYN is to encourage the development of a positive identity and belief in their potential, through linking cultural knowledges and values with technology. Studio 274, the lead studio in HTYN, is located on the Kia Aroha College campus. Proudly named with the prefix for telephone numbers in the Otara community, a number other communities actively try to avoid, Studio 274 is a connected learning and development network of affiliated High Tech Youth Studios focused on empowering young people aged 8–25 years to become more confident, resilient and creative life-long learners by linking cultural knowledge with advanced technology.

In a book about Studio 274 (Hancock & HTYN Contributors, 2015), the HTYN Trust Chairperson describes the story of Studio 274 as one with many strands and he talks in particular of the convergence of two main strands: "the whakapapa (genealogy) of High Tech Youth Network and the whakapapa of Kia Aroha College. We need to acknowledge these two strands equally because both are of equal importance. Both strands weave people and ideas into our story" (p. 46). Many other connections also add to the Studio 274 journey and its effectiveness, most importantly, the Studio staff, philanthropic benefactors, funders, and members, who now include youth from many other schools as well as Kia Aroha College. The achievements of Studio 274 could not be reality without the contribution and support of all of these stakeholders. However, as the HTYN Trust Chair explains in the opening pages of the book:

> This is the story about a predominantly Māori and Pasifika community in urban Aotearoa New Zealand where young people, their families and a school community chose to create a different tomorrow. It is a story of convergence; of restored memory of cultural tradition, values and beliefs, appropriate knowledge, information and technology, applied wisdom and spirituality. It is the story of Otara: where ancient and new technologies meet. (Chapman, in Hancock & HTYN Contributors, 2015, p. 5)

School Alienation, "Gaps" and Poverty

Programs such as the Waikato Tainui Strategy, and partnerships between other tribal areas and their local schools have a powerful potential to influence the endemic White spaces in our education system. However, these strategies will require the education system to relinquish its single-minded hegemonic hold on what counts as success and achievement, and require iwi groups to clearly define what "as Māori" or "as Waikato Tainui," for example, looks like for them. Without this understanding schools will default to the comfort zone that is their White space.

The alienation of Māori and Pasifika learners from school is not just an intermediate/middle or secondary school phenomena. Disengagement and dislocation from their cultural identity begins when children enter our schools' White spaces. Just because it takes some years for the impact of this dislocation to manifest itself does not absolve primary/elementary schools from their responsibility to respond differently. Nor is school alienation due solely to socio-economic status or poverty, although this is a contributing factor. The debilitating effects of poverty need to be put in context of the root causes of inequality, rather than attributed to individual and/or group pathologies (Ginwright & Cammarota, 2002, p. 82). Ginwright (2010) suggests that instead of asking, "What does this student need to academically succeed?" the question should be, "How can we eliminate inequities in the distribution of resources and power that shape academic outcomes?"

Yang (2009) points out that "the achievement gap is a mirror image to the punishment gap." He believes these are more aptly described as the "*exclusion rate*—the rate by which students are removed from the classroom—and the *inclusion rate*—the rate by which students matriculate to higher education" (p. 51). Yang states these rates should be key indicators in the assessment of overall school climate.

Kohn (2011) argues that demands to focus on closing the achievement gap and a single-minded focus on "raising the bar" serves to push low-income youth out of school and to develop curriculum and practice in which the emphasis is on "succeeding" rather than the questioning, arguing, collaborating more common in more affluent schools. This type of teaching has been called a "pedagogy of poverty" (Haberman, 2010)—the "'gold standard' for the way you are *supposed* to teach kids of color" (Kohn, 2011). Thus students living in poverty are exposed to a double dose of deprivation by virtue of poor teaching, teaching to the standards of imposed national expectations that lack depth and relevance and the capacity to engage students:

> Standardized exams serve mostly to make dreadful forms of teaching appear successful. As long as they remain our primary way of evaluating, we may never see real school reform—only an intensification of traditional practices, with the very worst reserved for the disadvantaged. (Kohn, 2011)

Bishop, Berryman, Cavanagh, and Teddy (2009, p. 736) agree that it is teachers who have the capacity to change the educational outcomes of Māori students. Hattie (2003) used reading results to confirm that the disparity between Māori and Pākehā learners was constant regardless of the socio-economic status (SES) of the schools they attended. He concluded that it is not socio-economic differences that have the greatest impact upon Māori student achievement and suggests that it is cultural and teacher/student relationships that make a difference (p. 7).

Is it poverty, or isn't it poverty? That's the question we seem to go back and forth about in New Zealand. Linda Smith (2013) sums up the popular discourse when she says, "'We' don't like to talk about it, or 'we' don't want to be told about it, or 'we' don't want to be reminded of it. In other words, poverty as described by the 'activists' doesn't exist" (p. 229). This also sums up our education system's "head in the sand" approach to the impact of poverty on the children we have marginalized and then failed to deliver equitable outcomes to.

The Kia Aroha College journey began in the 1990s, when the "blame the victim" view of the socio-economic status of Māori was the prevalent mindset. On one side of our thinking was the idea that if we accepted low socio-economic status (SES) as a reason for poor outcomes we ran the risk of accepting that the problem was too big for us, in our one school, to solve, so we could give ourselves a convenient excuse for not making much difference. That rationale totally rejected the low SES argument as a reason for poor achievement.

On the other side, the realities of poverty smacked us in the face at school every day, and challenged us to try harder. That choice was tempered with the sure knowledge that if we did manage to do better we gave the government of the day further excuses for denial of the urgent need for more funding, and better and different resourcing. After all, if a school could make a difference with limited resources, why provide more? Lurking in the background of both sides of this dilemma was our growing realization of what Thrupp (2007) calls education's "inconvenient truth," that schools, intentionally and unintentionally, reproduce the status quo of "persistent middle class advantage" (p. 254).[1]

To change the learning experiences and outcomes of children of color in our education systems we have to name the White spaces in our schools. We have to have to talk about White privilege and White supremacy without taking these terms personally. We have to ask the hard questions about the purpose of schools, whose knowledge counts, who decides on the norms we expect our youth to strive to achieve, who decides on literacy and numeracy as the holy grail and almost sole indicator of achievement and success? We have to understand the importance of relationships and the power of whānau. We have to name racism, prejudice, stereotyping, deficit thinking, policy and decision-making, power, curriculum, funding, community, school structure, timetabling, choice, equity instead of equality, enrolment procedures, disciplinary processes, poverty, and social justice. We have to reject framing culture as problematic and stop negating cultural identity within assimilationist terms such as multiculturalism and diversity. We have to challenge Eurocentric solutions that perpetuate the myth that "White is right," and that come from the perspective Stovall (2006) calls, "giving those poor people of color what they so desperately need" (p. 108).

Identity however is never a simple White/non-White binary. Coloring in the White spaces also requires us to look at the many shifting and changing identities young people must negotiate in our schools and in society if they are to navigate the White spaces successfully. The next chapter further examines the concept of cultural identity.

Note

1. The preceding four paragraphs are reproduced from: Milne, A. (2014). Colouring in the white spaces. In V. Carpenter & S. Osborne (Eds.), *Twelve thousand hours: Education and poverty in Aotearoa New Zealand* (pp. 223–230). Auckland: Dunmore. Reprinted by permission of the publisher. All rights reserved.

References

Akom, A. (2006). The racial dimensions of social capital: Toward a new understanding of youth empowerment and community organizing in America's urban core. In P. Noguera, S. A. Ginwright, & J. Cammarota (Eds.), *Beyond resistance! Youth activism and community change: New democratic possibilities for practice and policy for America's youth* (pp. 81–90). New York, NY: Routledge.

Alton-Lee, A. (2003). *Quality teaching for diverse students in schooling: Best evidence synthesis.* Wellington: Ministry of Education.

Apple, M. W. (1993). The politics of official knowledge: Does a national curriculum make sense? *Discourse: Studies in the Cultural Politics of Education, 14*(2), 1–16. http://doi.org/10.1080/0159630930140101

Apple, M. W. (2004). *Ideology and curriculum* (3rd ed.). New York, NY and London: Routledge Falmer.

Apple, M. W. (2006). *Educating the "right" way.* New York, NY: Routledge.

Bishop, R., Berryman, M., Cavanagh, T., & Teddy, L. (2009). Te Kotahitanga: Addressing educational disparities facing Māori students in New Zealand. *Teaching and Teacher Education, 25*(5), 734–742. http://doi.org/10.1016/j.tate.2009.01.009

Blackburn, M. V., & Clark, C. T. (2007). *Literacy research for political action and social change.* New York, NY: Peter Lang.

Bolstad, R., Gilbert, J., McDowall, S., Bull, A., Boyd, S., & Hipkins, R. (2012). *Supporting future-oriented learning & teaching—a New Zealand perspective.* Retrieved from https://www.educationcounts.govt.nz/__data/assets/pdf_file/0003/109317/994_Future-oriented-07062012.pdf

Bourdieu, P., & Passeron, J. (1977). *Reproduction in education, society and culture.* London: Sage Publications.

Darder, A. (1995). Buscando America: The contributions of critical Latino educators to the academic development and empowerment of Latino students in the U.S. In C. Sleeter & P. McLaren (Eds.), *Multicultural education, critical pedagogy, and the politics of difference* (pp. 319–348). Albany, NY: State University of New York Press.

Duncan-Andrade, J. (2006). Urban youth, media literacy, and increased civic participation. In P. Noguera, S. Ginwrigh, & J. Cammarota (Eds.), *Beyond Resistance! Youth Activism and Community Change* (pp.149–170). New York, NY: Routledge.

Duncan-Andrade, J., & Morrell, E. (2008). *The art of critical pedagogy : Possibilities for moving from theory to practice in urban schools*. New York, NY: Peter Lang.

Durie, M. (2001). *A framework for considering Maori educational advancement*. Paper presented at the Hui Taumata Matauranga II (Māori Education Summit). Turangi, Taupo, New Zealand.

Ess, C. (2004). *Questioning the obvious? Ethical and cultural dimensions of CMC and ICTs*. Springfield, MO: Drury University. Retrieved from http://funredesw.org/LC/documentos/Questioning_the_obvious.pdf

Fine, M. (2004). Witnessing whiteness/gathering intelligence. In M. Fine, L. Weis, L. P. Pruitt, & A. Burns (Eds.), *Off white: Readings on power, privilege, and resistance* (Vol. 12, pp. 245–256). New York, NY and London: Routledge.

Fitzsimons, P., & Smith, G. (2000). Philosophy and indigenous cultural transformation. *Educational Philosophy & Theory, 32*(1), 25–41.

Fryer, K., Kalafatelis, E., & Palmer, S. (2009). *New Zealanders' Use of Broadcasting and Related Media. Final Report*. Ministry for Culture and Heritage and Te Puni Kokiri. Wellington: New Zealand Government.

Gillborn, D. (2005). Education policy as an act of white supremacy: Whiteness, critical race theory and education reform. *Journal of Education Policy, 20*(4), 485–505.

Ginwright, S. (2010). Addressing root causes of health disparities: Promoting positive health & academic achievement among youth. In *Strengthening our practice: Refining our aim*. Keynote address. San Francisco, CA: National Professional Development (NPD) Conference.

Ginwright, S., & Cammarota, J. (2002). New terrain in youth development: The promise of a social justice approach. *Social Justice, 29*(4), 82–95.

Grace, P. (1985). *Books are dangerous*. Paper presented at the Fourth Early Childhood Convention, Wellington.

Haberman, M. (2010). The pedagogy of poverty versus good teaching (revisited). *Phi Delta Kappan, 92*(2), 81–87.

Hancock & HTYN Contributors. (2015). *Otara: where ancient and new technologies meet*. Otara: High Tech Youth Network.

Hattie, J. (2003). *New Zealand education snapshot: With specific reference to yrs 1–13*. Paper presented at Knowledge Wave 2003—The Leadership Forum. University of Auckland, Auckland.

Helfand, J. (2009). Teaching outside whiteness. In S. Steinberg (Ed.), *Diversity and multiculturalism* (pp. 77–96). New York, NY: Peter Lang.

Hohepa, M., Smith, L., & McNaughton, S. (1992). Te Kohanga Reo Hei Tikanga Ako i te Reo Maori: Te Kohanga Reo as a context for language learning. *Educational Psychology: An International Journal of Experimental Educational Psychology, 12*(3–4), 333–346.

hooks, B. (1989). *Talking back: Thinking feminist. Thinking black*. Boston, MA: South End Press.

Jobs, S. (1998). *Back on track*. Apple Special Event. USA: YouTube. Retrieved from https://www.youtube.com/watch?v=oxwmF0OJ0vg

Kamira, R. (2003). Te Mata o te Tai—The Edge of the Tide: Rising capacity in information technology of Maori in Aotearoa. *The Electronic Library 21*(5), 465–475 (2003).Kincheloe, J., & Hayes, K. (2007). *Teaching city kids*. New York, NY: Peter Lang.

Kohn, A. (2011). Poor teaching for poor children ... in the name of reform. *Education week*. Retrieved from http://www.alfiekohn.org/article/poor/

Kucukaydin, I., & Tisdell, E. (2008). The discourse on the digital divide: Are we being co-opted? *InterActions: UCLA Journal of Education and Information Studies, 4*(1). Retrieved from http://www.escholarship.org/uc/item/85m2z8j2

Lea, V., & Sims, E. J. (2008). *Undoing whiteness in the classroom: Critical educultural teaching approaches for social justice activism*. New York, NY: Peter Lang.

Leonardo, Z. (2002). The souls of White Folk: Critical pedagogy, whiteness studies, and globalization discourse. *Race Ethnicity and Education, 5*(1), 29–50. http://doi.org/10.1080/13613320120117180

Leonardo, Z. (2005). *Critical pedagogy and race*. Malden, MA and Oxford: Blackwell.

Leonardo, Z. (2009). Reading whiteness: Antiracist pedagogy against white racial knowledge. In W. C. Ayers, T. Quinn, & D. Stovall (Eds.), *Handbook of social justice in education* (pp. 231–248). New York, NY: Routledge.

Macedo, D. (1995). Literacy for stupidification: The pedagogy of big lies. In C. Sleeter & P. McLaren (Eds.), *Multicultural education, critical pedagogy, and the politics of difference* (pp. 71–104). Albany, NY: State University of New York Press.

McIntosh, P. (1988). *White privilege and male privilege: A personal account of coming to see correspondences through work in women's studies* (No. 189). Wellesley, MA: Wellesley College Center for Research on Women.

McLachlan, S. (1996). *The power of visual language: Māori in illustration in beginning readers* (Unpublished master's thesis). University of Auckland, Auckland.

McLaren, P. (2003). Critical pedagogy: A look at the major concepts. In A. Darder, M. Baltodano, & R. Torres (Eds.), *The critical pedagogy reader* (pp. 69–96). New York, NY: Routledge.

Milne, A. (2016). Where am I in our schools' White spaces? Social justice for the learners we marginalise. *Middle Grades Review, 1*(3). Retrieved from http://scholarworks.uvm.edu/mgreview/vol1/iss3/2

Morrell, E. (2007). Critical literacy and popular culture in urban education: Toward a pedagogy of access and dissent. In M. Blackburn & C. Clark (Eds.), *Literacy research for political action and social change* (pp. 235–254). New York, NY: Peter Lang.

Native Science Academy. (2007). *Is it possible to have Information Technology that reflects Indigenous Consciousness?* Learning Encampment in Chaco Canyon, Santa Fe, New Mexico. Retrieved from http://planetmaori.com/Files/Content/2014/IT4IndigenousConsciousness.pdf

Nieto, S. (2002). *Language, culture, and teaching*. Mahwah, NY: L. Erlbaum.

Radio Waatea. (2016). Technology to drive Tainui reo in Oz. *Interview with Rahui Papa*. Retrieved from http://www.waateanews.com/Waatea+News.html?story_id=MTI5MDM=&v=827#.VsV5IVyGlnx.mailto

Resta, P. (2011). *ICTs and indigenous people*. Moscow: UNESCO Institute for Information Technologies in Education. Retrieved from http://iite.unesco.org/files/policy_briefs/pdf/en/indigenous_people.pdf

Scheurich, J. (1998). Highly successful and loving, public elementary schools populated mainly by low-SES children of color: Core beliefs and cultural characteristics. *Urban Education, 33*(4), 451–491.

Sleeter, C. (2001). Preparing teachers for culturally diverse schools. *Journal of Teacher Education, 52*(2), 94–106.

Sleeter, C. (2008). Learning to become a racially and culturally competent ally. In K. Teel & J. Obidah (Eds.), *Building racial and cultural competence in the classroom* (pp. 82–96). New York, NY: Teachers College Press.

Smith, L. (1999). *Decolonizing methodologies: Research and indigenous peoples*. London: Zed Books.

Smith, L. (2013). The future is now. In M. Rashbrooke (Ed.), *Inequality: A New Zealand Crisis* (pp. 228–235). Wellington, New Zealand: Bridget Williams Books.

Stein, J. (2007). At Hyundai, "i" stands for inspiration, innovation. *Automotive News Europe*. Retrieved from http://europe.autonews.com/article/20070319/ANE/70315045/at-hyundai-%E2%80%98i%E2%80%99-stands-for-inspiration-innovation

Steinberg, S., & Kincheloe, J. (2001). Setting the context for critical multi/interculturalism: The power blocs of class elitism, white supremacy, and patriarchy. In S. Steinberg (Ed.), *Multi/Intercultural conversations* (pp. 3–30). New York, NY: P. Lang.

Stovall, D. (2006). Forging community in race and class: Critical race theory and the quest for social justice in education. *Race Ethnicity and Education, 9*(3), 243–259. http://doi.org/10.1080/13613320600807550

Tatum, B. (2003). *Why are all the Black kids sitting together in the cafeteria?* (Epilogue). New York, NY: Basic Books.

Thrupp, M. (2007). Education's "inconvenient truth": Persistent middle class advantage. *Waikato Journal of Education, 13*, 253–271.

Waikato Tainui. (2016). Tikanga Ora Reo Ora. Whakatupuranga 2050: The Tribal Development Strategy. Waikato Tainui. Retrieved from http://www.waikatotainui.com/wp-content/uploads/FINAL-TikangaOraReoOra_E-Doc.pdf

Wolfgramm, T. (2014). *[Re]Claiming our techological sovereignty through co-creating the Māori Innovation, New Technology, and ICT Sector*. Manukura, Planet Māori. Retrieved from planetmaori.com.

Yang, K. W. (2009). Discipline or punish? Some suggestions for school policy and teacher practice. *Language Arts, 87*(1), 49–61.

· 3 ·

CULTURAL IDENTITY

In New Zealand, the terms "ethnicity" and "culture" are in more common use than the word, "race." This is not always the case elsewhere, or in the literature, where often race, ethnicity, and culture are equated or conflated, or the terms and meanings change depending on the author or the context. Penetito (2010) suggests this preference in New Zealand educational discourses, "can be shown to be part of the ideological hegemony" (p. 63). He finds however, the Māori conceptual preference, historically and in the present, is to favor the term culture rather than ethnicity or race. He explains,

> The concept of culture as used by Māori tends toward including notions of biology, genetics, and inheritance, making it equivalent to the concept of race or ethnicity. When they think about culture, Māori are likely to be thinking of their identity, their whakapapa (genealogy), which carries with it the notion of determinism. (p. 64)

I have used the terms "ethnic group" or "ethnicity" to denote a person's racial heritage and the terms "culture" or "cultural" to describe the accumulated experiences of a people or group through social interactions in which values, beliefs, experiences and traditions are practiced and evolve. It is understood that other definitions may include culture in the terms "ethnicity" and "ethnic group." Statistics New Zealand use "ethnic group" and "ethnicity" in the official New Zealand Census to denote racial groups and these terms are also used in Ministry of Education statistics.

In Kia Aroha College a respected Samoan teacher explains their ethnicity to his Samoan students by saying, "You were born a Samoan, and when you die, no matter where you go, or what you do in between, you will still be a Samoan." He uses this statement to describe his students' Samoan racial heritage. His students learn about their Samoan culture, through their involvement in family events and practices, including those followed in their Samoan bilingual program at school. They also interact with other youth, with church, sport, music, technology and a wide range of groups outside school and home. All of these experiences shape the development of their cultural identity—which is a mixture of traditional Samoan practice, contemporary Samoan family practices in their New Zealand setting, and the identity shaped through the involvement of these young people in these many other social groups. This example clarifies the use of these terms in the school.

Cultural Identity

Cultural or ethnic identity refers to the degree to which a person feels connected with a racial or cultural group (Bennett, 2004, p. 862). Cultural identity is described by Phinney (1996, cited in Bennett, 2004) as a complex cluster of factors, "including self-labelling, a sense of belonging, positive evaluation, preference for the group, ethnic interest and knowledge, and involvement in activities associated with the group." Nasir and Saxe (2003) also argue that cultural practices—socially patterned activities organized with reference to community norms and values—are important arenas for the enactment and formation of identity. "It is in these cultural practices—as people 'do' life—that identities are shaped, constructed, and negotiated."

For students from indigenous and minority ethnic groups the development of a cohesive cultural identity is severely challenged in the school environment in which you spend the major part of your daily life, when your norms and values are not those of the dominant culture. This tension is exacerbated during the years of early adolescence when the formation of identity is occurring developmentally.

Grande (2000b) analyzes of her own identity development as an American Indian woman in the academy within the "prevailing theories of identity, namely those frameworks that have emerged from (left) essentialist, postmodern, and critical identity theories" (p. 347). The first two frameworks are discussed in the following sections, and critical theories of identity are discussed in terms of critical pedagogies.

Essentialist Frameworks

Stage Models

Root (2004) identifies the development of racial identity models within specific eras. Between the 1970s and early 1980s, alongside the civil rights and Black Pride movements in America of that time, stage models of racial identity development were popular. In general, Root observes, these models "suggest that there is an initial stage of internalization of a White reference group that necessarily is accompanied by internalization of devalued messages about Black people, values and cultures" (p. 114).

Banks' (2004) typology, which identifies six stages in the development of cultural identity is an example of a stage model, but this model has evolved from his earlier work (Banks, 1981). Rather than see these stages and descriptions as the ideal, Banks describes the typology as a "framework for thinking about and facilitating the identity development of students who approximate one of the stages" (p. 295). Banks suggests that in Stage 1 individuals may reject their own culture through internalizing the negative stereotypes and beliefs within the wider society about their particular ethnic group. This leads to low self-esteem. In Stage 2 individuals typically have newly discovered their ethnicity but still may have mixed feelings. They may try to limit themselves to their ethnic group and interact exclusively within it, considering the group superior to others. In Stage 3 individuals have developed an authentic pride in their ethnic group, have clarified their identity, and developed positive attitudes towards it. Individuals in Stage 4, "Biculturalism" have a healthy sense of their own cultural identity but are also able to participate successfully in another cultural community. Banks suggests at this stage people have "a strong desire to function effectively in two cultures." In Stage 5 individuals have clarified their positive personal, cultural and national identifications. They have developed positive attitudes towards other cultural groups. In Stage 6 individuals can function effectively in their own group, and in different ethnic groups nationally and globally—they have a commitment to all humanity. A prerequisite to developing this cosmopolitan stage is "strong, positive, clarified cultural identifications and attachments" (pp. 295–297):

> It is not realistic to expect Puerto Rican students in New York City to have a strong allegiance to U.S. national values or deep feelings for dying people in Afghanistan if they feel marginalized and rejected within their community, their school, and in their nation-state. (Banks, 2004, p. 297)

Banks believes teachers must be aware of and sensitive to students moving through these stages of cultural development in all their students and facilitate their identity development. Teachers then must play a central role but many teachers in schools are unaware of this responsibility.

Drawing on the stage model first proposed by Cross (1991), and the work of Helms (1990), Tatum (2003) describes five stages of racial identity development: pre-encounter, encounter, immersion/emersion, internalization, and internalization-commitment. As in Banks' typology, in Tatum's pre-encounter stage individuals take on negative stereotypes believing it is "better" to be White, seeking to assimilate into the dominant culture and rejecting their own. Typically, an event or a series of experiences of the impact of racism personally are the catalyst for transition to the "encounter" stage. While Cross suggests this stage usually happens in adolescence or early adulthood, Tatum identifies this change in Black junior high school students in predominantly White communities. Again, similar to Banks' model, this stage involves opposition to White culture and seeing their own culture as superior. Entering this stage of identity development can have a significant impact on school engagement and achievement (p. 55).

In the early part of Tatum's immersion/emersion stage individuals surround themselves with visible symbols of racial identity and in the latter part of this stage actively seek information about their cultural history. This develops an authentic sense of self. Taking this growing security in one's identity through to the internalisation stage, individuals can now establish meaningful relationships with their own and with other cultural groups. In Tatum's final internalisation-commitment stage, this translates into a personal commitment to the culture as a group, which is sustained over time. Helms (1990) points out however, that at this level a person is still continually open to new information and new ways of thinking about racial and cultural variables, and even at this stage particular situations can trigger old thinking and responses (p. 66).

Postmodern Frameworks

Ecological Models

Following the advent of civil rights and racial pride movements, stage models seem to have evolved into ecological models of identity which are not constrained by the time frame and structure of specific stages. Ecological models focus on social processes and variables that influence identity formation and suggest that different identities may be more flexible and reflect different individual or group needs (Root, 2004, p. 115).

Cerulo (1997) describes a shift, from the primary focus of sociologists on the individual's sense of self, to the collective sense of self. In post-modernism, identity is not unitary or essential. It is fluid or shifting, fed by multiple sources and taking multiple forms. We are all unique and we each have our own distinctiveness but we also have much in common. Postmodern thinking on identity represents the antithesis of the prescribed unitary linear identity development proposed in earlier stage models. For instance, a social constructionist approach to identity rejects any category that proposes essential or core features as the unique property of the members of a collective. Viewed from this perspective, the collective is a social artefact—an entity whose shape and direction is moulded by the predominant cultural scripts and centres of power (p. 387).

The literature abounds with explanations of processes to account for multiple and blended cultural identities. Acculturation and hybridity are two of these. Khanlou (2005) believes acculturation implies that acculturating individuals from minority cultures may help them acquire the mainstream culture but at the same time lose or weaken their original cultural identity (p. 13). Kraidy (2002) challenges the controversial status of hybridity, and suggests that one of the criticisms of the concept is that it is seen as a strategy of co-option used by the powerholders to neutralize difference (p. 323). These notions suggest that these constructs could further mask the processes of assimilation and loss of indigenous and already minoritized identities.

May (2009) discusses the challenges multiculturalism faces from postmodernist understandings of identity, and argues for a more critical conception of multiculturalism (see later in this chapter). He states that, "The challenge posed by postmodernist/left critics is this: how can multiculturalism, based as it is on a notion of group-based identities and related rights, avoid lapsing into reification and essentialism?" (p. 40). Hybridity theory is opposed to any idea of traditional or cultural "rootedness," emphasizing instead that multiple, shifting, and complex identities are the norm for individuals. However, May points out that one of the weaknesses of hybridity is:

> The considerable disparity between the intellectual celebration of hybridity and the reality of the postmodern world. The world *is* increasingly one of fractured and fracturing identities. But these identities are usually *not* hybrid; just the opposite in fact. Nation-states, as conservatives will be the first to tell you, are facing a plethora of ethnic, regional, and other social and cultural minority demands, many of which are couched in singular, collectivist terms. (p. 43)

Grande (2000a) makes this weakness explicit when she describes herself as, "the perfect postmodern subject, a no-size-fits-all kind of girl" (p. 345). With Peruvian Indian and Quechua (Spanish and French) ancestry, living away from her people in the United States she says, "I am differently perceived and named in all of my communities ... as I cross the literal border between the Americas a double invisibility takes place and I am absorbed into the nebula of American otherness." Quite certain of her identity and positionality when she entered the academy she soon realized that, nearly all of American Indian academe was besieged by the rancor of identity politics where the debate over who are the new Indians, who are the wannabes, who are the frauds, and who are the "real" Indians rages with great fury" (p. 345). In this environment Grande found that "gaining recognition as an American Indian scholar often comes at a price: that writings be accessible and pre-packaged for ready consumption by the Whitestream." Challenging the postmodernist critique of essentialist constructions of race and identity Grande believes postmodernist views of identity as "free-floating" present a real and significant threat to American Indian communities struggling to define their socio-political relationship to the United States:

> Unlike other subjugated groups, struggling to define their own local narratives within the democratic project, American Indians have not been working toward greater inclusion in the democratic imaginary but, rather, have been engaged in a centuries long struggle for the recognition of their sovereignty. This particular aspect of the Indigenous struggle completely transforms and reframes the identity question, moving it from the superficial realm of cultural politics to the more profound arena of cultural survival. (p. 351)

Paralleling the development of kaupapa Māori theory, Grande calls for the development of a "red pedagogy" and praxis founded on critical Indigenous theory of tribal identity and liberation. Contrary to postmodern thinking,

Grande believes there are, in fact, stable markers, and indicators of what it means to be Indian in American society and in this setting. She states, "Indigenous scholars cannot afford to perceive essentialism as a mere theoretical construct or academic choice and may, in fact, be justified in their understanding of essentialism as the last line of defense against capitalistic encroachment and Western hegemony" (p. 351).

Individual, environmental, and historical influences must be considered when examining the development of cultural identity. Using an ecological model framework, Khanlou (2005, p. 2) describes this as an "ecosystemic perspective" where it is the ongoing interaction between individual and the environment, made up of family, community, and society, that influences human development. She suggests the term, multiculturation, to imply that the development of cultural identity is not limited to a linear path, nor does it exclude the stage-oriented approach either. It recognises that in multicultural settings, a range of cultural identity development processes are possible and that such processes are influenced by context. As Grande argues, the context must consider indigenous perspectives as a safeguard against hegemonic imposition.

Adolescent Identity Development

Because the age of students in Kia Aroha College ranges from 11 to 18 years, an understanding of the specific importance of adolescence within the development of identity and ethnic or cultural identity is important. Houkamau (2006) defines identity as, "that aspect of the self-concept that relates to 'who' a person is and what that means relative to others" (p. 13). This is a crucial understanding for all adolescents but even more so for adolescents of color. Cunningham (2011) explains that "Māori concepts of adolescence are different than mainstream; the terms taiohi, taitamariki and rangatahi approximate but do not match the term 'adolescent'." He uses the term, "rangatahi development" (p. 145).

Erikson (1968) located the search for and development of one's identity as the critical psychosocial task of adolescence. Tatum (2003) explains that this search for identity in adolescence is not only about ethnic or cultural identity but can include such aspects as career aspirations, religious beliefs and values, and gender roles however, "for Black youth, asking 'Who am I?' includes thinking about, 'Who am I ethnically and/or racially? What does it mean to be Black?'" Because those around us shape our perceptions of ourselves when youth of color begin to encounter others outside their families and peer groups, the racial content of that message is heightened (p. 83).

In a three year longitudinal study, French, Seidman, Allen, and Aber (2006) looked specifically at two critical dimensions of ethnic identity development, *group esteem*—how one feels about belonging to one's ethnic group; and *exploration*—how much an individual tries to find out about what it means to belong to one's ethnic group. The study found that group esteem rose for both early and middle adolescents, but exploration rose only for the middle adolescent group. French et al. suggest that in order to have an achieved identity, one must go through a process of exploration and while early adolescents may have positive feelings toward one's group membership, "these are based solely on accepting what one is taught by one's family and not on the process of exploration" (p. 8). Schools are crucial sites for middle adolescents' exploration and development of an achieved, positive, ethnic identity.

Tatum (2003) explains that the concept of identity is complex and is shaped by the multiple experiences individuals, or the groups they identify with, family, social, political, and historical, encounter:

> Who am I? The answer depends in large part on who the world around me says I am. Who do my parents say I am? Who do my peers say I am? What message is reflected back to me in the faces and voices of my teachers, my neighbours, store clerks? What do I learn from the media about myself? How am I represented in the cultural images around me? Or, am I missing from the picture altogether? (p. 18)

This search for personal identity intensifies during adolescence. As children move from primary school to intermediate or middle school, as they experience puberty and enter adolescence they begin to ask the questions about who they are and where they fit into the society around them. Tatum (2003, p. 53) points out however, that while all adolescents look at themselves in new ways, not all adolescents have to think of themselves in racial terms. Why? Because this is the way the world sees them. Our perceptions of ourselves are shaped by the way others see us, and if we are not from the dominant culture, we are seen as being different from, or "diverse" compared with, society's accepted norms.

Critical Frameworks in Education

Debate about multicultural education, or education for "diversity" or "diverse learners," to use the more recent terminology, is nothing new and there is still little agreement about what this actually means. Steinberg and Kincheloe (2001, pp. 3–5) identify five positions in the discourse of the pedagogy of multicultural education. Particularly problematic are the pluralist position and practices, described by Steinberg and Kincheloe as the "mainstream articulation of multiculturalism," and the "left-essentialist" multicultural education position and practice. Grande (2000a) describes left-essentialism as:

> Merely a permutation of essentialist theory in which the categories of race, gender, and other social groupings are viewed as stable and homogeneous entities, or as if the members of such groups possess some unique or innate set of characteristics that sets them apart from "Whites". ... An essentialist discourse that remains fixated on the individual fails to conceive the sociopolitical whole and, in this way, leaves little room for social transformation and revolutionary coalition. (p. 347)

Grande (2000a) describes the confusion she struggled with against the construct of the "essential or authentic American Indian—as a pure-blood pedigreed individual raised in a reservation community," which located the struggle for identity in self. Constructions of American Indians as stereotypical, "teepee dwelling, buckskinned warriors, and exotic maidens" (p. 347), or similar exotic constructions of Māori and Pasifika cultures have no place within culturally-located, critically conscious classrooms. Unfortunately a "benevolent multiculturalism" (May, 1994) perpetuates these stereotypes and is often misconstrued by schools who believe that slightly "shading in" the White spaces is a good enough response. These approaches were the basis of the early popular "taha Māori" or Māori dimension policies of the 1980s in New Zealand. Expressions of these policies continue to persist in the "one-off" cultural weeks, ethnic meals, ethnic costume days, and in the "dial-a-Māori" pōwhiri (welcome ceremony) many schools view as a sufficient response to the ethnicities and cultures of their students. Such activities represent those aspects of culture and tikanga Māori that Whitestream teachers can feel comfortable with for specific, and short, periods. Slightly "shading" the White spaces in this way actually diminishes and demeans Māori and Pasifika children because these activities contribute to trivializing, belittling, and marginalizing Māori and Pasifika cultural values.

Steinberg and Kincheloe (2001) advocate for *critical* multiculturalism. Many of the characteristics of critical multiculturalism are consistent with those of critical race theory in that, "the power wielders who contribute to the structuring of knowledge, values and identity" are named:

> The power of white supremacy is seen as an important target of critical multiculturalism, with its phenomenal ability to camouflage itself to the point of denying its own existence. Whiteness presents itself not only as a cultural force or a norm by which all other cultures are measured, but as a positionality beyond history and culture, a

non-ethnic space. Thus, in a culture where whiteness as an ethnicity is erased, critical multicultural educators receive strange looks when they refer to their analysis of white culture. (p. 5)

May and Sleeter (2010) also see critical multiculturalism as the best way to prioritize a structural analysis of unequal power relations, "including, *but not necessarily limited to* racism." They argue that:

A structural analysis via critical multiculturalism frames culture in the context of how unequal power relations, lived out in daily interactions, contribute towards its production, rather than framing it primarily as an artefact from the past. Culture and identity are understood here as multilayered, fluid, complex, and encompassing multiple social categories, and at the same time as being continually reconstructed through participation in social situations. (p. 10)

While critical multiculturalism specifically examines race, White supremacy, gender and patriarchy, socioeconomic class, and privilege, a concern is that indigenous perspectives might be overlooked in this all-encompassing examination of identity and power. Brayboy (2005) identifies this issue in his development of a Tribal Critical Race Theory in education (TribalCrit). TribalCrit, Brayboy states, is rooted in "a belief in and a desire to obtain and forge tribal autonomy, self-determination, self-identification, and ultimately tribal sovereignty" (p. 433). In TribalCrit notions of culture, knowledge, and power are those that "have been circulating among Indigenous peoples for thousands of years." Brayboy explains that from this perspective culture is simultaneously fluid or dynamic, and fixed or stable.

Indigenous Perspectives

Our biggest Hawaiian question this last century, How can we be more like them? has become slowly, Why do we want to be more like them? Someone has rolled down the window. The breeze of identity rushes toward my skin as the aroma of ocean air fills our memory. (Aluli-Meyer, 2001, p. 125)

Macedo, in his introduction to the 30th anniversary edition of *Pedagogy of the Oppressed* (Freire, 2006) describes the struggle to transcend "a colonial existence that is almost culturally schizophrenic: being present and yet not visible, being visible and yet not present." He writes that through first reading this book in 1971 he finally had the critical tools and language to understand, "the process through which we came to know what it means to be on the periphery of the intimate yet fragile relationship between the colonizer and the colonized" (p. 11). This is a common experience for indigenous people throughout the world.

In 2009, I visited schools and listened to the experiences of La Raza in Tucson, Arizona, First Nations people in Vancouver and on Vancouver Island in Canada, and indigenous Hawaiian educators. I also met long-term Aboriginal activists and academics from Australia and was able to compare the struggle of Māori with these international indigenous counterparts. To discuss indigenous identities is to discuss identity as if it were a memory, something lost that is grieved for, and also to discuss anger and resistance over generations.

In Tucson I was told, "We didn't cross the border, the border crossed us." Many spoke of impact of what they referred to as, "The 1C" on their parents and grandparents. Initiated in Southern Arizona in the early 20th century, the 1C program segregated generations of language-minority students, for the next 45 years, often with tragic results. Spanish was forbidden in the classroom or on the playground and the program's goal was to "fix" the linguistic and academic deficiencies of Mexican children who, regardless of their ability, had to follow this low level education track that focused on vocational and homemaking skills. The memories of families who had been involved in "The 1C" were still very raw.

In Port Alberni on Vancouver Island, I was welcomed with ceremonial drums by the Nuu-Cha-Nalth Tribal Council and was afforded a wonderful meal of salmon caught in the river right outside the traditional House of Hupacasath where I had been invited to present a talk to community elders and district educators. Over lunch, Hupacasath elder and artist, Ki-Ke-In (Ron Hamilton), talked about the residential schools and the experiences of the 370 people interviewed in his research for his contribution to the report, *Indian Residential Schools: the Nuu-Chah-Nulth Experience* (Nuu-Chah-Nulth Tribal Council, 1996). People told him about the loss of family ties, culture, language, the physical and sexual abuse, and a mistrust in the present systems designed to support Nuu-Chah-Nulth children, families, and communities. His research shows how the schools failed to prepare the students for life outside of school, while stripping the children of their cultural knowledge and identity. He told me that a whole generation of First Nations people—those who had been in the schools, didn't know how to be parents, because they had been removed from their families and had no parents as role models. As the youngest of a family of eight and the only one who wasn't taken away to residential school he described his guilt, and the anger he suspected his siblings felt, that his experience had been better than theirs.

Edward "Tat" Tatoosh, musician, cultural teacher, and elder from the Hupacasath First Nation spoke of the loss of a language, the loss of respect from young people, the loss of traditional skills, and the loss of his Nation's history. Without your own language you are forced to use the tools of the colonizer to think, record and interpret your experience. Loss of language makes it more difficult to think and act within your own world view. "It's very hard." he said, "It's a constant battle to just survive. A lot of what happened is not even published." There was a sense of Macedo's "being present and yet not visible" in his words, "I got my linguistics degree at the University of Victoria in 1977, but I'm not really recognized as a linguist a lot of times."

I was privileged to visit the Haahuupayak Independent School, situated within the traditional territory of the Tseshaht First Nation, and on the Tseshaht Reserve. The school's building, the culturally rich classroom environments, the language spoken, the activities I saw the children engaged in, all strongly represented cultural identity and pride, which was also embedded in their mission statement, "… to provide an education that meets the needs of today in a manner consistent with nuuchahnulth cultural teachings."

I spoke with Dr. Bob Morgan, then Conjoint Professor at Wollotuka, the School of Aboriginal Studies at the University of Newcastle in New South Wales in Australia. Morgan chaired the 1993 World Indigenous Conference in Education (WIPCE) and following that conference, initiated the Task Force that drew up the now famous *Coolangatta Statement on Indigenous Peoples Rights in Education* (World Indigenous Peoples' Conference on Education, 1999). Morgan spoke of the "Stolen Generation" and of being lined up with all the other Aboriginal children at his primary school and being told by the "whitefella" teacher that they would never be capable of learning. When he recounted this experience to his mother, "his greatest teacher," she told him he could live the teacher's dream or he could live his own dream.

Through the forcible removal of children from families or through policies such as assimilation, integration, multiculturalism, biculturalism, and mainstreaming, the politics of difference and diversity, and globalization, indigenous peoples have been stripped of their identities in spite of their long resistance to these hegemonic practices. Linda Smith (1999) explains:

> While the West might be experiencing fragmentation, the process of fragmentation known under its old guise of colonization is well known to indigenous peoples. We can talk about the fragmentation of lands and cultures. We know what it is like to have our identities regulated by laws and our languages and customs removed from our lives. Fragmentation is not an indigenous project, it is something we are

recovering from. While shifts are occurring in the ways in which indigenous peoples put ourselves back together again, the greater project is about recentring indigenous identities on a larger scale. (p. 97)

Shape-Shifting: Identity Changing, Identity as Resistance

For an example of the typical "shape-shifting" identity faced by many families, I need look no further than my own four children. On my side of the family their forebears are Pākehā, my parents both being descendants of early settlers from England and Scotland, who arrived in New Zealand in the late 1800s. On their father's side; a mother, with one Samoan and one English parent, and a father whose parents were also English and Scots—or so the family thought, until well after his death when a direct Māori whakapapa (genealogy) to Ngai Tahu and a network of relatives, was discovered in his father's family through my own research into our children's family history. While this whakapapa was undoubtedly known, it was never told to his children.

If we were to attempt to quantify my children's ancestry, it is predominantly Pākehā, on both sides of the family. However, my four children identify first and foremost as Māori. If you ask them about their cultural identity they will tell you emphatically it is Māori. This is evident in their daily lives, socially and politically, and in their choices for their children. My grandchildren and great grandchildren are being educated in Māori immersion or bilingual settings and are all becoming fluent speakers of Māori. Two great granddaughters, immersed in Māori language from birth, speak almost no English, the deliberate choice of their parents that they will be fluent and articulate Māori speakers first. How has this evolved?

In our case there is clearly no kaumātua or kuia (elders) in our whānau passing down cultural knowledge, and their father was unaware of his Māori heritage until well after our children were born. The answer is partly due to my own upbringing in a rural Māori community, my choice to involve our children in Māori activities from an early age, and my long term involvement with Māori education, as a student, a teacher, and a school principal. None of us can recall any family discussions about, or any deliberate influence on, our children's choice to "be Māori." This was something that just evolved in our experience. This has not meant that their other cultural identities are denied. They are comfortable and competent in Pākehā and Samoan settings, however they choose to "live as Māori" (Durie, 2001).

The influence of my choices aside, there is a much more important explanation for my children's decisions to identify as Māori first and foremost. Bishop (1996) describes the similar story of the loss of his family's whakapapa and the "inexorable process of Europeanisation" that had overtaken his family, as a "vignette of New Zealand's history" (p. 36). Not only had this same process caused my children's paternal grandfather's Māori ancestry to disappear altogether from the family's knowledge, it also caused their paternal grandmother to deny her Samoan heritage and to prevent her children from any involvement with Samoan language or custom. The extent of this denial became clear to me on the day I found her massaging my days-old daughter's nose to ensure it didn't remain "too flat" and identify her features as Samoan. Having taken real pride in the fact she had married a "palagi" (White person) she was horrified to later learn of his Māori heritage, which she then also strenuously denied.

Within just two generations, through this denial of their Māori and Samoan heritage, the "Whitening" of our children could have been complete. Their commitment to resist, reject, and reverse this process through their strong identification as Māori is something I celebrate. The results of this resistance are evident in the next generations, my grandchildren and great grandchildren.

Wijeyesinghe (1992) identifies several factors that can significantly impact the process of establishing biracial identity. They are biological heritage, sociohistorical context of society, early socialization experiences, culture, ethnic identity and heritage, spirituality, individual awareness of self in relation to race and racism, and physical appearance, as well as other personal social identities. Many of these factors can be identified in my family's story.

However, just as my children choose to identify themselves primarily as Māori, if I search the enrollment information of the children in the schools in this story, parents rarely provide more than one ethnic group in their enrolment details. This is in spite of the fact that the enrolment form provides spaces for several ethnic groups and I know that large numbers of students are from mixed ethnic backgrounds and cultures. May and Sleeter (2010) observe that identity choices are a product of power relations, inevitably shaped by one's position in society. They suggest that the notion of multiple or hybrid identities presupposes "that everyone has an equal opportunity to pick and choose freely from the mélange of identities available to them. But this is simply not the case" (p. 5). It seems the reality is that people make a choice and the context allows identities to "shape-shift" according to need and situation. Pollock (2004) calls this process of daily wrestling with race categories, "race-bending."

Identity Lost: Social Toxins

Originating with Garbarino (1995) the idea of a society that is toxic to children and young people, draws on a conceptual framework from Bronfenbrenner (1977) and ecological systems theory. According to Garbarino, "the mere act of living in our society today is dangerous to the health and well-being of children and adolescents ... the social world of children, the social context in which they grow up, has become poisonous to their development" (pp. ix, 4). Garbarino finds the elements of social toxicity are easy enough to identify:

> violence, poverty and other economic pressures on parents and their children, disruption of relationships, nastiness, despair, depression, paranoia, alienation—all the things that demoralize families and communities. These are the forces in the land that pollute the environment of children and youth. (pp. 4–5)

This concept underpins the acclaimed seven part California Newsreel documentary series, *Unnatural Causes: Is inequality making us sick?* (Adelman, 2008), exploring racial and socioeconomic inequities in health in the United States of America. Evidence presented in this series suggests that more equitable social policies, secure living-wage jobs, affordable housing, racial justice, good schools, community empowerment, and family supports are health issues just as critical as diet, tobacco use, and exercise. Episode 3 of the series titled, *Bad Sugar*, explores the reason for the poor health of the Tohono O'odham American Indian people who have the highest incidence of Type II diabetes in the world. The causes lie, not in the routinely expected poor diet and limited exercise, drugs and medical care, but in economic, political and social structures:

> They may be hard to see, yet they can be powerful determinants of our health. Pacific Islanders, African Americans, Aboriginal peoples in Australia, all suffer from Type II diabetes at rates double or triple the national averages. ... They have totally different histories. They are all different populations, and yet they all have the same manifestation ... what's going on? What's the common denominator? And in every case, we're talking about people who have been dispossessed of their land and of their history. They haven't been able to re-create it. In all these far-flung parts of the world the social circumstance of being ripped from roots ends up with the same manifestation of disease. (Adelman, 2008)

Similarly, Shields, Bishop, and Mazawi (2005, p. 3) link pathologizing practices and policies to education (deficit thinking, teacher dominant pedagogies, schooling itself as a tool of colonization and assimilation are examples), and describe the damage these cause to Navajo, Māori and Bedouin Arab children in education systems that would, at first glance, seem to be literally worlds apart.

Fullilove (2004), links this issue to cultural identity, using the gardening phenomenon of "root shock" to describe the impact of the dislocation of people from their communities, their cultures and identities—their very roots. An ecosystem in nature relies on achieving a perfect balance for its wellbeing and survival, and loss or change to any part of the ecosystem causes this to be disrupted, often permanently. The same effect can be seen in groups of people who have been removed from their environments through policies of urban renewal, gentrification, and racism. The impact and stress suffered through root shock can last for generations:

> Root shock undermines trust, increases anxiety about letting loved ones out of one's sight, destabilizes relationships, destroys social, emotional, and financial resources, and increases the risk for every kind of stress-related disease, from depression to heart attack. (p. 14)

Duncan-Andrade (2011) connects root shock to education, positioning school classrooms as ecosystems where pain suffered by one student in the ecosystem can be transferred to others. Conversely healing can also be transferred. We have to be able to identify external toxins that come into our ecosystem in schools in order for us to attempt to heal them.

In New Zealand we have the same health discrepancies, which we for the most part, seem to attribute to the victims' "choice" of lifestyle. However, look further into the statistics and inequity soon surfaces. Robson, Purdie, Cram, and Simmonds (2007) looked at the age-standardized measure used to compare health statistics in New Zealand. An age-standardized rate is a summary measure of a rate that a population would have if it had a standard age structure, however because the age structure of Māori is substantially younger than that of non-Māori the World Health Organization (WHO) standardized measure is not valid. Using a kaupapa Māori (Māori world view, philosophy) analysis the researchers observe that, "The use of the WHO standard thus privileges the colonial population's mortality experience, potentially influencing prioritising decisions and perceptions of disparities between the two populations" (p. 7).

In 2004, in response to a political debate over health funding, Professor Tony Blakely, Director of the Health Inequalities Research Program (HIRP) at the University of Otago, decided to pre-release findings of an unpublished study that looked at mortality rates in terms of both ethnicity and income levels. The results, he said, were too critical to leave until they were formally published. The findings of the New Zealand Census-Mortality Study (Ministry of Health and University of Otago, 2006) when it was released, showed clearly that Māori still had a higher death rate, regardless of how much they earn. The study shows that disparities in mortality between Māori and non-Māori persist within income groups and, for people aged 25–59 years, the mortality rates for Māori with high incomes were similar to, or higher than, mortality rates for non-Māori in the low-income group (p. 17). Ballard (2008), citing this report, describes "a racialised social order" in which health inequalities are the result of inequalities of resources and power.

For young people the cost of the loss of identity can be more immediate than disease in later life. The suicide death rate for Māori youth (15–24 year olds) in 2012 was 2.8 times the non-Māori youth rate. Young Māori males are most at risk with 25.6 per 100,000 suicide deaths compared to 16.3 per 100,000 for young non-Māori males. Young Māori females died by suicide at twice the rate of non-Māori females in 2012 (Ministry of Health, 2015). Coupe (2000; 2005) finds that not being connected to Māori culture is a key risk factor associated with attempted suicide among Māori and recommends that it is vital that cultural identity be further explored in relation to Māori suicide.

Schools and Cultural Identity

It would be expected then that schools would take seriously the need to develop cultural identity as a crucially important foundation for students' well-being. This is not the case. In 2011, Massey University in New Zealand conducted a research project that aimed to develop an understanding of how young people think of themselves in terms of national identity (Walshaw, Andrews, Bell, Butler, & Tawhai, 2012). The research sought to identify what national identity looks like in New Zealand, how it is fostered, and how young people experience it in everyday life. Researchers surveyed 787 Year 12 (Grade 11) students, from 56 schools located within 13 different regions across New Zealand. Students were also asked to respond to questions about how they identified themselves in terms of ethnicity, why they identified in that way, and how they felt about a series of questions about ethnic identity. Students could select more than one ethnicity if they preferred.

One of the researchers chose to follow up the survey with Kia Aroha College student participants for her doctoral research (Butler, in process). She explains that in examining the survey data around ethnic identity Kia Aroha College stood out as different from the other participating schools. When asked why they identified with their ethnic group or groups, 37.5% of respondents from Kia Aroha College specifically mentioned the role of the school in helping them to support or foster their cultural identity. In comparison, only five students (0.8%) of the 771 other students who responded to the survey, mentioned "school" or "kura" in their response to the question. In every question of the survey Kia Aroha College students came out significantly more positive about their identity than all other 54 schools.

This first section of the book has identified and named the White Spaces in our education systems and our schools. Many schools can identify the causal factors contributing to a loss of identity and alienation from learning. It is much more difficult to construct a comprehensive response to address this issue, and which is embedded in all aspects of a school's practice. The next section explains Kia Aroha College's approach in detail to show that it is possible to change the color of these White spaces. Dei, Karumanchery, and Karumanchery-Luik (2005) point out that the very fracturing of cultural and community identity that this first section has named has effectively erased community and cultural solidarity and the supports needed to fight that fragmentation. They believe that the development of a "critical anti-racist consciousness is intrinsically important to our ability to reclaim that commonality":

> As we move from *spaces of Whiteness* to *places of Color*, our eyes become opened to the commonality of our experiences, the commonality of our oppression and the commonality of our struggles. In other words, we start to recognize the patterned interactions and relations of power that frame our opprsession. (p. 166)

How can a school and a community fight back, to reclaim cultural identity and solidarity in a system designed to remove those crucial supports?

References

Adelman, L. (2008). *Unnatural causes: Is inequality making us sick?* California Newsreel. Retrieved from http://www.unnaturalcauses.org/transcripts.php

Aluli-Meyer, M. (2001). Our own liberation: Reflections on Hawaiian epistemology. *The Contemporary Pacific, 13*(1), 124–148. http://doi.org/10.1353/cp.2001.0024

Ballard, K. (2008). *Teaching in context: Some implications of a racialised social order*. Keynote address, University of Waikato, New Zealand. Te Kotahitanga Voices Conference.

Banks, J. (1981). *Multiethnic education: Theory and practice*. Boston, MA: Allyn and Bacon.

Banks, J. (2004). Teaching for social justice, diversity, and citizenship in a global world. *The Educational Forum*, 68(4), 296–305. http://doi.org/10.1080/00131720408984645

Bennett, C. (2004). Research on racial issues in American higher education. In J. Banks & C. McGee Banks (Eds.), *Handbook of research on multicultural education* (2nd ed.). San Francisco, CA: Jossey-Bass.

Bishop, R. (1996). Collaborative research stories: Whakawhanaungatanga. *Academic Monograph No 20*.

Brayboy, B. M. J. (2005). Toward a tribal critical race theory in education. *The Urban Review*, 37(5), 425–446.

Bronfenbrenner, U. (1977). Toward an experimental ecology of human development. *American Psychologist*, 32(7), 513–531.

Butler, P. (in process). Multiple ethnic identities in senior secondary students in New Zealand. Ph.D Thesis (in process), Massey University.

Cerulo, K. A. (1997). Identity construction: New issues, new directions. *Annual Review of Sociology*, 23, 385–409.

Coupe, N. (2005). *Whakamomori: Māori suicide prevention* (Unpublished PhD thesis). Massey University.

Coupe, N. M. (2000). The epidemiology of Maori suicide in Aotearoa/New Zealand. *South Pacific Journal of Psychology*, 12(1), 1–12.

Cross, W. E. (1991). *Shades of black: Diversity in African-American identity*. Philadelphia, PA: Temple University Press.

Cunningham, C. (2011). Adolescent development for Māori. In P. Gluckman (Ed.), *Improving the transition: Reducing social and psychological morbidity during adolescence*. A report from the Prime Minister's Chief Science Advisor. Wellington: Office of the Prime Minister.

Dei, G. S. J., Karumanchery, L. L., & Karumanchery-Luik, N. (2005). *Playing the race card: Exposing white power and privilege*. New York, NY: Peter Lang Publishing.

Duncan-Andrade, J. (2011). The principal facts: New directions for teacher education. In A. Ball & C. Tyson (Eds.), *Studying diversity in teacher education* (pp. 309–326). New York, NY: Rowman & Littlefield.

Erikson, E. H. (1968). *Identity: Youth and crisis*. New York, NY: Norton.

Freire, P. (2006). *Pedagogy of the oppressed*. (30th anniversary edition). New York, NY: Continuum.

French, S. E., Seidman, E., Allen, L., & Aber, J. L. (2006). The development of ethnic identity during adolescence. *Developmental Psychology*, 42(1), 1–10. http://doi.org/10.1037/0012-1649.42.1.1

Fullilove, M. T. (2004). *Root shock*. New York, NY: One World/Ballantine Books.

Garbarino, J. (1995). *Raising children in a socially toxic environment*. San Francisco, CA: Jossey Bass.

Grande, S. (2000a). American Indian geographies of identity and power: At the crossroads of Indígena and Mestizaje. *Harvard Educational Review*, 70(4), 467–499. http://doi.org/10.17763/haer.70.4.47717110136rvt53

Grande, S. (2000b). American Indian identity and intellectualism: The quest for a new red pedagogy. *International Journal of Qualitative Studies in Education, 13*(4), 343–359.

Helms, J. E. (1990). *Black and white racial identity: Theory, research, and practice.* Westport, CT: Greenwood Press.

Houkamau, C. (2006). *Identity and socio-historical context: Transformations and change among Māori women* (Unpublished PhD thesis). The University of Auckland, New Zealand.

Khanlou, N. (2005). Cultural identity as part of youth's self-concept in multicultural settings. *International Journal of Mental Health and Addiction, 3*(2), 1–14.

Kraidy, M. (2002). Hybridity in cultural globalization. *Communication Theory, 12*(3), 316–339.

May, S. (1994). *Making multicultural education work.* Clevedon: Multilingual Matters.

May, S. (2009). Critical multiculturalism and education. In J. Banks (Ed.), *The Routledge international companion to multicultural education* (pp. 33–48). New York, NY: Routledge.

May, S., & Sleeter, C. (Eds.). (2010). *Critical multiculturalism: Theory and praxis.* New York, NY: Routledge.

Ministry of Health. (2015). *Suicide facts: Deaths and intentional self-harm hospitalisations 2012.* Wellington: Ministry of Health.

Ministry of Health and University of Otago. (2006). *Decades of disparity III: Ethnic and socio-economic inequalities in mortality, New Zealand 1981–1999.* Wellington: Ministry of Health.

Nasir, N., & Saxe, G. (2003). Ethnic and academic identities: A cultural practice perspective on emerging tensions and their management in the lives of minority students. *Educational Researcher, 32*(5), 14–18.

Nuu-Chah-Nulth Tribal Council. (1996). *Indian residential schools: The Nuu-Chah-Nulth experience: Report of the Nuu-Chah-Nulth Tribal Council Indian Residential School study, 1992–1994.* Port Alberni, BC: Nuu-Chah-Nulth Tribal Council.

Penetito, W. (2010). *What's Māori about Māori education?* Wellington: Victoria University Press.

Phinney, J. (1996). When we talk about ethnic groups, what do we mean? *American Psychologist, 51*(9), 918–927.

Pollock, M. (2004). Race wrestling: Struggling strategically with race in educational practice and research. *American Journal of Education, 111*(1), 25–67. http://doi.org/10.1086/424719

Robson, B., Purdie, G., Cram, F., & Simmonds, S. (2007). Age standardisation—An indigenous standard? *Emerging Themes in Epidemiology, 4*(3).

Root, M. (2004). Multiracial families and children: Implications for educational research and practice. In J. Banks & C. A. M. Banks (Eds.), *Handbook of research on multicultural education* (2nd ed., pp. 110–126). San Francisco, CA: Jossey-Bass.

Shields, C. M., Bishop, R., & Mazawi, A. E. (2005). *Pathologizing practices.* New York, NY: Peter Lang.

Smith, L. (1999). *Decolonizing methodologies: Research and indigenous peoples.* London: Zed Books.

Steinberg, S., & Kincheloe, J. (2001). Setting the context for critical multi/interculturalism: The power blocs of class elitism, white supremacy, and patriarchy. In S. Steinberg (Ed.), *Multi/intercultural conversations* (pp. 3–30). New York, NY: Peter Lang.

Tatum, B. (2003). *Why are all the Black kids sitting together in the cafeteria?* (Epilogue). New York, NY: Basic Books.

Walshaw, M., Andrews, R., Bell, A., Butler, P., & Tawhai, V. (2012). *National identity and cultural diversity: A research project that looks at what Year 12 students say about identity in New Zealand*. Massey University. Retrieved from http://mro.massey.ac.nz/handle/10179/4213

Wijeyesinghe, C. (1992). *Towards an understanding of the racial identity of bi-racial people: The experience of racial self-identification of African-American/Euro-American adults and the factors affecting their choices of racial identity*. Doctoral Dissertation, University of Massachusetts. Retrieved from http://scholarworks.umass.edu/dissertations/AAI9305915

World Indigenous Peoples' Conference on Education. (1999). *The Coolangatta statement on indigenous peoples' rights in education*. Retrieved from http://ankn.uaf.edu/iks/cool.html

PART TWO

COLORING IN THE WHITE SPACES

· 4 ·

KIA AROHA COLLEGE

Kia Aroha College is located in the suburb of Clover Park, in the wider community of Otara, a southern suburb of Auckland, New Zealand's largest city. In the immediate school community, 91.1% of the population is either Māori (17.4%) or Pasifika (73.7%),[1] 0.7% are Asian, and 10.2% are Pākehā (European/White). The community has a median age of 26.9 years, 11 years lower than the national median (Statistics NZ, 2015).

This local concentration of Māori and Pasifika families is a significant factor for Otara schools where less than 1% of students in all 18 schools in the community are Pākehā. In Otara schools, approximately one third of students are Māori and two thirds are Pasifika—predominantly Samoan (34.6%), Cook Islands Māori 16.3%), and Tongan (16.1%). The only schools that break this pattern are Kia Aroha College, where the 49% Māori roll is drawn to the Māori bilingual program, named Te Whānau o Tupuranga, and Te Kura Kaupapa Māori o Piripono where all 59 students are Māori (Ministry of Education, 2015).

The continual negative media spotlight on "South Auckland" is a fact of life for our young people and their families, and those who have worked in the community for many years. However, all would attest that Otara is nonetheless a rich, diverse, vibrant and proud community with assets that are rarely recognized or publicized.

Born Out of Struggle

The question that visitors to Kia Aroha College ask most often is how did the school develop its philosophy, and how has it sustained its difference in the face of systemic opposition and an education climate that has become more and more about school compliance? This chapter outlines the history of the school's struggle which is significant to understanding the community's commitment to the school's approach.

There have been three prolonged efforts by parents in the Clover Park, Otara, community, over a span of more than two decades, to resist and reject alienating school environments in favor of a more relevant model of schooling. Three different school names, and three official changes of status have featured in the school's journey since it opened in 1981 to its current form in 2016. Each of these changes took almost five years of battling bureaucracy to achieve, and each successful outcome solidified the community's understanding that change was possible, if you didn't give up.

The Schools

Clover Park Middle School

Clover Park opened as a traditional two-year New Zealand Intermediate (Grades 6–7) school in 1981. In the early 1980s the school had made efforts to include a Māori perspective, as far as education policy at the time would allow, and had established the first Māori bilingual program at this age level in the country. In 1995, after a five year struggle, Māori parents won approval to extend the two-year Clover Park Intermediate School to a four-year middle school, then named Clover Park Middle School. However, by this time we had already retained Years 9 and 10 (Grades 8–9) students in the school from 1990 through a variety of arrangements, some with, and some without the Ministry of Education's knowledge.

Parents wanted continuity of the Māori whānau (extended family group), learning environment and te reo Māori (Māori language). They wanted teachers who knew their children well and with whom both students and whānau could establish a relationship of trust. They wanted high academic outcomes and consistently high expectations. They wanted their children to have clear boundaries and they worried about their children's safety and learning in a secondary school system where Māori values and knowledge had little worth and where they had to relate to many different adults each day. Many families spoke from the bitter schooling experience of the parents themselves and also of older siblings in the family.

At the time, in the early 1990s, we had no knowledge of middle schooling as a concept, we simply looked for ways to keep the children in the bilingual whānau for longer than the two traditional Intermediate school years. We were unprepared for the opposition we faced from the Ministry of Education in response to what parents felt was a logical and simple request, and were surprised at its intensity. We found later, through professional reading and study as a staff, that what our Māori parents were asking for was closely aligned with the basis of middle school philosophy and the core developmental needs of the emerging adolescent, 11–15 years age group. These included: a sense of competence and achievement, self-exploration and definition, identity, supportive social interaction with peers and adults, challenging and rewarding physical activity, meaningful participation in school and community, routine limits and structure and diversity of experience (Dorman, 1984; Lipsitz, Mizell, Jackson, & Austin, 1997; McKay, 1994). These goals became the foundations of our learning program, with the development of a secure identity as Māori, Samoan, Tongan, and Cook Islands Māori at the center.

Te Whānau o Tupuranga

In 2001 the Board of Trustees of Clover Park Middle School received a request from a delegation of parents and former students of the four-year middle school program, to explore ways to allow these young people to return to Te Whānau o Tupuranga. Again, they cited continuity of the Māori learning environment and strong relationships as their reason for wanting to return. Five further years of struggle ensued. Key events in this protracted process included a visit to the Minister of Education in Wellington late in 2001, threat of legal action and many tense meetings with local Ministry officials, directives to place the students elsewhere, and warnings to parents by these officials that Clover Park would disadvantage their children's academic progress (missing the point that this had already happened elsewhere).

Again, with the Ministry of Education's reluctant knowledge, but no funding, we simply retained the 14 students from the original delegation and this number grew each year as parents of students graduating from Year 10 argued that their children should not have to first experience alienation in another school before they were entitled to be in the class. The outcome of this struggle was the establishment of Te Whānau o Tupuranga as a stand-alone, bilingual, Year 7–13 (Grades 6–12) high school, situated on a shared site with the existing Clover Park Middle School. Te Whānau o Tupuranga opened in 2006 and towards the end of 2008 students moved into new school buildings purpose-built for the way we wanted to teach and learn—flexible open learning spaces based on Māori and Pasifika ways of learning and engaging.

But there was no rest space between issues this time. A group of Samoan, Tongan and Cook Island Māori parents had already asked the Board to find ways to keep their children learning bilingually in their languages through to the end of their schooling. The Board of Trustees had expected this. The Ministry of Education had not, and so the community embarked on a third struggle to simply, they thought, extend the middle school to senior year levels. The community's vision was two Year 7–13 (Grades 6–12) small secondary schools, one Māori, one Pasifika, working together as we had always done, sharing facilities on a shared campus. Parents argued that this was already the situation, as Pasifika students in Clover Park Middle School who graduated from Year 10, were simply enrolling in Te Whānau o Tupuranga and joining the Māori bilingual program, in preference to leaving the campus to enroll in other schools.

It seemed a logical and simple argument to us, but this was not the case. This third battle, initiated by Pasifika parents in August 2007, was sustained through two phases of Ministerial rejections, opposition from other secondary schools in the local community, a change of government, and the consequential change of the Minister of Education. When it became clear, even to us, that our vision of two schools on the one site was not going to be approved, the board changed their strategy and agreed to the then Minister of Education's suggestion that the two schools should merge, thus giving Pasifika students the right to remain in the school through to the end of their schooling. Given that the suggestion came in the same letter from the Minister, delivered in person by Ministry of Education officials, that rejected their proposal, the board had good reason to believe that the Minister was simply softening the blow, and would expect them to resist this idea. They decided, in their words, to "call her bluff."

Having fought for so long to establish Te Whānau o Tupuranga as a school in its own right however, the Board of Trustees was unsure if the Māori community would easily agree to cede that autonomy in the proposed merger. They guaranteed Māori parents that Te Whānau o Tupuranga would not lose its name, or its unique identity. The Board need not have worried. Māori parents implicitly understood the struggle and its importance and, in the survey of 312 families or individuals in the community, 96% of responses supported the proposal.

Finally, in September 2010, the combined Board of Trustees of Te Whānau o Tupuranga and Clover Park Middle School received approval from the Minister of Education to merge to become one Year 7–13 designated-character school, named Kia Aroha College. In the new structure Te Whānau o Tupuranga continued to be the Center for Māori Education and Fanau Pasifika is the Center for Pasifika education, specifically for Samoan and Tongan bilingual programs.

While the ultimate goal of Kia Aroha College's bilingual or dual immersion programs in Māori, Samoan and Tongan is that children will be bilingual and biliterate in their home or heritage language and English, there are a number of variables in the school's approach towards this goal. Students enter Kia Aroha College from Year 7 (Grade 6) aged 11–12 years. Many students also enroll for the first time at higher year levels. In the enrolment information provided by parents of the 300 students attending the school in 2016, parents state that English is the first language for all but two students. Of the 160 Māori students, only 13 have previously been enrolled in Māori language immersion programs, mostly in Kura Kaupapa Māori where Māori was the language of instruction, prior to enrolling at Kia Aroha College. Ten students (four Samoan, four Tongan, one Cook Island Māori and one Sri Lankan) qualify for additional ESL/ESOL funding to support their English language acquisition. However, almost all of these students claim English is their first language on their enrollment forms. This decision by parents to claim English, even when that is not the case, is not surprising. Maxwell (2015) exposes backlash racist and negative attitudes in New Zealand society towards the decision made by her research participants to raise their children immersed in Māori language (p. 100). All of her participating families had experienced negative attitudes towards their choice, which many members the public felt it was their right to express. Pacific parents are enrolling in a bilingual school, but with a long history of sending their children to school to acquire English. That thinking originated in a time when their children already spoke their home language fluently. This is no longer the case, but the mindset is hard to shift. As May, Hill, and Tiakiwai (2004) observe, "Bilingualism (and language more broadly) can never be examined in isolation from the social and political conditions in which it is used" (p. 7).

The reality is that the majority of our students are monolingual, in English, when they enroll in Kia Aroha College. A small number are fluent in both their home language and English—those who have attended Kura Kaupapa Māori or other Māori language immersion programs, and those who have been raised speaking their own language at home. An even smaller number have recently immigrated to New Zealand and are monolingual in their home language. Across all of these different abilities, a further reality is that while some students may have conversational proficiency in the target language, very few have the academic language proficiency required for cognitive or classroom-based discourse (May et al., 2004, p. 53). This reality requires a multi-pronged approach. All approaches are additive, where students are "adding" a second language, at no expense to the first, and aim to achieve, foster and/or maintain longer-term student bilingualism and biliteracy. These programs vary according to student proficiency and include dual medium immersion where fluent speakers are mixed with non-speakers, and developmental maintenance approaches where students are taught through the medium of two languages, depending usually on time or place, or the teacher.

In order to enroll in Kia Aroha College, families must agree to accept and support the school's designated character in which adherence to Māori, Samoan, Tongan customs, languages and knowledge are the norm. In practice however, the school accepts all students who seek enrollment and, although there is no such official model in New Zealand's education system, it has become a "magnet" school, sought out by agencies, including the Ministry of Education, to take students who have become disengaged in their previous school/s. In addition to experiencing extreme behavioral difficulties, these students typically also experience serious learning difficulties, usually exacerbated by long periods of time when they have not attended school at all. It is not uncommon to be told by these families that their child has been refused entry into several schools before seeking enrollment in Kia Aroha College. A growing trend is seen in the enrollment of students who have been out of school for months, and often one to three years. Inevitably, the child or the family are described as the problem by agencies.

Winning the War

Every school in New Zealand is required to have its own charter. When a board applies to establish a school with a designated or special character, they have to specify how the proposed school will be different from general Whitestream schools. In the first application to establish Te Whānau o Tupuranga one of the Board of Trustees' goals was, "To honor the Treaty of Waitangi and uphold tino rangatiratanga (self-determination)." The board was advised by the Ministry of Education to remove any reference to tino rangatiratanga if we wanted the first application to succeed. Maaka and Fleras (2000) discuss the controversy that surrounds the term, "tino rangatiratanga" in New Zealand. They explain that for many non-Māori, "the expression is often dismissed as offensive or an affront, since references to rangatiratanga challenge the foundational myth of 'he iwi kotahi tatou' (we are one people)." In contrast, Māori perceptions of tino rangatiratanga, "conjure up a host of reassuring images for restoring Māori as a people to their rightful place in a post-colonising society" (p. 99). Obviously the concept of tino rangatiratanga was a step too far for the Ministry of Education.

In the third application, to extend the range of year levels at Clover Park Middle School, two of the proposed goals were (1) to give students participation in decision-making in curriculum content and planning to address real world issues through the lenses of empowerment and social justice and (2) to empower students to become catalysts of change in their communities and society. After the objection to tino rangatiratanga in the second struggle with education officials, it was no surprise when an email arrived from the Ministry of Education, advising the board that, "national office have slightly reworked the designated-character statement to more clearly define the difference between yourselves and a regular state school" (Ministry of Education, personal communication, August 2, 2010).

Empowerment and social justice were removed and these goals reworded. The goal of empowering students to become catalysts of change was deleted completely. In other changes to the 12 goals, references to cultural identity were narrowed down to specific Māori, Samoan, Tongan and Cook Islands "cultural practices." The goal, "to enable children to live as who they are at school, to develop the skills and knowledge to actively participate as citizens of the world to enjoy good health and a high standard of living," based on Durie's (2001) research was not acceptable, even though Durie's recommendations are the cornerstone of the vision of the Ministry of Education's strategic plan for Māori education. In the revised form, deemed acceptable by the Ministry of Education, the school's designated-character objective states that Māori and Pasifika children will draw on their cultures, identities and languages, so that they "gain the knowledge and skills necessary to do well for themselves, their communities, Aotearoa New Zealand, the Pacific region and the world." We were never sure what "do well for themselves" actually meant.

The revised objectives, supposedly changed, "to more clearly define the difference between yourselves and a regular state school," left us with goals one would hope would be the intent of any regular New Zealand school that was serious about valuing Māori and Pasifika learners. Through 20 years of resistance however, the Board of Trustees had learned to concede some battles in order to win the war. The board therefore opted to agree to the Ministry-revised designated-character statement on paper so as not to further delay an outcome to the application, in the certain knowledge this would not change our actual philosophy or practice in the school at all.

In the 20 years between 1990 and 2010 there were only six years when the community was not involved in a fight for educational sovereignty. Through these three different, and bitterly fought, struggles, the community refused to back away from their goals, no matter what obstacles education officials put in the way. The reason the community managed to achieve what they did was simply because the Board of Trustees listened the first time and the community was empowered by that experience. When they asked to bring back senior students in 2000, and the board said they thought that would be an impossible task, the community quite rightly told them they had done it before. They were correct, and the board agreed to support their action.

Unfortunately, each initiative was met with exactly the same opposition from education authorities. These objections had very little to do with the education of this community's youth and everything to do with maintaining the status quo in the national network of existing schools. In official minds the country's state-funded schools already provide an education relevant to all students and they have too much invested in that concept to give it up easily.

Through Aroha

Manulani Aluli-Meyer's (2008) work in Hawaiian epistemology describes the intelligence of aloha, "the intelligence of compassion, empathy and care" (p. 221). Aluli-Meyer says true intelligence, comes from self-knowledge, not from a test score. She cites the unpublished writings of Halemakua (2004), "truth is the highest goal, and aloha is the greatest truth" (p. 258).

The Māori equivalent of aloha is aroha. The choice of the name *Kia Aroha* was an intentional statement about what the community and the Board of Trustees strongly believe about education. Loosely translated by the school community as "through aroha," a literal translation of the word "kia" is "be, or let be, indicating it is desirable for something to occur (Moorfield, 2011), as in kia kaha (be strong) and kia ora (be well). In this sense the school name makes clear that aroha is our expectation.

Firstly, "Kia Aroha" was the motto of Clover Park Intermediate School when it opened in 1981, and the motto was retained when the school became Clover Park Middle School in 1995. It was the name chosen by kaumātua (Māori elders) in 1998 as the name of the school marae, so is an integral part of Te Whānau o Tupuranga's history as well. Using this name therefore took a piece of all three schools into the merger. Much more important though, is the meaning of the name, and its connection to our pedagogy and practice. This is encapsulated in this definition of aroha from a study of Māori leadership:

> Aroha is the wellspring of generosity and giving, and opens up to be caring, empathetic and accountable in such a way that we are willing to see, listen and respond to others as they truly are—and not only to human others, but to all living others. Aroha is an expansive relational experience that is an invitation for leaders to consider the highest expression of humanity in all that they do. (Spiller, Panoho, & Barclay-Kerr, 2015)

Note

1. Where a person reports more than one ethnic group in the NZ Census, they are counted in each applicable group. As a result percentages do not add up to 100 (Statistics NZ).

References

Aluli-Meyer, M. (2008). Indigenous and authentic: Hawaiian epistemology and the triangulation of meaning. In N. Denzin, Y. Lincoln, & L. T. Smith (Eds.), *Handbook of critical and Indigenous methodologies* (pp. 217–232). Los Angeles, CA: Sage.

Aluli-Meyer, M. (2013). The context within: My journey into research. In D. Mertens, F. Cram, & B. Chilisa (Eds.), *Indigenous pathways into social research: Voices of a new generation* (pp. 249–260). Walnut Creek, CA: Left Coast Press.

Dorman, G. (1984). *Middle grades assessment program*. University of North Carolina, Centre for Early Adolescence.

Durie, M. (2001). *A framework for considering Maori educational advancement*. Paper presented at the Hui Taumata Matauranga II (Māori Education Summit). Turangi, Taupo, New Zealand.

Lipsitz, J., Mizell, M. H., Jackson, A., & Austin, L. M. (1997). Speaking with one voice. *Phi Delta Kappan*, 78(7), 533–540. Retrieved from http://search.proquest.com/openview/2dd7beb0aa6e5220ab166db871de1367/1?pq-origsite=gscholar

Maaka, R., & Fleras, A. (2000). Engaging with indigeneity: Tino Rangatiratanga in Aotearoa. In D. Ivison, P. Patton, & W. Sanders (Eds.), *Political theory and the rights of indigenous peoples* (pp. 89–110). Cambridge, England: Cambridge University Press.

Maxwell, K. (2015). *Walking in two worlds: Parents raising tamariki in Te Reo Māori as their first language in Aotearoa/New Zealand* (Unpublished Master's Thesis). Te Whare Wānanga o Awanuiārangi.

May, S., Hill, R., & Tiakiwai, S. (2004). *Bilingual/immersion education: Indicators of good practice.* Wellington: Ministry of Education.

McKay, J. A. (1994). *Schools in the middle: Developing a middle-level orientation.* The practicing administrator's leadership series. Retrieved from http://eric.ed.gov/?id=ED383094

Ministry of Education. (2015). *Education counts: School rolls.* Retrieved from https://www.educationcounts.govt.nz/statistics/schooling/student-numbers/6028

Moorfield, J. (2011). *Te Aka Māori-English, English-Māori dictionary and index* (3rd ed.). Auckland, New Zealand: Longman/Pearson.

Spiller, C., Panoho, J., & Barclay-Kerr, H. (2015). *Wayfinding leadership: Ground-breaking wisdom for developing leaders.* Huia Publishers. Retrieved from https://books.google.com/books?id=5VR6CwAAQBAJ&pgis=1

Statistics NZ. (2015). 2013 *Census QuickStats about a place: Clover Park.* Retrieved from http://www.stats.govt.nz/Census/2013

· 5 ·

CHANGING THE LENS

> There can be no authentic Māori education without a context in which te ao Māori can find its true expression. There can be no authentic Māori education without its encompassing wairua manifest in te reo Māori. There can be no authentic Māori education that does not set out from the beginning to enhance and strengthen he tuakiri tangata (a Māori identity). (Penetito, 2010)

Penetito explains that "there are many ways to 'be' Māori, but one constant is that the collective has priority over the individual" (p. 269). That is the polar opposite of Western perspectives on learning that value and reward individual achievement. Penetito observes that an educational philosophy has to spell out in detail those experiences that count towards what it means to "be" Māori and adds that, "this is the dimension with which mainstream schools and teachers are least successful in dealing with Māori students" (p. 267).

Kia Aroha College's philosophy is clear. To be Māori in the school means that "as Māori" and "being Māori"—your cultural identity, have to be embedded in every aspect of the school day, no matter what the subject area, no matter what the activity, no matter whose class you are in. It has to be in school policy, in the budget, modelled by those who have leadership roles, intentionally taught in classes and underpinning all curriculum contexts for study. You can't do "as Māori" or develop cultural identity on Tuesdays and Thursdays, or in "one-off" cultural weeks during the year. "As Māori" can't be left to timetabling so that students can be who they are in those spaces or classes but have to leave that identity at the door the rest of the time.

In the early stages, in the 1990s, we had changed the language of instruction to introduce Māori, Samoan, Tongan, and Cook Islands Māori dual medium bilingual learning. By the late 1990s we had realized that simply adding a language, no matter how important that was, wasn't enough to change students' attitudes towards "being" Māori, or Samoan, or who they were. Our further changes to school organization and pedagogy are described in this section of the book. Our Pacific staff and communities have always been very clear that the changes over time in the three schools respected the status of Māori as tangata whenua (indigenous, people of the land) first. Because of this acknowledgement, Te Whānau o Tupuranga has always taken the lead, and Pasifika languages and programs have been developed based on the lessons learned from the Māori experience within the schools. While examples in this section therefore are predominantly about Māori learners and Māori initiatives, this thinking has paved the way, and been adapted by Pasifika staff to suit their respective cultural norms and customs.

Truth-Telling: Auditing Schools' White Spaces

How did we color in our spaces? Firstly, we had to be brutally honest. In my work with schools and teachers, I suggest that we first audit our spaces to explore our implicit assumptions and practice through a critical lens. We cannot change our White spaces if we don't know they exist, if we don't name them truthfully, or if we try to defend them. For us, the "space" starts outside the school gate and continues through all places and spaces that make up the school. One of our most powerful professional development activities in the early days of our journey was to assemble all of our staff in the street outside the school and to "walk through" the campus trying to see the school through critical eyes. We have since repeated this activity with students carrying out the evaluation. Each time, we learned and discovered spaces that we had not realized had crept back in. The default White space is seductive. It develops from our White teacher training and it becomes our comfortable space. Staying outside this comfort zone takes vigilance and honesty. Typical audit questions are:

- What does your school signage say?
- How are you greeted in the school office, on the phone, by teachers, and by students?
- How are children's names pronounced?

- What is clearly valued, in classroom displays, in the environment?
- How is this reflected in the curriculum, in assessment practice, in pedagogy, in adult and student behavior?
- What languages do you hear, and where do you hear them?
- What is your student "graduate profile"—your expectations for your graduating learners?
- Have you "spelled this out" in ways other than academic achievement outcomes, in terms that reflect cultural ways of knowing and being?
- Can Māori or Pasifika, or other ethnic groups see themselves *first* and *specifically*, in those expectations?
- Are these values explicit in school documentation, in the school prospectus, in formal school reports to parents, on the school website, in school newsletters, in the school's library collection, articulated and supported by the Board of Trustees, school leadership, and staff?

If you are a Māori child:

- What images, symbols, practice, and contexts, do you see *most* in front of you every day, in all of the spaces you learn in, and in your regular classroom environment?
- What images, symbols, practice, and contexts, do you see *sometimes*, depending on the space and the activity?
- What images, symbols, practice, and contexts, do you see *on special occasions*?

If you are a Māori family:

- How do you see your children reflected in the everyday practice of the school?
- How do you have a voice for Māori knowledge and learning—how are your aspirations for your child to learn "as Māori" collected, received, understood, met?
- How does the school lead in this aspect of your child's learning? (or do you have to ask?)
- Is this embedded or on the surface—is it authentic? How do you know?

Designing a School

From the time of the approval, in May 2005, to establish Te Whānau o Tupuranga as a brand new school on a shared site with the existing Clover

Park Middle School, the Board of Trustees, staff and students were involved in the process of designing an environment to specifically support the school's learning philosophy. The official design team included members of the board, staff, and students, however in practice; anyone who wanted to come to any of the many meetings was included in the design team. The team felt it was important for the architects and project managers to spend time, on the school marae and in classes, and their willingness to do this was the start of a genuine partnership and commitment to create a unique learning environment.

Whānau Involvement

In the early stages of the process, our Māori school community voiced concerns that the original building that had housed Te Whānau o Tupuranga since its inception as a bilingual program in 1988, might be demolished. This was certainly in the architects' project brief. The whānau (the school's Māori community) demanded a meeting with the Board of Trustees, which was attended by many parents, former students, staff, the architects, and project manager. Whānau were not happy and this was a very important lesson for the architects who learned that the buildings were just not bricks and mortar in the minds of the whānau. Following this meeting, the board was able to come up with some clear directives, which were presented to the architects in April 2006.

The board pointed out that some buildings were sacrosanct in that they held special historical and spiritual significance. While they could be refurbished, they could not be radically altered. These included the Wharenui (carved meeting house) on the school marae (meeting complex). The original Tupuranga classroom building also had special importance. It was originally a split-level design due to the contour of the site. A large floor space at the top level, always called the "landing," was connected to the lower level by wide right-angled steps. Two generations, and thousands of young people had sat on those steps over the previous 20 years the whānau had told us, and the steps had to stay, as did a large exposed beam that whānau saw as the "tāhuhu" (backbone) of Tupuranga. They acknowledged that the new school would mean that some changes had to be made to the original building but it was important that the entrance, the landing and steps, the tāhuhu, the footprint and foundations of the old building remained undisturbed. This presented some major design problems for the architects, and some significant budget implications for the project managers, but whānau were heard and the cultural integrity and significance of the buildings were respected and maintained.

A further area that required special attention was a grove of seven trees, planted at the time of a 15-year reunion of Te Whānau o Tupuranga in 2001. Six of these trees commemorated students who had passed away, some through illness or accident and some through violent circumstances. The seventh tree, named "Te Hunga Wairua," was planted to honor students' family members or those close to the school who had passed away, and to respect the loss of any members of the whānau in years after the reunion. Ngā Rākau (the trees) are an integral part of Te Whānau o Tupuranga and a song has been composed about their importance. It was paramount that these be protected.

Learning Spaces

Other design features were important to the board and whānau. The whole campus had to look and feel Māori and Pasifika. We wanted an open plan design not too different from the original 1980s variable teaching spaces concept that was popular at that time, but which had since been phased out of school building design. Computers had to be available as a tool in the classrooms, there as and when needed, and not placed in separate computer rooms. In our learning model teachers are facilitators and rarely "stand and deliver" learning from the front of the class. We wanted no such thing as a "front" of the classroom spaces. That meant all equipment had to be moveable and multipurpose. Classrooms have no interior walls or doors and are arranged in pods of four, around the periphery of a very large common "hui" (meeting) space in the center that allows students to mix, meet, and collaborate. This also allows teachers to work together as a whānau—teaching cooperatively, sharing planning and assessment and grouping students in a wide variety of organizations depending on the current topic or inquiry.

When we asked students what they wanted in the new school, they said they wanted mirrors. This made perfect sense. Mirrors are of vital importance to young people consumed with a desire for excellence in Māori and Pasifika performing arts. In the Performing Arts Center the rear wall of the large stage is a wall of mirrors so students can perfect their performances.

We visited a number of new schools across the Auckland region as our design ideas progressed. Each of these had elements we thought we wanted to incorporate—and many we did not like at all. These all helped to refine our thinking. One of our sticking points was the design of the learning spaces for technology and science. The Ministry of Education expected science laboratories and technology workshops. We wanted multipurpose areas, which included the equipment needed for science and technology but allowed us to include these subject areas as part of an integrated curriculum approach. "We don't want to have to 'do technology' just because it's 11.00 a.m. and it's Tuesday," we tried to explain, but it was clear this explanation wasn't working. One of our board members, a very wise kaumatua, finally was moved to tell one of the legendary stories those of us who know him well are always prepared for.

"I heard this story from an Aboriginal mate," he said, "when I asked him how Australian farmers prevent their stock from straying on those vast Australian outback cattle stations, which are too big to fence. What do you think his answer was?"

Ministry property officials and architects were nonplussed. "They sink wells, and the cattle come to the water, because that's where they want to be," he said. "We are trying to tell you we want to sink technology wells." We won the argument. There were to be many more times during the design process that we had to repeat what became our mantra, "If you build us a school that looks like all the others, you'll force us to learn the way everyone else does!"

Cultural Spaces

The school marae, *Kia Aroha*, is the hub of the campus. New carvings were commissioned to give the marae presence and mana (prestige) at the entrance of the school. The original carvings, erected in 1989, were preserved and now form a waharoa (a carved "gateway") over the students' entrance to Te Whānau o Tupuranga's classrooms. The Wharekai (marae dining hall) was completely remodelled to allow for the preparation of meals on the many occasions students and whānau, or visiting groups, are hosted or sleep overnight there. The commercially equipped Wharekai kitchen became the new school's food technology area where students learn about food and nutrition in an authentic Māori setting and learn to cook for large numbers, catering for our many visitors. This is very different from traditional food technology classrooms.

The former Clover Park Middle School staffroom became the Fale Pasifika to give the Pasifika community their own traditional space for meeting, gathering, and sharing food. The Whānau Center, run by the school's social worker, has its own entrance and provides spaces for families to access help and a wide range of support in confidence, without having to go through a public process at the school reception office.

External Spaces

Outside, the environment is designed to be an extension of the learning program. It includes paved Māori navigation pathways, a traditional Māori star compass used in navigation, tukutuku (traditional lattice-work) patterns in the paving and Māori and Pasifika designs on concrete planters and seating. At the front entrance of the school four giant "pou" (posts) each represent one of the school's four main cultures, Māori, Samoan, Tongan and Cook Islands Māori and vertical battens represent the palisades of a pā (Māori fortified village) site. The whakataukī (proverb) from which Te Whānau o Tupuranga's name is derived is featured in the pre-cast concrete wall at the entrance to the school campus and every sign on the campus, internal, external, and in the school library collection, include all four languages, as well as English.

The school's buildings and landscape design have won national architectural awards. In 2011 Te Whānau o Tupuranga's buildings were featured in a national television series *Whare* Māori (Scottie Productions, 2011) featuring Māori buildings. Teacher, William Ropata, captured the essence of the facilities and their importance to staff and students alike in his interview in this episode:

> Open plan learning, open plan teaching is a very strong feature of the entire campus. Those ideas around whānau (family), manaakitanga (caring for others), the sharing of information, and that philosophy of everybody is a learner; everybody is a teacher—that's really important.
>
> ... All you have to do is look at our learning space and you get this immediate realisation that we are part of a tikanga (Māori custom) learning pathway. The colors on the walls, the motifs we have on the windows that acknowledge who we are, as Māori.
>
> ... The landscaping is such an important concept. It's Papatūānuku (the Earth Mother), and it reminds our kids every day that our spiritual connect is not only inside, it's outside, so the landscaping reflects that. The plants that are there, the motifs around the boxing, the colors, they are all part of who we are. (English translations inserted)

Changing the Lens

We believed we could develop a counter-narrative to the common experience of Māori and Pasifika learners in New Zealand schools by linking a strong academic identity with a secure cultural identity. We had found that including students' heritage languages into our program and restructuring the school differently to better reflect Māori and Pasifika values, were both important stages in our journey, but we knew that wasn't enough. The essence of this thinking is captured in the observations of Adam Driver (2015), a New Zealand teacher who selected Kia Aroha College as "an exemplar of a culturally responsive school" to explore Māori and Pasifika students' cultural leadership. He was told, "You can't live as Māori unless you're political," and found that:

> At Kia Aroha College there is a consistent and highly visible counter-story to the dominant one; to the extent that mainstream schools have a dominant narrative it is unlikely to be as coherent, or recognized by most educators as political. ... For Kia Aroha, the "critical" in critical pedagogy includes looking after cultural knowledge, having the keys to access it, and living it. The seeds of cultural and political knowledge are planted at the school by the adults, but the students are not the equivalent of bonsai trees. Ultimately, what the students choose to do and think is their decision to make, as the idea of self-leadership implies, and as the students understand. (p. 105)

Kia Aroha College describes its philosophy and practice as "whānau-based, bilingual, critically conscious, culturally responsive, social justice education." It seems a long-winded description however, every word is intentional, and to use any one of these descriptors on its own is not enough to describe the school's approach. Driver found that, "Students are activists for social justice when representing the school, which champions social justice as the right to a culturally responsive and critical education for Māori and Pasifika youth" (p. 103).

Duncan-Andrade and Morrell (2008) identify three goals of critical pedagogy as empowered identity development, academic achievement and action for social change. This is consistent with Ladson-Billings (1994) three criteria for culturally relevant teaching: "an ability to develop students academically, a willingness to nurture and support cultural competence, and the development of a sociopolitical or critical consciousness" (p. 483). Castagno and Brayboy (2008) argue that "scholarship on culturally responsive schooling rarely includes discussions of racism and how racism might relate to the need for and the effectiveness of culturally responsive practices" (p. 950). Kia Aroha College believes that the single focus on academic achievement, typical of many schools and certainly the priority of New Zealand's education system, that ignores, or even negates, the other two goals, and does not name and challenge racism, cannot possibly be 'success' or excellence for Māori and Pasifika learners. In the next section, I describe the overarching learning model that the school developed and adopted in 2004 (Figure 5.1). The three lenses in this model are aligned with the Duncan-Andrade and Morrell's three goals:

- Empowered identity development: The Self-Learning Lens
- Academic achievement: The School-Learning Lens
- Action for social change: The Global-Learning Lens

The Power Lenses Learning Model

In the *Power Lenses Learning Model* (Milne, 2004) another whole body of legitimate knowledge (self-learning) sits alongside what is mandated in the curriculum or "school learning." Children's languages, their cultural norms, how they "live as Māori," how they can learn and succeed "as Māori," or as Samoan, Tongan, or who they are, how they develop a strong cultural identity, their wairua (their spirituality), whanaungatanga (relationships, their connectedness) are all high status learning, valid in their own right. We need to value this "self-learning" just as highly as we value "academic" learning.

The most important part of the model is the critical, social justice practice at the center—the toolkit young people need in order to challenge and change a system, whose single-minded focus on Western/European outcomes tells them they are failing. The six relationships in the center of the Power Lenses Learning Model (Figure 5.1) are adapted from the work of Otero and Chambers-Otero (2002), whose relationships framework identifies five critical learning/educational relationships: the learner or leader' relationship to self, to content/subject matter, to instructor/teacher/boss, to peers/other learners/other leaders, and to the wider community/context/situation.

Given the powerful influence of peers in adolescence and the alienation that Māori and Pasifika families traditionally experience from both their own and their children's schooling, Kia Aroha College staff felt the home-school and peer relationships had to be an integral part of our pedagogical approach, and had to be specifically relevant to the experiences and understanding of our Māori and Pasifika learners and communities. As a result the Power Lenses Learning Model used in Kia Aroha College is based on these six key relationships:

1. The student's relationship to self (cultural identity, who am I, where do I "fit?")

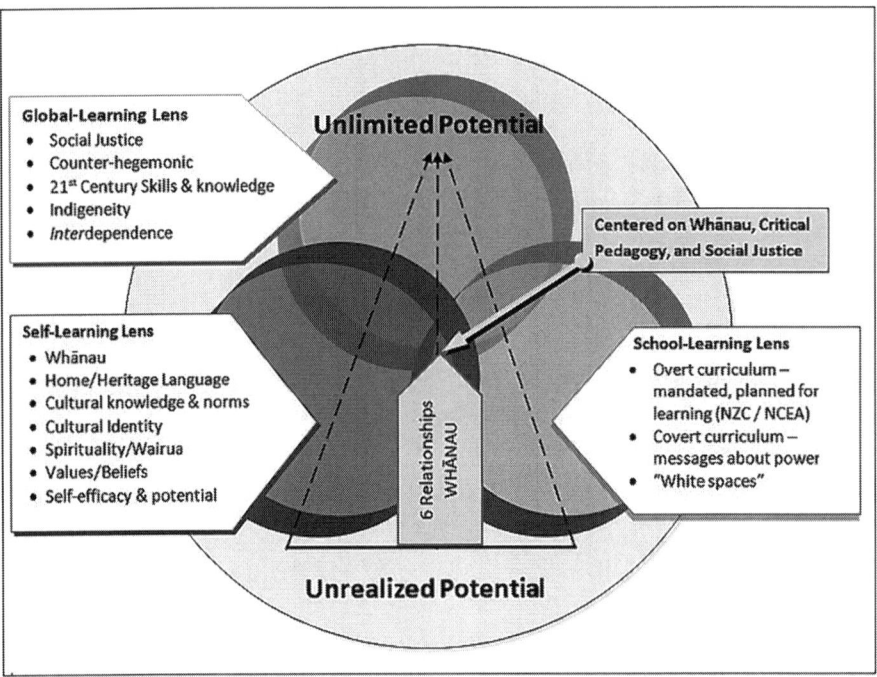

Figure 5.1. The Power Lenses Learning Model
Source: (Milne, 2004)

2. The student's relationship to their learning (its relevance to students' backgrounds)
3. The student's relationship to other students (positive peer influence and support, empathy)
4. The student's relationship to the wider world (anti-racist, critical)
5. The student's relationship to the teacher (mutual respect, high expectations, support, solidarity)
6. A reciprocal relationship between home and school (mutually beneficial, reciprocal partnership)

In this model the student and peer relationships are about developing a secure cultural identity which answer the questions, "Who am I?" and "Where do I fit?"—into my ethnic group, into my peer group, in my extended family, in my community, in society, and in the worlds I navigate beyond school. The relationship with learning has important questions for students and teachers such as:

- How relevant is this learning to students' background experiences, as Māori and Pasifika youth in this community?
- How will they be able to relate this learning to further learning?
- How ready am I for learning about this?
- Am I able to negotiate and participate in deciding contexts for learning that are relevant to me?

The relationship between Māori students and teachers is the central focus of the *Te Kotahitanga* research (Bishop et al., 2003) which exposes the impact of teachers' strongly held deficit views of Māori students. In *Te Kotahitanga* and in the Power Lenses model this relationship is seen as one that is reciprocal, with mutual respect and high expectations—from the teacher to students, and vice versa. It is also a whānau relationship, based on trust and authentic caring. In Kia Aroha College students call teachers "Whaea," "Matua," and "Nanny" (or their respective Samoan, Tongan, or Cook Islands Māori equivalents), accompanied by their first names, as they would address parents, aunts or uncles and grandparents. The relationship is supportive with clear guidelines and boundaries for behavior.

The home-school relationship is also based on reciprocity. Māori and Pasifika parents have legitimate reasons to mistrust the education system in general and schools specifically. This relationship therefore must be an authentic partnership that is of mutual benefit to both whānau and school. Too often these relationships are controlled by schools who offer guidelines and instructions to families which are designed to make children "fit" the school environment:

> This idea of reciprocal relationships is very different from the common school practice which develops relationships with the community characterized by school needs and demands. We ask parents to help, expect them to attend school functions, support the school in ensuring their children follow our rules, behave in ways we decide, complete school tasks and assignments and ensure they attend every day. We may be required by legislation to "consult" with our communities but consultation merely implies that we will receive input—not necessarily act on it. How then can we expect dialogue and interaction with families to have a positive impact on young people when the Eurocentric "rules of the game" are set by the school? (Milne, 2004, p. 171)

The remaining relationships; school learning, self and peers, and the wider world are explained in following chapters. However, in summary, in the context of Kia Aroha College, peer relationships, are based in whanaungatanga and are collective, as opposed to individual relationships. The wider world relationship takes into account all of the other groups and environments our students navigate and traverse in their lives outside school, and those they will encounter in the future, including understanding and connecting to wider struggles for social justice. This wider world relationship includes church, extended whānau, youth groups, and participation in sports, music, and other activities. An important focus of this global lens is on the tools, in particular the technologies and critical thinking that our youth need to go forward into the global world. This relationship adds to our students' understanding of society through conscientization, resistance and transformative praxis.

The Power Lenses Learning Model is about empowerment, and viewing learning through multiple lenses. The approach intentionally rejects labels like "special needs," "gifted and talented" or "at risk." We describe all our young people as being on a journey from unrealized to unlimited potential. As teachers it is our job to find out where each child is on that continuum and match our program to their specific needs. Describing young people's progress in terms of potential is an approach described by Durie (2006) in this way:

> The "potential approach" encompasses wellbeing, knowledge, influence and resources and the desired outcome is one where Māori succeed as Māori. Built on the complementary pillars of rawa (wealth), mātauranga (knowledge) and whakamana (autonomy and control), the focus is away from deficit and failure towards success and achievement. (p. 14)

We are always aware that what we think we teach and what young people actually learn are not the same and the background hegemonic White space, the "hidden" covert curriculum, is always present. The following eight key assumptions about learning are integral to all three lenses in the Power Lenses Learning Model, and they serve to drive school organization and learning practice in both schools. The ways these assumptions guide practice in classrooms are explained in detail in following chapters:

1. Learning is integrated—across subject areas and with students' lives and realities.
2. Learning is negotiated—by students, with teachers.
3. Learning is inquiry-based and student-driven.
4. Learning is critical—it provides young people with the power and the tools to understand and challenge inequity and injustice and to make change in their lives.

5. Learning is whānau-based—it is collective, cooperative, collaborative and reciprocal. This means learning is shared—you receive it, you share it, and you give back to other learners.
6. Learning is located within strong relationships—with self, with each other, with teachers, with the learning itself and its relevance, with the world beyond school and between home and school.
7. Learning is culturally located and allows you to live your cultural norms throughout the school day.
8. All students are at different places on the Unrealized to Unlimited potential continuum and this position is always identified.

In the next three chapters Kia Aroha College's practice and vision for learning through each of the three lenses is described in detail.

References

Bishop, R., Berryman, M., Richardson, C., & Tiakiwai, S. (2003). *Te Kotahitanga: The experiences of Year 9 and 10 Māori students in mainstream classrooms*. Report to the Ministry of Education. Wellington: Ministry of Education.

Castagno, A. E., & Brayboy, B. M. J. (2008). Culturally responsive schooling for indigenous youth: A review of the literature. *Review of Educational Research, 78*(4), 941–993.

Driver, A. (2015). *Cultural leadership: the reciprocities of right relationship at Kia Aroha College*. Auckland: Auckland University.

Duncan-Andrade, J., & Morrell, E. (2008). *The art of critical pedagogy : Possibilities for moving from theory to practice in urban schools*. New York, NY: Peter Lang.

Durie, M. (2006). *Whānau, education, and Māori potential*. Paper presented at Hui Taumata Mātauranga V. Taupo, New Zealand.

Ladson-Billings, G. (1994). *The dreamkeepers: Successful teachers of African American children*. California: Jossey-Bass.

Milne, A. (2004). *"They didn't care about normal kids like me." Restructuring a school to fit the kids* (Unpublished masters thesis). Massey University, Palmerston North.

Otero, G., & Chambers-Otero, S. (2002). *Relationa learning: Toward a human ecology in 21st century schools*. Retrieved from http://relationalearning.com/wp-content/uploads/2013/09/RL-Position-Paper-PDF1.pdf

Penetito, W. (2010). *What's Māori about Māori education?* Wellington: Victoria University Press.

Scottie Productions. (2011, July 24). Whare Wananga [Episode 11]. In *Whare Māori., 2011*. Auckland: Māori Television.

· 6 ·

COLORING IN THE SCHOOL-LEARNING SPACE

The School-Learning Lens

This chapter describes the school's practice through the school-learning lens, the lens through which Kia Aroha College views the mandated national curriculum. The chapter describes the pedagogical practices within the school that intentionally "color in" the school-learning White space and specifically describes a critical pedagogy of whānau in practice. It emphasizes however that practice viewed through the school-learning lens is predicated on the belief that not only do we have to view learning differently, through lenses that include self-learning and global learning, but there is still very much work to be done to review the practice in our education system within this school lens. Within school-learning experiences there must be room for "opposition scholarship" (Calmore, 1992, p.2161), that challenges the narrow focus of Western academic learning and has a legitimate and equal place, not alongside the lens, but *centered within it*.

Culture at the Center

Over the past two decades, both in New Zealand and internationally, there has been an increasing realization of the central role of students' cultures in classroom practice. In New Zealand, the school's role in connecting school-learning to students' cultures was highlighted by Bishop and Glynn (1999) who developed the idea that, "culture counts" explaining that classrooms should be "places where learners can bring to who they are to the learning interactions in complete safety, and their knowledges are acceptable and legitimate" (p. 163).

The relationship between students and teachers is a crucial factor in this interaction. In order for teachers to help students become culturally competent, they first must become aware of their own culture and its role in their lives and become culturally competent themselves. Evident in both international and New Zealand research with indigenous and minoritized students is the crucial importance of a positive, respectful and reciprocal relationship between teacher and student (Bishop, Berryman, Richardson, & Tiakiwai, 2003; Delpit, 2006; Ladson-Billings, 1994). However, there is also ample evidence that the majority of teachers bring to their relationships with students a "pedagogy of whiteness" (Adkins & Hytten, 2001; Levine-Raskey, 2000) that maintains the teacher's knowledge as the point of reference and the lens through which the relationship is perceived and developed.

In the *Te Kotahitanga* research project, Bishop et al. (2003) developed an Effective Teaching Profile (ETP), to address the need for teachers to reject deficit theorizing about Māori students' achievement and to accept professional responsibility for changing their practice. The ETP includes teachers caring for students as culturally located individuals, teachers having high expectations of their students, and teachers building caring and learning relationships and interactions with Māori students. The "Culturally Responsive Pedagogy of Relations" developed through *Te Kotahitanga* (Bishop, Berryman, Cavanagh, & Teddy, 2007), is an approach that merges the concepts of culturally responsive pedagogy (Gay, 2000; Ladson-Billings, 1994; Osborne & Cooper, 2001), with a pedagogy of relations (Bingham & Sidorkin, 2004; Shields, Bishop, & Mazawi, 2005; Sidorkin, 1999, 2002).

Kia Aroha College's changes to restructure the school as a whānau also meant conscientizing teachers. Sleeter (2008) states, "There is ample evidence that White people enter the teaching profession bringing little or no understanding of race and racism, but well-armed with misinformation and stereotypes learned over the years" (p. 82). This misinformation is not only the domain of White teachers. Penetito (2002) comments, "Pākehā teachers and a significant proportion of Māori teachers have habitually steered away from doing anything that was too seriously Māori" (p. 182).

The requirements for teachers in Kia Aroha College, included raising their own awareness of their own cultures so they could better understand others, exploring their knowledge and experience of social justice, and culturally responsive, critical, pedagogy. That soul-searching is necessary for the fundamental shifts teachers need to make to work in our school. That requires reading, talking, reflecting, questioning, researching and higher level study. The outcome of this conscientization of teachers is the Critically Conscious, Culturally Responsive, Teacher Profile (CCCRTP) developed by our teachers in 2008 and adopted by all as their job description. Alongside the mandated national professional teaching criteria, the CCCRTP includes requirements that a teacher:

- practices a critically conscious, culturally responsive, pedagogy that understands the relationship between power and knowledge;
- shows evidence of ongoing learning and developing of their pedagogy in the areas of social justice, solidarity, and critical thinking;
- shows commitment to becoming secure in their own cultural identity;
- understands the cultural backgrounds of students;
- understands of the concept of whānau and its importance as the fundamental concept underpinning all school organisation and practice; and
- is visibly involved in the cultural aspects of the school's program and practices including hosting and looking after visitors, parents, and whānau.

Conscientizing teachers also meant helping teachers to reject deficit thinking and replace that with a model that envisages unlimited potential in all children. This fits with the principles of authentic deep caring, and a pedagogy of whānau which carry with them the implicit understanding that these are "our kids," not "other people's children" (Delpit, 2006). This change in thinking shifts the focus from low, self-fulfilling, expectations of youth of color, to expectations of high learning outcomes in both Western "academic" learning and cultural knowledge and competence.

Students' connectedness, however, needs to go beyond a positive learner-teacher relationship. Students need to not only to be connected to who they are as culturally located individuals, but need also to see where they fit in the world. This is consistent with Banks (2004) framing the necessity to develop a balance of cultural, national and global identifications. Otero and Chambers-Otero (2002) advise, "drop curriculum, drop subjects, teach connectedness, our survival depends on it," and comment further:

For schools to be effective with today's young people, it will be crucial to have a sense of self and a sense of how to relate to 12 billion other selves. Ironically, to succeed in a global society, the personal and local must become the focus. The major challenge will be an examination and redefinition of the relationship between the individual and the collective.

The Concept of Whānau

Bishop (1996) discusses the range of uses of the word whānau from its literal meaning of extended family, people linked by blood to a common ancestor, to Metge's (1990) concept of metaphoric whānau to refer to collectives of people working for a common end, who may not be connected by kinship, let alone descent (p. 217).

Moeke-Pickering (1996) believes that the sense of collective affiliation from the concept of whānau with its obligatory roles and responsibilities plays a major role in forming and maintaining a pathway through which Māori identities can be formed and developed, in spite of urbanization and dislocation from these traditional ties experienced by many Māori. Moeke-Pickering suggests this separation does not necessarily mean that Māori are neglecting their whānau cultural practices. Instead, many Māori have become adept at maintaining a balance between their Māori and their contemporary worlds. Bishop (2005) agrees, "It seems to me that, in practice, Māori cultural practices are alive and well and that, when used either literally or metaphorically, they enable Māori people to understand and control what is happening" (endnote 8).

Māori students in New Zealand schools, however, seldom have this choice of continuing to "live as Māori" (Durie, 2001), while pursuing academic learning at school. Bishop and Glynn (1999) suggest, the principles of Kura Kaupapa Māori and *Te Aho Matua*[1] provide "metaphors for a new awareness of theorising and addressing educational relationships" (p. 168). To achieve authenticity in this culturally located learning model however, Kura Kaupapa Māori had to withdraw from the state education (Whitestream) system. Similarly, very few Pasifika students have the opportunity to enjoy a culturally connected learning environment within the state school system. Year 11 student 'Aisea's research identifies the issue from a Tongan learner's perspective:

> There were over 17,500 Tongan students in New Zealand schools in 2014. One hundred and seventy-nine of us were learning for more than 50% of our time in the

Tongan language. Sixty-nine of us were students in Kia Aroha College, the only secondary school in the country to give us this option, and the remaining 110 students were in two primary schools. (Ministry of Education, 2014)

It's hard to see then how our own language is a priority for the Government, or schools, in spite of the great rhetoric of the Pasifika Education Plan (Ministry of Education, 2013). The experience of many of our Pasifika students is captured by a Tongan student research participant who said that he felt accepted at Kia Aroha College and he credited the school with changing his future. In his description of his experience in his previous school, he said:

We never really learn about who we are and that. Just go and chuck you in a class. I was never really put in the same class as one of my brothers. I was never in a class with another Tongan. I was always in a class with heaps of White people, and I was always being mocked because of that. That's why they called me the bully when I was back there, because they kept mocking me and all that mocking just angered me more. But once I came here, all that bullying and that was gone. That's why all the teachers say I'm a changed man. ('Aisea, in Pirini-Edwards et al., 2015)

Smith (1997) states that a Kaupapa Māori paradigm in education is founded on three key themes; the validity and legitimacy of Māori are taken for granted, the survival and revival of Māori language and culture are imperative, and the struggle for autonomy over their own cultural well-being and over their own lives is vital to Māori struggle.

He describes Kaupapa Māori theory and praxis as being the response by Māori to the State/Pākehā dominated interests through conscientization and resistance to transformative action. Freire's (1972) model of change argues that conscientization leads to action or struggle; when people learn to read the word and read the world of injustice they will then act against it. Kaupapa Māori contends that this change is not necessarily a linear progression. Smith (2004) suggests that all of these components are equally important and all need to be held simultaneously. The elements are better understood as a cycle which individuals and groups can enter from any position without necessarily having to start at the point of "conscientization" (p. 50). Smith (2003) uses the example of parents who may have enrolled their child in a Kōhanga Reo (Māori language pre-school) because it was the only early childhood option in the town, but this later led to the parents becoming, "conscientized about the politics of language revitalization and highly active participants in resistance movement." Smith explains there can be simultaneous engagement with more than one element or engagement can be in any order. According to Smith, all Māori can be plotted somewhere on the cycle—"the point is that every Māori is in the struggle whether they like it or not, whether they know it or not" (p. 13).

Smith (2003) asserts that the lessons learned from the Māori experience and kaupapa Māori theory do have relevance and meaning in other indigenous contexts. There is certainly interest from Pasifika communities in the Kaupapa Māori model. However, Smith also advises caution in adopting these strategies uncritically or without proper consideration of the specific cultural context in which they are being reapplied:

> There is much to inform other indigenous contexts from this situation, in particular, the need to focus on the process of "transforming", and on the transformative outcomes—What is it? How can it be achieved? Do indigenous people's needs and aspirations require different schooling approaches? Who benefits? Such critical questions, which relate to the task of teachers being change agents, must not only inform our teacher education approaches, they must also ensure the "buy in" from the communities they are purporting to serve. (p. 14)

Aluli-Meyer (2001) articulates the issues for Pasifika learners in education systems that alienate indigenous learners:

> It has been a confusing travelogue with regard to schooling and indigenous knowledge. I was and still am a back-seat passenger in this car called Education. I have sat like a good daughter on some long cross-continental haul, trying to behave, but because I have begun to question acultural and thus apolitical assumptions in the art of teaching and the science of learning, I am in essence changing my own destination. The hermeneutic hazing has begun. It is a strange world indeed, to wake up and realize that everything I have learned in school, everything I've read in books, every vocabulary test and jumping jack, every seating arrangement and response expectation—absolutely everything—has not been shaped by a Hawaiian mind. (p. 124)

It is little wonder, Meyer explains, that Hawaiian understanding of this process has come slowly, "dulled by the guessing game of another culture," still believing, "that literacy is the best indicator of intelligence," and "always at the short end of a smaller and smaller identity stick." Hawaiian epistemology, Meyer writes, "is a long-term idea that is both ancient and modern, central and marginalized" (p. 126), that is both constant and changes, according to time and influence. She identifies seven ways of experiencing this "ocean of knowing":

1. Spirituality and Knowing—the cultural contexts of knowledge.
2. That Which Feeds—physical place and knowing.
3. The Cultural Nature of the Senses—expanding the idea of empiricism.
4. Relationship and Knowledge—self through other.

5. Utility and Knowledge—ideas of wealth and usefulness.
6. Words and Knowledge—causality in language and thought.
7. The Body-Mind Question—illusions of separation.

Tongan academic, Thaman (1995) argues, "For over one hundred years, we have promoted (or at least accepted) a view of education that is diametrically opposed to our traditional notions of *ako* (learning and teaching), *'ilo* and *poto*"[2] (p. 731). In recent years, indigenous Pacific scholars have investigated Pacific epistemologies and ways of doing and being. Their work documents and interprets efforts by local communities they are associated with or part of, to validate and explore their own epistemologies and to renegotiate development on their own terms (Huffer & Qalo, 2004, p. 88). Sanga (2002) describes the disconnected worlds in which most Pasifika students interact as "In-School" [IS] and "Out-of-School" [OS]:

> The world of IS and that of OS are seen as distinct entities. ... The IS world is one of conflicting value systems, of cultural intrusion, of identity denial, of pretensions and of compelling aspirations for things not theirs. ... [The world of OS] is the world of non-compartmentalisation, of being always tentative, of frequent doses of grace, of learning and working together, of competing in fun and of purposive socialisation. (Sanga, 2002)

These studies show that the importance of indigenous Pasifika knowledges and identities in education and school is gradually being recognised by Pasifika people in their home nations. Pasifika students in New Zealand schools, where the disconnection is even greater, find it even harder to build secure identities against the backdrop of New Zealand culture. Pasifika youth are, what Meyer refers to as, "links in this chain of cultural continuity." That continuity is threatened when the chain is broken, and when schools see no reason for it to be reconnected. In all of these worldviews, relationships are central.

A Critical Pedagogy of Whānau: Whanaungatanga in Practice

The word "whānau" is often used in a wide variety of contexts in school settings. Kia Aroha College staff explored questions about how whānau actually work out interaction, respect, expectations, responsibilities, and support, while dealing with mixtures of ages and maturity. In your whānau at home, do you work in age levels? Do bells ring to tell you to stop and change what you are doing every 45 minutes? Do you get new adults every period, or every year? The answers often brought up further issues. What about power? Who makes the decisions? Samoan staff told us, for example, that in their families children would have no part in decision-making.

The concept of whānau, with its associated concepts of cultural principles, values and obligations is central to Māori conscientization, resistance and transformation. Smith (1995) aligns the concept of whānau with knowledge, pedagogy, discipline, and curriculum in the school setting. These understandings guided our decisions about all of these aspects of Kia Aroha College's program and practice:

The whānau concept of knowledge is that knowledge is regarded as belonging to the whole group or whānau, rather than being private or belonging to the individual. It is a shared resource for the ultimate benefit of the total group, and is not essentially a credential for capital gain.

The whānau concept of pedagogy, comprises core Māori values that are taken as "given." It incorporates tuakana-teina as part of pedagogical framework, requiring that those with knowledge assist those needing and wanting to learn, and it mixes local wisdom with global knowledge. It is not simply a retreat to the past.

The whānau concept of discipline, positions the total school as constituting a single whānau. It regards all parents as "parents" to all children in the school whānau. It involves teachers being called papa (father), matua (father or uncle), whaea (mother or aunty), kōka (senior woman or aunty). It regards learning and behavior difficulties as a shared responsibility, and emphasizes that needs for discipline and types of discipline are different, depending on the child and the circumstances.

The whānau concept of curriculum requires that the Māori community has some measure of influence over what counts and what is included in curriculum. The curriculum is reorganized to connect with the interests and backgrounds of Māori learners, to "be Māori" is taken as "normal"; and the Māori worldview is reflected and reproduced within the school (Smith, 1995).

School Spaces as Whānau Spaces

The way the school is organized reflects our final decisions about what we meant by whānau, and whanaungatanga (relationships). In all parts of the school, several age levels work together throughout the day, in the same classes and stay with the same small group of teachers for at least four years. Students work within their own ethnic groups, usually with teachers fluent in their languages, and learn bilingually—in English and Māori in Te Whānau o Tupuranga, in Samoan and English in Lumana'i, in Tongan and English in Fonuamalu.[3] Te Whānau o Tupuranga students work predominantly in two levels, vertically grouped Years 7–10 classes and Years 11–13 classes multi-levelled according to senior NCEA levels of study.

The Māori concept of tuakana-teina is a key learning process—older students are expected to be responsible for younger ones, more able students are expected to support less able, learning is cooperative and collaborative, sometimes independent, but rarely individual. Teachers work across several classes of students in a flexible team-teaching organization. Students work in small groups on tasks that are usually inquiry-based, and which give them a wide range of choices and options. Timetabling is also flexible and teachers typically allow time to work intensively on the current study. There is minimal whole-class, teacher directed instruction. Senior staff, in a group interview in 2011, comment on the school's pedagogy of whānau in practice:

> It's having a different attitude like we have in our school about the whole, these are our kids and not other people's children sort of thing, and that all of us have a personal responsibility which is not the same as a professional responsibility. I think that many other schools are able to stop at a professional responsibility but we all take on the personal. ... I think in my experience in other schools there is no requirement to move into that personal space, you can just stay in the professional realm and it doesn't really matter if they succeed or don't succeed—you can put it in a box and think that is all I can do. (Haley)

> In other schools we talk about whānau a lot but from my experience whānau to them is just like the grouping of sports teams or whatever school competition they run the in—that's their form of whānau, or they stick a few Samoans in a class together and they call it a whānau, when they have no real concept of that, whereas we have actually looked deeper. We validate our kids' cultures so we haven't just held on to the power to say to our kids, by the way, you are still going to learn this because we say so. (Eneli)

> They are still saying our kids are failing. Why? Because of their system—there is nothing in place for our people. If only they would give us a chance with our own way of dealing with our people, for example in Lumana'i we have kids who are good in palagi (English) and we get them to work with kids that are good in Samoan and they share that but in most schools they don't do that. (Eliu)

Authentic Critical Caring

These teachers are identifying the roles related to whānau. Whanaungatanga imposes on whānau members, a series of rights and responsibilities, commitments, obligations, and supports that are fundamental to the group. Bishop (1996) calls these "the tikanga of the whānau," attributes which "can be summed up in the words aroha (love in the broadest sense), awhi (helpfulness), manaaki (hospitality), tiaki (guidance)" (p. 218).

Duncan-Andrade (2007) describes the decision of teachers in his research to be committed to a consistent presence in the school community and in the lives of the students and their families. The teachers explain their actions as part of a commitment to solidarity with their students, as opposed to empathy (p. 629). That shift in perspective is crucial in whanaungatanga. It marks the shift from seeing students as victims, to one of empowerment and authentic caring – *aroha* in Māori terms, *alofa* in Samoan, *'ofa* in Tongan and *aroa* in most Cook Islands Māori dialects. It is important not to see these concepts as a "soft" option. With every privilege inherent in whanaungatanga comes corresponding responsibilities, expectations and accountability. Macfarlane, Glynn, Grace, Penetito, and Bateman (2008) define aroha as referring to "the manner of responding positively to the *hā* (essence) of people by accepting their individuality, together with their whānau connections, their strengths and their self-worth" (p. 110).

The Spanish language equivalent of aroha is *cariño*, which Duncan-Andrade (2006) describes "is more a concept than a word. It is the foundation of relationships among the poor and working classes—often the only thing left to give, in families raising children on substandard wages" (p. 451). He cites Valenzuela's (1999) description of *cariño* in the context of schooling as *authentic caring*. This is a concept distinctly different from what she calls *aesthetic caring* (italics in original) "a culture of false caring, one where the most powerful members of the relationship define themselves as caring despite the fact that the recipients of their so-called caring do not perceive it as such" (Duncan-Andrade, 2006, p. 451). Valenzuela (2005) clarifies this distinction by explaining, "teachers expect students to *care about* school in a technical fashion before they *care for* them, while students expect teachers to *care for* them before they *care about* school" (p. 83).

Noddings (2003) also uses the term "aesthetical caring" for caring about things and ideas and associates caring with the action of, "stepping out of one's own personal frame of reference into the other's" (p. 24), as opposed to projecting one's own reality on to the other person. Thompson (1998) strongly critiques the colorblind assumption of caring as an emotion-laden practice characterized by low expectations motivated by taking pity on students' social circumstances. Antrop-Gonzáles and De Jesús (2006) agree with Thompson and advance a theory of critical caring:

> Notions of educational caring are not colorblind or powerblind and communities of color necessarily understand caring within their sociocultural context. This context must be acknowledged in order to forge a new caring framework that privileges the cultural values and political economy of communities of color as a foundation for education. (p. 413)

Beauboeuf-Lafontant (2002) examines the pedagogy of exemplary black women teachers who exhibit "womanist caring." She draws on three central points that support womanism: the understanding that oppression provides all people with varying degrees of penalty and privilege, the belief that individual empowerment combined with collective action is the key to lasting social transformation, and a humanism that seeks the liberation of all, not just themselves (p. 72). She connects the caring of these women teachers to the mothering of their own children and cites one teacher who established her own school based on a premise of care and accountability, "If the school was going to be good enough for other children it had to be good enough for my own" (p. 73). This is an often-stated belief among staff of Kia Aroha College where, when we counted in 2010, nine staff members had made the deliberate choice to enrol their children, grandchildren, or nieces and nephews in the school. Beauboeuf-Lafontant describes the African-American teachers' attitude towards mothering as a community responsibility. This same cultural connection is very evident in the practice of all staff in the different cultural settings in Kia Aroha College.

Macfarlane et al. (2008) link the construct of whanaungatanga with rangatiratanga (self-determination, Māori authority) and highlight this as a major difference in values between a Western/European construct of the individual "self" and individual achievement, and Māori and other indigenous peoples' worldviews on human development and education. They state:

> In a Māori worldview, qualities such as personal autonomy, independence, leadership, and prestige are all learned and exercised within a social context in which people share a powerful collective identity. Personal autonomy, strength and leadership are always exercised within the context of whanaungatanga, of nurturing and caring relationships. ... Part of achieving rangatiratanga (chiefly) status involves

striving for individual excellence while at the same time providing and caring for the community, and receiving the respect of the community. (pp. 118–119)

These learning opportunities have to be embedded in the way the school operates and is structured. In a White Space, you can't see manaakitanga (caring for people) if your youth don't look after others daily, or tautoko (support) if they work independently and individually, you can't see whanaungatanga and aroha if whānau isn't at the center, you can't see expertise in tikanga (Māori customary beliefs) and Māori performing arts if your performance group is assembled to entertain your visitors and then vanishes again. You can't see action for social change if you don't address all the barriers our whānau face.

Students' Experience of Whanaungatanga

The following responses from former students of Te Whānau o Tupuranga, in an online survey and face to face interviews in 2011 identify what they felt were the key features of the school, and the differences between these and other schools they had attended. They show the importance of whānau and the authentic critical caring described in the previous section. The use of first names or anonymity respects the participant's choice:

> Te Whānau o Tupuranga works with the whānau for the whānau. ... The kaiako (teachers) are like your parents, you can ask them for anything day or night and they will do all that they can to give you what you need. (Participant A)

> I like the way we try to fight stereotypes. I also like the way that people don't give up on you, and don't say, "Next school. Away you go." They keep trying to help you improve yourself. I like the way you are accepted as who you are. You don't have to impress anybody here. (Ngawai)

> Whakawhanaungatanga: Being able to relate to every person as your brother, sister, aunty, uncle and even Nan. I don't know of any other kura (school) that has this type of vibe. (Kylie)

> It felt so comfortable being here. Everything you did, it just seemed normal. I didn't ever feel the need to leave. It was just like being back home, or being at home really. When you are here you know who you are and where you are from, you know your history and your whole identity pretty much, and then you go somewhere else and there are people who don't even know where they are from, and that's weird. I still feel Māori, no doubt about that. I'm going to be Māori anywhere, but when I'm somewhere else

besides here, it's like I have to change who I am to understand everyone else or they don't take me seriously. It feels I always have to prove myself. (Ngawai)

It is much harder to fail, or suspend from school, children who belong to the whānau, and not to "other people." It requires genuine partnership and solidarity with families and a commitment that goes beyond teaching. This means that the practice of whanaungatanga in school requires rethinking usual school policies. In Kia Aroha College it means inclusion, so students with special learning or behavior needs remain in the classroom and are not withdrawn. It means support for parents, grandparents, siblings, and other family members, and the employment of a social worker, and a youth health nurse. The establishment of a Whānau Center, the school marae, and Fale Pasifika (Pasifika Center) demonstrate that commitment. It means accepting all students and, having accepted them, not giving up on them. It means being in solidarity with our students, outraged at inequity and injustice and being determined not to perpetuate these in school decision-making and policy. In 2004 we made a decision that if we were serious about whānau we would no longer stand-down or suspend students from school. In the discussion with staff prior to implementing this policy, staff were asked, in order to fulfill this goal, how would the behavior and thinking of the adults in the school have to change? Over a decade later apart from a very small number of exceptions, when a decision has been made by the school and family together, this policy has been upheld.

The commitment required from teachers to retain children in school is part of whanaungatanga. Although at different times each school has trialed a series of set consequences for identified behaviors, these have been discarded in favor of a process that utilizes the strong relationships between teachers and students, students and students, and school and home to develop an appropriate response to each situation as needed.

In keeping with the whānau concept of discipline (Smith, 1995), Yang (2009) warns against a universal discipline policy in favor of a "nurturing Classroom X," and advocates, "Schools should not invest in a great discipline policy, but rather in a genuine discipline praxis" (p. 59) that is geared towards developing teachers' practice and involves sustained, serious self-critique and reflection. Yang sees "Classroom X" as a learning environment with a critical X-factor:

> Classroom X operates as a highly structured apprenticeship, rather than a rule-bound reformatory, as a space for rigorous creativity rather than for free expression. Although safe, it is not a "safe" space, but rather a community of risk-taking, of

> setbacks, of difficulty. This classroom engages the learner in these risks, but also provides the structure to do so. Although collaborative, it is not equalitarian—the teacher exercises authority without becoming an authoritarian (Lisa Delpit, 1988). In this classroom, everybody swims. (p. 55)

In Kia Aroha College inappropriate behavior might result in other staff taking that child for a fixed time to give the teacher and child time out. It involves family first, rather than last when all else has failed. Students who disrespect others or the school's expectations are made aware of the impact of their behavior, and are required to be part of the solution to fix the harm they have caused and to face the consequences of their actions. Often this involves mentoring by older students and always the response assumes there is a shared responsibility taken for the actions and decisions of a member of the whānau. This meant for example, when a female Samoan teacher reprimanded a new Māori student to the school and was deliberately jostled by him as a result, Tupuranga staff asked senior students to discuss with Samoan teachers the appropriate Samoan cultural process to make an apology. The total Tupuranga staff and student population then seated themselves silently outside the Samoan bilingual unit and waited to be invited in, where senior students and staff then apologized to the Samoan teacher and their apology was formally accepted. This was a powerful lesson to the offender of the widespread impact of his behavior—and a lesson to everyone else involved as well. These are many more options than being able to avoid the issue by leaving the school either temporarily or permanently. Former students comment:

> A key feature of Tupuranga was definitely the kaiako [teachers]. They were awesome! We knew they would go the extra mile for us and be there when we needed them. Also if we were out of line they wouldn't have to say much for us to get the idea and tune ourselves back up. They built their respect within us first and so it was like being told off by Aunty. (Kingi)

> Kaiako listen to the students. If there was a fight they would listen to all sides of the story before they started dishing out consequences. … Kaiako notice things. Say, like all of a sudden I went from a excellent student to a haututū (troublesome) student because there were problems going on at home. The kaiako would pick up that something was wrong and then would want try and help me out. (Kylie)

Student-Driven Learning

Placing culture at the center of curriculum design meant changing to a curriculum that is integrated, not just across subject disciplines, but across students' lives and realities (Beane, 1997). This integrated curriculum approach, already built around issues of social concern which are specifically relevant to students' families, communities and cultures, later widened to incorporate youth participatory action research (Akom, Cammarota, & Ginwright, 2008; Duncan-Andrade & Morrell, 2008; Romero et al., 2010), and learning through a critical, social justice framework. This critical lens in itself has been instrumental in raising teacher awareness of the need to reflect on their practice and particularly to consider the pervasiveness of White privilege in their training and in their experience, regardless of their own ethnicity.

In practice, contexts are identified through a range of activities both at the beginning of the year and at different stages throughout the year. All students are involved in this process. Teachers continually "frontload" topical issues as they occur to ensure students' questions do not become routine and repetitive. All events provide rich contexts for questioning and study. At the beginning of 2016, Year 10 students joined the march in Auckland City, to protest against New Zealand's signing of the Trans-Pacific Partnership Agreement (TPPA), after studying the impact of this free trade agreement on Māori. Many Māori protested this policy on the grounds that Māori did not cede sovereignty under the Treaty of Waitangi and therefore the government did not have the right to negotiate away deeply held Māori beliefs and Māori rights. This was an example of the use of a topical issue, studied from an indigenous perspective, by one group of students.

Other contexts are school-wide, and studied by all year levels. These might start with a single question. After examining Dr. Manulani Aluli-Meyer's (2008) assertion that "aloha is our intelligence," teachers posed the question, "If aroha (ofa, alofa) is our intelligence, how intelligent are we?" Students explored traditional knowledge and how knowledge was valued. The topic took on a Science and Health curriculum perspectives as students investigated traditional medicines and healing, the use and knowledge of the sea and Māori concepts of seasons. Central to the study for Māori students was the Māori belief in the "three baskets of knowledge." These provided a framework for students to ask how these traditional knowledges and intelligences had changed, and what were their modern day equivalents?

At times, the overall topic is studied through different contexts, with year levels groups taking on a different aspect. In an investigation entitled "Reading the World," the whole school studied majoritarian stories, defined by Love (2004) as, "the description of events as told by members of dominant/majority groups, accompanied by the values and beliefs that justify the actions taken by dominants to insure their dominant position" (p. 229).

Students investigated a movement that demonstrated a counter-story and then explained, why this was a counter-story, and what majoritarian story it exposed. Using this knowledge, they then investigated a counter-story from their own iwi, whānau, or village to answer the same questions. Years 7 and 8 Māori students investigated the counter-story of "Nga Tamatoa" a Māori activist group that promoted Māori rights, and fought racial discrimination throughout the 1970s. Ngā Tamatoa was instrumental in raising New Zealand's awareness of Māori rights and fought for the teaching of Māori language in schools. Pasifika Years 7–9 students investigated the Pasifika diaspora, asking why Pasifika people had left the Pacific Islands to live and work in New Zealand, and how that had impacted on Pasifika society, both in their home islands and in New Zealand. Years 10 and 11 across the school explored the "Idle No More" movement, originating with First Nations people in Canada in protest against parliamentary acts that threatened to erode Indigenous sovereignty and environmental protections, without consultation. The movement, called on "all people to join in a peaceful revolution, to honour Indigenous sovereignty, and to protect the land and water" (Idle No More, 2013). Senior students in Years 11–13, studied the Mexican-American Studies program in Tucson, Arizona, and the banning of this successful program, and the banning of books by Arizona education officials.

At the same time as students were studying majoritarian and counter-stories, staff professional development required teachers to investigate a counter-story that demonstrated their own critical consciousness. These stories were to be presented to the whole staff in any way each teacher chose. The stories could be the same as those their students were studying, or they could be any other story, including personal stories. The outcome of this professional development was powerful. Teachers created displays, made movies and power-point presentations, wrote stories, songs and haka, and created art pieces. The methods of delivery and presentation were as varied as the stories themselves. One story told of the successful retention of the pronunciation of their family name in spite of every effort on the part of schools to anglicize it. Another story was a display about the importance of reading taught by a teacher's grandmother (complete with books from childhood and a bone-china cup of tea). There were stories about fighting back after damage caused by schooling, about reclaiming language and identity. Parents told stories of pride in their children's achievements, and there were stories about turning lives around. Some of these memories were painful, and when teachers asked to be excused from presenting these two colleagues, their request was respected. It was an important lesson in conscientization, which mirrored the learning of students and gave teachers insight into their students' learning journey.

Most often, this learning ends with a "performance of knowledge" which might be a presentation, a speech, a written piece of work, or a display. Sometimes there is an "Expo"—a large-scale presentation of work to a variety of audiences, including other classes, families, and communities. Audiences might be the class, the whole school, families, visitors, or conference and speech contest forums. The importance of kapa haka (Māori performing arts) and Pasifika performing arts in this demonstration of learning is discussed in the next chapter.

Five typical student-negotiated contexts and the learning that evolved from them, are explained in detail in the following section, and typify the practice understood through the school-learning lens. The examples are chosen from a ten-year time span that shows continuity of this pedagogy over time, and throughout the three schools' changes of status and structure.

Student Context 1: Citizenship

Prior to Manukau City's amalgamation into the Auckland super-city structure Te Whānau o Tupuranga students regularly attended Manukau City Council citizenship ceremonies each month as the Māori support group for the city's Mayor. The group received a donation from the City Council for this duty, and this funding directly contributed to the costs of the school marae, which is heavily used by the school. These regular public performances also enhanced the school's profile and were an opportunity for our youth to give service to the community. However, students had questions about immigration, and the impact of the hundreds of new citizens they saw each month, on jobs for Māori whānau. This questioning led to a major study of citizenship by Years 7–10 students—not from the usual perspective of what constitutes a "good citizen" but from a critical Māori viewpoint. Students' questions included:

- Does the government make sure new citizens understand the Treaty of Waitangi?
- How do we retain our tuakiritanga (identity) as Māori?
- If New Zealand changes because of immigration, what are we prepared to compromise (if anything)?
- What happens to culture in citizenship?
- Is there ever a time when citizenship should be revoked and if so, when?

- What was the concept of citizenship in the past and how has this changed?
- Do you become colonized when you become a citizen?
- Pākehā think they own the land, but to Māori the land owns us because it is where our tupuna (ancestors) came from. What do immigrants think?

One of the outcomes of this study was a significant reduction in the number of times we agreed to support the city's citizenship ceremonies as a form of resistance to what students felt were decisions that overlooked Māori rights and interests.

Student Context 2: Māori Education

In 2007, senior staff received an invitation to attend an education conference in Manukau City, with the theme of *Connecting Education and Community*. The purpose of the conference was to help to shape the development of a Manukau Education Strategy. We decided to register our Year 13 students as full delegates to the conference.

The students spent several days in intense preparation prior to the conference. A set of discussion papers distributed to registered delegates proved a rich source of information and "front loading" about what to expect and what they wanted to find out—Who was the conference for? Who was consulted? What was presented? Who were the presenters? What did they focus on? Who decided what to include? Whose values counted? What was insinuated or suggested? What was left out? They learned about discourse analysis, they drafted questions about the papers, and researched the background of some of the initiatives featured.

At the conference, they took photos and notes. As the only young people there, very visible in their formal school uniform, they were approached by many principals and community leaders who asked why they had come, and who were taken aback when the students said they had come to critically analyze the conference from the perspective of Māori learners in Manukau. The students didn't miss the fact that it was 2.30 p.m. before the word "Māori" was mentioned, only once, and then in relation to the problem of diabetes, or that the only session run by Māori was at 4.30 on Friday afternoon, or that most people arrived for the first session after the pōwhiri (Māori ceremonial welcome).

Back at school, the students were outraged at the marginalization of Māori education in the conference format and the city's Strategic Plan. Each chose a specific aspect of the conference to produce a research paper and a multimedia presentation. Lita used critical discourse analysis and, in her presentation, she first explained what this was:

> As an example, if a school newsletter tells parents that they are having a Māori Language Week and a Pacific Languages Week, critical discourse analysis would make us realise that, if there are 38 weeks in the school year, what they are really saying is that they have 36 English Language Weeks. The newsletter makes us feel the school is focusing on Māori and Pacific languages. Critical discourse analysis helps us see that the school's real focus is English.

She then analyzed a paper and presentation by the Ministry of Education on schooling improvement initiatives in Manukau:

> Using critical discourse analysis I can say that, with the use of "raising" and "improvement" so frequently, it is insinuated that there was a problem in the first place that needed to be fixed, and literacy is the only solution. Look at me! Do I look like a problem waiting to be fixed? That's a rhetorical question!
>
> I believe that what you focus on becomes your reality. If the Ministry's focus is only on improvement and raising achievement as defined by Pākehā, they won't recognise the unique talents and skills we, as Māori learners, have to offer. The effect of this type of education is cultural genocide, the destruction of our identity. My analysis showed that there is little chance that this will be understood by the leaders of our education in Manukau City. (Lita)

Wikitoria decided to explore the question of "Whose knowledge counts?"

> Whose values count when questions are raised about the purpose of education? Mainstream values, in other words Pākehā values. Where is there a place for Māori values? Tomlins-Jahnke (2007, p. 6) says, the term mainstream is a "code" word for schools that privilege a western-Eurocentric education tradition. And so I ask again, what is knowledge? Can we focus on one culture's learning and leave out the other? I don't think so! It's not fair and it doesn't work! (Wikitoria)

Lawrence focused on hegemony. "Hegemony is insidious," he said. "It creeps up on you." He was later to use his understanding of hegemony in the impromptu speech that won him the regional and national titles in the prestigious *Ngā Manu Kōrero* speech competitions.[4] He gave his investigation the title, "What's the use of all this culture stuff?"

> By 2050 when it is predicted Pākehā will be in the minority in Aotearoa, will Māori hegemony have a voice? I doubt it from the way our voice was not heard in the conference about the future of education in Manukau. Paulo Freire (1982) says, "The silenced ... are the masters of inquiry into the underlying causes of the events in their world. In this context research becomes a means of moving them beyond silence into a quest to proclaim the world." That means, if they had asked us, we would have been the experts in telling them what was needed for our education—but they didn't! (Lawrence)

Maurice analyzed the photos he took at the conference to show that the majority of people at the conference, and almost all of the presenters, making decisions about education in Manukau City, were White. He then took photos at the Manukau City Center shopping mall to contrast the ethnic mix of people who live in the community with those who attended the conference. He confirmed this by requesting a list of delegates from the organizers. He later went on to analyze NCEA statistics and school Education Review Office reports on local secondary schools to produce a report on the lack of educational provision for Māori students in Manukau:

> The conference was in Manukau City, the audience were mainly Pākehā and the people talking about what education should be were Pākehā, but the conference was supposed to be about rangatahi (youth) like us. So what does that mean for us as young Māori learners in Manukau City? To me I think it's no wonder so many Māori students leave school before they are even 16 and hardly any of us make it to Year 13. (Maurice)

The topic was to become a year-long, in-depth study for this group. Together we mapped out an NCEA credentials pathway built around the theme of hegemony and the marginalization of Māori. By the end of the year, the students had presented their findings to a wide range of audiences including the Minister of Education, Members of Parliament, Ministry of Education and City representatives and staff, who formally assessed their work. Their questions prompted a response from conference organizers that the students felt was a poor attempt to cover up the omission of Māori from the proceedings. They had good reason to believe that a Māori education forum, hastily convened after the event, was in part due to their presentations and questioning.

Video clips from their presentations were used in my own presentations throughout the country and when possible, the students accompanied me and spoke to audiences in person. They had read and reviewed a wide range of texts that related to this theme, including an Australian film, a novel by a Māori author, speeches by Malcolm X and Steve Biko, academic papers by

Māori researchers, and a series of newspaper articles about police raids on the Tūhoe people. They had produced extended transactional writing using four different genre, produced a short film from their work using professional industry-standard movie-making software, and used computer graphics to advertise the film premiere.

The NCEA standards, chosen by the students with input and advice from teachers, covered social studies, sociology, English, computing and media studies. They covered the 42 credits required from prescribed subjects for a University Entrance qualification. Together with credits from Māori Performing Arts and te reo Māori, as well as some individual subject choices, such as mathematics, they provided students with all the credits required to achieve NCEA Level 3.

The Manukau Education Conference and the marginalization of Māori from these proceedings immediately caught these students' attention and kept them engaged and highly motivated. Having been so closely involved in the design, the planning and the choice of contexts within the broad topic, which they had also chosen, these students became predominantly self-directed, requiring only facilitation and support from their teachers who were also co-members of the learning whānau. The learning and achievement that came from students' lived experiences in this context is the powerful learning that results from a genuine critical pedagogy of indignation (Freire, 2004).

This indignation and outrage is well-founded. The following year, in her first year of university study for a Bachelor of Education degree, one of these four students sent me a copy of her first essay, on the topic of diversity. She wrote about hegemony and dominant/subordinate identities. She quoted a wide range of sources including Freire, Gramsci, and Ladson-Billings, as well as Māori and Pasifika research. Her lecturer's reaction was to ask for a meeting and to question her closely about how she could possibly know so much about hegemony? The very clear implication was she must have had help or had plagiarized material in order to write in this way so soon after leaving school. Her answer that she had learned this at school was met with disbelief. Her essay stated:

> Throughout the eight years I spent at my secondary school, I was given opportunities to learn in a culturally relevant learning environment, I was given opportunities and expected to lead and assist the younger members in our whānau. Unlike many other students in secondary schools, my experience of learning has enabled me to develop my cultural identity, validate my cultural beliefs and learn about the world in an environment that allowed me to live and think as a young Māori woman. (personal communication, April 27, 2009)

Other students studying at tertiary level have reported similar incidents, and this same student was to face a second serious accusation of plagiarism, for the same reason, before she successfully completed her degree.

Student Context 3: Social Toxins

In 2009, "social toxins" was the theme for the year, in both middle and senior levels of the school. The spark that engendered student questions about social toxins was the visit in September 2008 of Dr. Jeffrey Duncan-Andrade and Dr. K. Wayne Yang. Senior students participated in all the seminars these two visiting professors delivered to educators at our school marae. They also worked with these visitors in classes. All staff also attended their workshops and seminars.

Throughout the 2009 year, students explored the question, "Is inequality making us sick?" (Adelman, 2008). Groups investigated the phenomenon of root shock in ecosystems and the impact of many different aspects of this trauma when it is applied to people, from the transience of families, to the loss of land, language, culture, and identity due to colonization, assimilation and integration policies. Te Whānau o Tupuranga middle school students walked to the Manukau City Centre to participate in the march arranged by Māori groups to protest the government's proposal to merge Auckland's cities into one super-city. Senior students looked at gentrification and the impact of council policies like this on communities like ours. Tongan students asked the question, "Who has the power?" in relation to the government's decision to amalgamate the five cities in the Auckland region. Cook Islands Māori students explored the loss of the Cook Islands Māori language and asked about freedoms, racism, and privilege. Samoan students debated whether the goal of their parents and grandparents to seek a 'better' life by bringing their families to New Zealand has actually been fulfilled. They studied the "root shock" of immigration and asked is your life really "better" if, as a result of those decisions, you have lost your language and identity?

Student Context 4: My Culture Defines Me

Towards the end of 2011 senior students were engaged in a social studies investigation on the topic; "My culture defines me." A critical question arising from this topic was, "but who is defining my culture?" A group of five students in Years 11, 12 and 13, decided to investigate how schooling had impacted on their culture, and to explore whether their experience of schooling in Kia Aroha College was any different from that of their parents and their peers who had been Māori or Pasifika learners in other schools. They drew on their long term involvement in the school as their starting point and, with input from several staff members, they developed these questions:

1. How is my culture defined by schooling in New Zealand?
2. Why has this happened?
3. What is my family's experience of this?
4. What is Kia Aroha College's response to this?
5. How is that response working for us as rangatahi (youth)?

The group decided to conduct a survey about people's experience of school. They chose to survey family members, community members, teachers, past students and current students, both those who had been students in Te Whānau o Tupuranga since Year 7, and those who had enrolled later, after spending time in other secondary schools. They also surveyed students who were not enrolled in Te Whānau o Tupuranga. Altogether, they surveyed 100 people, 66% of whom were either current or past students and 74% of whom were under the age of 20. By the end of 2011 the student group had developed rich data from these sources and had decided to select some of the survey participants to conduct in-depth video interviews.

The students also had access to research from other sources, independent of the schools, which included Education Review Office reports, a research report on whanaungatanga in practice following a 2-year study of the school by the New Zealand Families Commission (O'Sullivan et al., 2011), and the 2011 National Identity and Cultural Diversity Study (Walshaw, Andrews, Bell, Butler, & Tawhai, 2012) by Massey University which Year 12 students had participated in.

Earlier in 2011 I had been invited to present a paper at the 2012 American Education Research Association (AERA) Conference in Vancouver in a Symposium entitled, *Reclaiming Education: Youth Counter-Narratives in the Neoliberal Reform Era*. As the student group presented their early work to fellow students and staff it became very evident to me that their research could replace what I had intended to present in this forum. This possibility sparked off wider research by the group into the schooling experiences of First Nations youth in Canada, and they were able to make comparisons with their findings.

In April 2012, with the full support of their families, the staff, and the Board of Trustees, the five students and three staff members traveled with me to Vancouver where the students presented their research. They received a standing ovation and brought some audience members to tears. They extended their knowledge by attending an indigenous research conference at the University of British Columbia, by attending other sessions at the AERA Conference, by spending time with First Nations community members on Vancouver Island, and visiting a primary school on a First Nations reserve.

On their return this group delivered their conference presentation to the whole school and their whānau, and then presented their work in many forums with me as co-authors and co-researchers. Their research is a powerful collaborative counter-story and their presentations invariably led to further invitations to share this work with wider audiences. Two of the students sum up the group's findings with these statements:

> There is little doubt from our evidence about the importance of whānau to us in our school, which should be no surprise. In Kia Aroha College teachers use Lisa Delpit's (1995) term, that we students are "their kids, not other people's children." Our research confirmed that feeling. That's what whānau means. 70% of the youth we surveyed, who had been long term students on our campus, told us that the school worked as a whānau all the time in everything we did. However the students we surveyed from other schools said their participation in Māori Performing Arts was the predominant way they experienced "being Māori" at school. (Koha, Year 11)
>
> Our research shows that, from our perspective as young people, it is possible to develop a counter-narrative to our dominant White system where most interventions and reforms have their origin in deficit thinking, and continue to alienate us as Māori and Pasifika learners. The counter-story for us has been whānau—and enabling us to develop the tools we need to challenge that system and to change it. (Deazel, Year 13)

Student Context 5: Speaking Out "as" Us

In 2015, we received an invitation from the national Māori Principals' Association, *Te Akatea*, asking for a group of students to speak at their national conference in Auckland. I asked teachers to choose some students and offered to work with them to prepare. It soon became obvious that we had not chosen wisely. Some students were too busy with other commitments to put in the intensive time this required, and we were running very short of time. Soon I only had two of the original five left and I explained to them that we needed new group members. Within 10 minutes they appeared in my office with three new "recruits." None of the new members would have been on my selection list so, once again, I learned a valuable lesson about what our youth can teach us. When I later asked the original members the reasons why they had chosen the new additions to the group, they had perfect explanations that included abilities that I was unaware of like: not being easily distracted, an ability to not distract others which they felt was a much-needed attribute given our short time frame, a sense of humor they felt would get good audience reaction, an avid reader who was "not shy" to ask questions, one person's reluctance to speak, which they felt they could help overcome, and Māori knowledge they respected. Of course, the students were right, and the group's 20 minute conference presentation was a huge success.

During our preparation one of our staff, who was writing his thesis for his Master's Degree in Indigenous Studies, was visited by his supervisor. The teacher asked the group to explain their research to his visitor. He was so impressed with their analysis that he invited them to present their research in a 90 minute symposium at the New Zealand Association for Research in Education (NZARE) national conference which was to be held later in the year. The group then learned about submitting a conference proposal, which was later accepted. They also learned that a 90 minute presentation was markedly different from their original 20 minutes. Again, they had solutions, and they arrived one morning with an extra group member, explaining that this new person, who was Tongan, would allow them to include a Pasifika viewpoint which they hadn't included in their earlier presentation to Māori principals. The new member also brought advanced technology skills, particularly in video-editing, and they felt this was going to be extremely useful because they could produce video interviews with their participants and thus extend their time. Again, they were right. The six students in the group ranged from Year 10 (Grade 9) to Year 13 (Grade 12).

The original presentation to Māori principals had focused on the government's vision for Māori education; "Māori children enjoying educational success and achievement, as Māori," Now the government's strategy for Pasifika education, *The Pasifika Education Plan*, also came under their scrutiny. They decided on three research questions:

1. What does success or achievement "as Māori"—or as Tongan, as Samoan, actually mean?
2. Are rangatahi (youth) really experiencing that type of success in our schools?
3. If we are, what does that look like—to *us*?

They conducted two surveys with students, ex-students and staff of Kia Aroha College as well as parents, grandparents, and staff and students from other schools. Ages of the 83 survey participants in the survey about Māori education ranged from 12 to over 60, and 90% were Māori. The Pasifika education survey focused on 64 current students of Kia Aroha College, in our Samoan or Tongan bilingual units. Thirty of these students had also attended other intermediate or secondary schools prior to coming to Kia Aroha College.

The group also asked Māori educators and researchers what those two words "as Māori" mean to them and examined Ministry of Education and Education Review Office documents. They checked the online reports of the 82 Auckland schools who were reviewed by ERO between February and August 2015 for the answers to the ERO question: "How effectively does the school promote educational success for Māori, as Māori?" Excerpts from their findings have been quoted in earlier chapters but the following comments and observations from the group demonstrate the depth of their research and thinking. Throughout, they refer to their adult sources of information using the terms of respect; "Whaea" and "Matua":

> The story of Kia Aroha College is a counter-story of resistance and transformation. We perform a haka called, *Taniwha Wāwāhi Mā*—about the White spaces in our education system, we sing waiata (songs) about our daily karakia (prayer) we call *Te Ara Tino Rangatiratanga*, the pathway to self-determination. We wanted to hear the stories of Māori and Pasifika secondary school students, and also tell our own stories, and the story of Kia Aroha College.
>
> Whaea Leonie Pihama told us that firstly "as Māori" means that within Aotearoa there are two different societies, Pākehā society and Te Ao Māori. They co-exist on Māori land. However, they do not co-exist equally. The focus for everyone is to participate in Pākehā society, with little validation of Te Ao Māori. She says that what Sir Mason Durie has always advocated is that living "as Māori" means we can "be Māori" in any place and space in Aotearoa. As a Year 11 Māori learner I strongly believe those places and spaces have to include our schools. Our research shows us that is not the case. (Matthew, in Pirini-Edwards et al., 2015)

Ebony's story, from her personal experience, described a scenario all too familiar, of low expectations, deficit and racist attitudes towards Māori students. Similar experiences are often related by students enrolling after they have been excluded or have become disengaged in their previous schools:

> *Ka Hikitia* was updated and revised for 2013–2017. It begs the question then, what progress has been achieved in the seven years since its inception? Right here, right now, I'm going to say, not a lot. But why? I have good reason to think this way due to my own experience.

> I came to Kia Aroha College at the beginning of this year—moving away from my home and my whanau. Last year I was in Year 12 in a secondary school in the north, where I had completed 103 NCEA Level 1 credits and almost no Level 2 credits. This was due to the low expectations, and assumptions I believe teachers made about my capabilities based on my ethnicity and what they thought they knew about other members of my extended whanau. Did I imagine this? Might I have been wrong? No! A teacher once told me to go home to get a pen, in spite of the fact half of the class had no pens. He added that I should call in to WINZ[5] on my way home to tell them how much of a loser I was. That's a direct quote!
>
> I was told at the end of last year that I could not be in Year 13 this year, "because I wouldn't be able to handle it," and that I would need to repeat Year 12. At Kia Aroha College, 10 months later, I am four credits away from completing the NCEA Level 3 I was told I "couldn't handle," and I will complete University Entrance requirements by the end of the year. I am here, speaking to you at a national research conference, and my applications to enroll in conjoint Bachelors' degrees in Laws and Arts have been accepted by both Victoria University and the University of Waikato. Not too bad for the "loser" my previous teacher saw! What is the difference? I am able to be Māori at Kia Aroha College, and my teachers have high expectations of me in everything I do. There has never been any expectation that I would fail! (Ebony, in Pirini-Edwards et al., 2015)

The Education Review Office (ERO) is the New Zealand government department that evaluates and reports on the education of students in schools and early childhood services. Gayleen examined the Education Review Office reports of over eighty Auckland schools reviewed in 2015 to work out what ERO thinks "Māori enjoying education success as Māori" means. She concluded that the Education Review Office's single focus on the literacy, numeracy, and NCEA achievement *of* Māori learners, cancels out all of the achievement and success Māori students could enjoy *as* Māori. What schools have to measure is what schools treat as important, no matter how many resources there are. She also asked questions about the capacity of ERO reviewers to make these decisions, then focused on what was left out of ERO reports:

> We've heard what matters to the Government, through the Ministry of Education. We've seen what matters and what is considered effective to ERO, but what else matters, and what matters to us? Our student surveys told us clearly that relationships matter, that cultural identity matters, that language matters—and that these matter *first* and matter most! However, what else matters, and what else is *not* mentioned in Ministry or Education Review Office reports? Two weeks ago, the *New Zealand Herald* ran a series of articles on equity in New Zealand schools, using Auckland schools as examples (Johnston, 2015). One article quotes the book, *Twelve Thousand Hours: Education and Poverty in Aotearoa New Zealand* (Carpenter

& Osborne, 2014), where Massey University academics Ivan Snook and John O'Neill have concluded that home background is responsible for up to 80 per cent of a child's school success.

> Our Minister of Education doesn't agree with this. In the same article, she said, that although the impact low socio-economic factors have on student outcomes is a concern, she thinks that these factors are often overstated. Our group read the articles and held a debate. The moot was: "Poverty matters to our learning." The boys took the affirmative and we girls had to argue the negative. Although I hate to say it, the boys won, because our hearts just weren't in our side. We all agreed in our discussion later, of course poverty matters to every one of us. (Gayleen, in Pirini-Edwards et al., 2015)

Kiwa contacted well-known Māori academics and elders to find out what Māori think "as Māori" means. He brought his own experience as a student previously in a Kura Kaupapa Māori, and his fluency in Māori language to his view. He asked, "What good is an education that completely diminishes your cultural right to know who you are, what you are, where you're from and what blood runs through your veins?"

> I think the Government definitions make it perfectly clear that our people are still assimilated in Whitestream schools achieving at Pākehā academic standards, mostly with no clue of their cultural heritage, or little importance placed on this by their schools. But we don't realize this because we trust that the goals for success and a better chance of wellbeing for our whānau lie in our modern education system. I am not saying that people are blind to the depth of what really is happening to young Māori in schools, but what I am saying is that to live "as Māori" in the education system should be to fully understand both Pākehā society and Te Ao Māori, and your education should enable you to continually become stronger in the knowledge of your cultural heritage and identity.
>
> In our history, the introduction of Western ideas of individualism marginalized Māori whānau—and education was a devastating tool in this practice. Dr. Linda Tuhiwai Smith (1986) refers to New Zealand's "Native School" system as a "Trojan Horse"—schools built inside Māori communities which deliberately targeted Māori whānau as a site of colonization. The colonization and assimilation which targeted our ancestors, and our grandparents, continued in our parents' generation—and in ours. (Kiwa, in Pirini-Edwards et al., 2015)

Jacob, the youngest member of the group, asked, "So how can schools counter that hegemony? That thinking that sneaks into our heads and makes us also put Māori or Pasifika knowledge on a lower level—or just not think about it at all?" He presented the outcomes of the group's student surveys, and also examined research about Kia Aroha College by independent researchers.

So did our students come to school already strong in their understanding of Māori knowledge? Not according to our survey. In fact it seems 61% of students in our survey came into Te Whānau o Tupuranga with very little understanding of their Māori identity and state strongly that the way we work, our whānau environment, our relationships with teachers and the way we learn, strengthened and continues to develop our identity "as Māori". Far fewer of the students in other schools had this experience.

Kia Aroha College's special character is whānau-based, Māori and Pasifika-centered education. It sets out how we are different from regular state schools, but I think it's about how we are fighting to be fully human. What does being fully human mean you ask? We learned about Paulo Freire who argues that oppression relies on a process of dehumanization. Changing that, means our education has to be about full control over what we want to do, think and most of all it has to be about self-determination/Tino Rangatiratanga. Our Graduate Profiles make very clear what success "as" Māori, looks like at Kia Aroha College. What we hope we are showing you today is the outcome of our Graduate Profile—warrior-scholars, make warrior-researchers! (Jacob, in Pirini-Edwards et al., 2015)

The students summarized their findings in the form of an achievement assessment of everyone they had investigated. Their report cards on "the efforts and effectiveness of those who think they are delivering education achievement and success "as Māori" or "as Pasifika"" used the Ministry of Education's own National Standards' terminology—finding the Ministry of Education and the Government "well below standard" and schools and the Education Review Office, "below standard." The long-lasting impact of this high level of engagement cannot be underestimated as Ebony's feedback, printed in the NZARE magazine shows:

As a member of the senior Warrior-Researcher team it was an honor and privilege to attend and present our research at the annual NZARE Conference, hosted by Te Whare Wānanga o Awanuiārangi. Upon reflection, I am moved to comment that it was a great opportunity for a group of young students to connect with information and research that both informs what we do at school and the potential for future leadership for myself. My interest in future researching for academic purposes was significantly strengthened after attending both the session of Tā Hirini Moko Mead and Dr. Arnetha Ball, along with the other researchers. I appreciated the perspectives they shared around the ineffectiveness of the modern education system. I now feel that I am quite accustomed to working under-pressure and speaking in front of large audiences, after presenting at the conference and speaking at The Quay restaurant with conviction. I am sure my experience at the NZARE will benefit my future work as a lawyer, to speak with confidence, argue with passion, and to understand with compassion. (New Zealand Association for Research in Education [NZARE], 2016)

A national survey of secondary schools' practice and perspectives (Wylie & Bonne, 2016) found however that this type of learning was the approach New Zealand secondary schools used *least*. In fact, having students "work together on a project/activity that will make a difference to their class/local environment or community" (p. 10) was the learning experience that received the lowest ratings for both importance and frequency. Only 14% of students in low-decile schools were given this type of learning opportunity, rising to 31% in high-decile schools.

Notes

1. *Te Aho Matua* is the foundation document for Kura Kaupapa Māori. It lays down the principles by which Kura Kaupapa Māori identify themselves and structure learning.
2. Tongan: poto may be defined as the positive application of 'ilo (knowledge and understanding).
3. Fonuamalu is the name of the Tongan bilingual unit, established in 2003, meaning a safe shelter.
4. Ngā Manu Kōrero is an annual national Māori speech competition for secondary students.
5. Work and Income New Zealand—the government unemployment agency.

References

Adelman, L. (2008). *Unnatural causes: Is inequality making us sick?* San Francisco, CA: California Newsreel. Retrieved from http://www.unnaturalcauses.org/transcripts.php

Adkins, A., & Hytten, K. (2001). Thinking through a pedagogy of whiteness. *Educational Theory*, 51(4), 433–450.

Akom, A., Cammarota, J., & Ginwright, S. (2008). Youthtopias: Towards a new paradigm of critical youth studies. *Youth Media Reporter*, 2(1), 108–129. Retrieved from http://cci.sfsu.edu/files/Youthtopias.pdf

Aluli-Meyer, M. (2001). Our own liberation: Reflections on Hawaiian epistemology. *The Contemporary Pacific*, 13(1), 124–148. http://doi.org/10.1353/cp.2001.0024

Aluli-Meyer, M. (2008). Indigenous and authentic: Hawaiian epistemology and the triangulation of meaning. In N. Denzin, Y. Lincoln, & L. T. Smith (Eds.), *Handbook of critical and Indigenous methodologies* (pp. 217–232). Los Angeles, CA: Sage.

Antrop-González, R., & De Jesús, A. (2006). Toward a theory of critical care in urban small school reform: Examining structures and pedagogies of caring in two Latino community-based schools. *International Journal of Qualitative Studies in Education*, 19(4), 409–433.

Banks, J. (2004). Teaching for social justice, diversity, and citizenship in a global world. *The Educational Forum*, 68(4), 296–305. http://doi.org/10.1080/00131720408984645

Beane, J. (1997). *Curriculum integration: Designing the core of democratic education.* New York, NY: Teachers College Press.

Beauboeuf-Lafontant, T. (2002). A womanist experience of caring: Understanding the pedagogy of exemplary black women teachers. *Urban Review, 34*(1), 71–86.

Bingham, C. W., & Sidorkin, A. M. (2004). *No education without relation.* New York, NY: Peter Lang.

Bishop, R. (1996). *Collaborative research stories: Whakawhanaungatanga.* Palmerston North, New Zealand: Dunmore Press

Bishop, R. (2005). Freeing ourselves from neo-colonial domination in research: A Kaupapa Māori approach to creating knowledge. In N. Denzin & Y. Lincoln (Eds.), *The SAGE handbook of qualitative research* (3rd ed., pp. 109–138). Thousand Oaks, CA: Sage Publications.

Bishop, R., Berryman, M., Cavanagh, T., & Teddy, L. (2007). *Te Kōtahitanga phase 3 Whanaungatanga: Establishing a culturally responsive pedagogy of relations in mainstream secondary school classrooms.* Wellington: New Zealand Ministry of Education Research Division.

Bishop, R., Berryman, M., Richardson, C., & Tiakiwai, S. (2003). *Te Kotahitanga: The experiences of year 9 and 10 Māori students in mainstream classrooms.* Report to the Ministry of Education. Wellington: Ministry of Education.

Bishop, R., & Glynn, T. (1999). *Culture counts: Changing power relations in education.* Palmerston North: Cengage Learning Australia.

Calmore, J. (1992). Critical race theory, Archie Shepp, and fire music: Securing an Authentic Intellectual life in a multicultural world. *Southern California Law Review, 65,* 2129–2231

Carpenter, V., & Osborne, S. (2014). *Twelve thousand hours: Education and poverty in Aotearoa New Zealand.* Auckland, New Zealand: Dunmore Publishing.

Delpit, L. (2006). *Other people's children: Cultural conflict in the classroom* (1st ed.). New York, NY: The New Press.

Duncan-Andrade, J. (2006). Utilizing Cariño in the development of research methodologies. In J. Kincheloe, K. Hayes, K. Rose, & P. M. Anderson (Eds.), *The Praeger handbook of urban education* (pp. 451–460). Westport, CT: Greenwood Publishing Group.

Duncan-Andrade, J. (2007). Gangstas, Wankstas, and Ridas: Defining, developing, and supporting effective teachers in urban schools. *International Journal of Qualitative Studies in Education, 20*(6), 617–638. http://doi.org/10.1080/09518390701630767

Duncan-Andrade, J., & Morrell, E. (2008). *The art of critical pedagogy: Possibilities for moving from theory to practice in urban schools.* New York, NY: Peter Lang.

Durie, M. (2001). *A framework for considering maori educational advancement.* Paper presented at the Hui Taumata Matauranga II (Māori Education Summit). Turangi, Taupo, New Zealand.

Freire, P. (1972). *Pedagogy of the opressed.* Harmondsworth: Penguin.

Freire, P. (2004). *Pedagogy of hope: Reliving pedagogy of the oppressed* (1st ed.). London: Continuum International Publishing Group.

Gay, G. (2000). *Culturally responsive teaching.* New York, NY: Teachers College Press.

Huffer, E., & Qalo, R. (2004). The contemporary emergence of pacific theoretical thought. *The Contemporary Pacific, 16*(1), 87–116.

Idle No More. (2013). The vision. Retrieved from http://www.idlenomore.ca/vision

Johnston, K. (2015, November 8). Education investigation: The great divide. *New Zealand Herald*. Retrieved from http://m.nzherald.co.nz/nz/news/article.cfm?c_id=1&objectid=11539592

Ladson-Billings, G. (1994). *The dreamkeepers: Successful teachers of African American children*. San Francisco, CA: Jossey-Bass.

Levine-Raskey, C. (2000). Framing whiteness: Working through the tensions in introducing whiteness to educators. *Race, Ethnicity and Education, 3*(3), 271–292.

Love, B. (2004). Brown plus 50 counter-storytelling: A critical race theory analysis of the "Majoritarian Achievement Gap" story. *Equity & Excellence in Education, 37*, 227–246.

Macfarlane, A., Glynn, T., Grace, W., Penetito, W., & Bateman, S. (2008). Indigenous epistemology in a national curriculum framework? *Ethnicities, 8*(1), 102–126. http://doi.org/10.1177/1468796807087021

Metge, J. (1990). *Te Kohao o Te Ngira: Culture and learning*. Wellington: Learning Media, Ministry of Education.

Ministry of Education. (2013). *Pasifika Education Plan 2013–2017*. Wellington: Ministry of Education. Retrieved from http://www.education.govt.nz/ministry-of-education/overall-strategies-and-policies/pasifika-education-plan-2013-2017/

Ministry of Education. (2014). *Pasifika Language in Education*. Wellington, N.Z: Ministry of Education. Retrieved November 6, 2015, from http://www.educationcounts.govt.nz/publications/schooling/6846

Moeke-Pickering, T. (1996). Māori identity within Whānau: A review of literature. Retrieved from http://researchcommons.waikato.ac.nz/bitstream/handle/10289/464/content.pdf?sequence=1

New Zealand Association for Research in Education (NZARE). (2016). Through the eyes of students. *He Pātaka Tuku Kōrero, 38*(1), 4. Retrieved from http://www.nzare.org.nz/portals/306/images/Files/Input Feb 2016final.pdf

Noddings, N. (2003). *Caring, a feminine approach to ethics & moral education* (2nd ed.). Berkeley, CA: University of California Press.

Osborne, B., & Cooper, D. (2001). Culturally responsive pedagogy: First steps towards culturally relevant pedagogy. In B. Osborne (Ed.), *Teaching diversity & democracy* (pp. 261–290). Victoria: Common Ground.

O'Sullivan and Action Inquiry Contributors. (2011). *Thriving in practice: Connected—reflective—effective*. New Zealand Families Commission: Auckland, New Zealand. Retrieved from http://www.superu.govt.nz/sites/default/files/TPRACTICE_Resource_0.pdf

Otero, G., & Chambers-Otero, S. (2002). *RelationaLearning: Toward a human ecology in 21st century schools*. Retrieved from http://relationalearning.com/wp-content/uploads/2013/09/RL-Position-Paper-PDF1.pdf

Penetito, W. (2002). Research and a context for a theory of Māori schooling. *McGill Journal of Education, 37*(1). 89–109.

Pirini-Edwards, E., Tukutau, A., Katipa, M., Ropitini-Fairburn, K., Harris-Kaaka, J., & Bellamy, J. (2015). *Speaking out "as" us: Māori and Tongan secondary students investigate our education system's vision for Māori and Pasifika learners*. Whakatane, NZ: Symposium presented at New Zealand Association for Research in Education (NZARE) Conference.

Romero, A., Cammarota, J., Dominguez, K., Valdez, L., Ramirez, G., & Hernandez, L. (2010). The opportunity if not the right to see: The social justice education project. In J. Cammarota & M. Fine (Eds.), *Revolutionizing education: Youth participatory action research in motion* (pp. 131–151). New York, NY: Routledge.

Sanga, K. (2002). Beyond access and participation: Challenges facing pacific education. In F. Pene, A. M. Taufe'ulungaki, & C. Benson (Eds.), *Tree of opportunity: Re-thinking pacific education* (pp. 52–58). Suva, Fiji: University of the South Pacific, Institute of Education.

Shields, C. M., Bishop, R., & Mazawi, A. E. (2005). *Pathologizing practices*. New York, NY: Peter Lang.

Sidorkin, A. M. (1999). *Beyond discourse*. Albany, NY: State University of New York Press.

Sidorkin, A. M. (2002). *Learning relations*. New York, NY: Peter Lang.

Sleeter, C. (2008). Learning to become a racially and culturally competent ally. In K. Teel & J. Obidah (Eds.), *Building racial and cultural competence in the classroom* (pp. 82–96). New York, NY: Teachers College Press.

Smith, G. (1995). Whakaoho whānau: New formations of whānau as an innovative intervention into Māori cultural and educational crises. *He Pukenga Korero: A Journal of Māori Studies*, 1(1), 18–35.

Smith, G. (1997). *The development of Kaupapa Māori: Theory and praxis* (Unpublished Doctoral dissertation). University of Auckland, Auckland.

Smith, G. (2003). *Kaupapa Māori theory: Theorizing indigenous transformation of education & schooling*. Presentation to the Kaupapa Māori Symposium. NZARE/AARE Joint Conference, Auckland.

Smith, G. (2004). Mai i te māramatanga, ki te putanga mai o te tahuritanga: From conscientization to transformative praxis. *Educational Perspectives*, 37(1), 46–52.

Smith, L. (1986). Is Taha Maori in schools the answer to Maori school failure? In *Nga Kete Waananga: Maori Perspectives of Taha Maori*. Auckland: Auckland College of Education.

Thaman, K. H. (1995). Concepts of learning, knowledge and wisdom in Tonga, and their relevance to modern education. *Prospects: Quarterly Review of Education*, 25(4), 723–733.

Thompson, A. (1998). Not the color purple: Black feminist lessons for educational caring. *Harvard Educational Review*, 68(4), 522–554.

Valenzuela, A. (1999). *Subtractive schooling: U.S. Mexican youth and the politics of caring*. Albany, NY: State University of New York Press.

Valenzuela, A. (2005). Subtractive schooling, caring relations, and social capital in the schooling of U.S. Mexican Youth. In L. Weis & M. Fine (Eds.), *Beyond silenced voices* (Revised, pp. 83–92). Albany, NY: State University of New York Press.

Walshaw, M., Andrews, R., Bell, A., Butler, P., & Tawhai, V. (2012). *National identity and cultural diversity: A research project that looks at what year 12 students say about identity in New Zealand*. Massey University. Retrieved from http://mro.massey.ac.nz/handle/10179/4213

Wylie, C., & Bonne, L. (2016). *Secondary schools in 2015: Findings from the NZCER national survey*. Wellington: New Zealand Council for Educational Research. Retrieved from http://www.nzcer.org.nz/

Yang, K. W. (2009). Discipline or punish? Some suggestions for school policy and teacher practice. *Language Arts*, 87(1), 49–61.

· 7 ·

COLORING IN THE SELF-LEARNING SPACE

The Self-Learning Lens

Aluli-Meyer (2001) explains that, "Everything I have learned in school, everything I have read in books, every vocabulary test and jumping jack, every seating arrangement and response expectation—absolutely everything—has not been shaped by a Hawaiian mind." She says realization of this fact came slowly to indigenous Hawaiians, "dulled by the guessing game of another culture, still believing that literacy is the best indicator of intelligence," and "always at the short end of a smaller and smaller identity stick" (p. 124). This understanding has developed to realizing that Hawaiian education does not need to be seen in relation to Western norms, but must be seen in relation to knowledge that is organically Hawaiian:

> There it is. How do we educate our youth for the challenges of the next millennium? We surround them with our community, we give them meaningful experiences that highlight their ability to be responsible, intelligent, and kind. We watch for their gifts, we shape assessment to reflect mastery that is accomplished in real time, not false. We laugh more, plant everything, and harvest the hope of aloha. We help each other, we listen more, we trust in one another again. We find our Hawaiian essence reflected in both process and product of our efforts. That is Hawaiian education, and understanding our Hawaiian epistemology is our foundation, our *kumupaʻa*. So,

let it be said and let it be known: We *have* what we need. We *are* who we need. (Aluli-Meyer, 2001, p. 146)

What Is Success?

Ehara taku toa i te toa takitahi engari he toa takitini.
My strength is not that of the individual but of the many.

The very divergent Māori and Pākehā attitudes to success and achievement, described earlier, are evident in this Māori proverb. For Māori, success as an individual is important when that success or learning benefits "the collectives of whānau, hapū, iwi"[1] (Wilkie, 2010, p. 34). However, in our New Zealand state education system success is seen as the individual pursuit of qualifications and academic achievement. Penetito (2001) observes succinctly that the ongoing difficulty faced by Māori in education was that "the New Zealand education system has always operated as though its clients were either Pākehā or wanted to become Pākehā; Māori had much to learn from Pākehā but Pākehā had little to learn from Māori" (p. 18).

Wilkie (2010) uses the metaphor of the multi-levelled steps of the poutama[2] to analyse the many factors that make up these opposing worldviews and to provide a culturally relevant tool to describe success in Māori terms. The continual and spiral nature of learning is captured is this explanation:

> Traditionally, poutama teaches us that learning begins before birth, continues through life, and after death. Poutama teaches us that the mana of a learner is equal to all other [learners], ahead of them and behind them, on the learning pathway. Poutama teaches us that knowledge is gained in steps, and implies the perseverance needed to progress upwards. Poutama reminds us that knowledge is built layer upon layer, and for Māori the foundations of this knowledge begin with our tipuna and before them eternally, with Papatūānuku, the land. (p. 262)

In a personal communication to Wilkie, Māori elder, Tuahine Northover explained that "there are only five steps on the learning poutama: *Kua Tīmata*, the first step; *Kua Mārama*, enlightened; *Kua Kaha*, confident; *Kua Mōhio*, knowledgeable; *Ko Te Taumata*, the pinnacle." Learning is not completed on reaching Te Taumata, but continues with the first step on the next level. Northover states, "Traditionally there is no concept of either success or failure in Te Ao Māori. Those who 'never aim to be successful also never fail; they just don't reach the taumata, they don't fail'" (Wilkie, 2010, p. 36).

This is a concept that is diametrically opposed to the widely alleged notion of Māori students' "failure" in schools and to the Western concept espoused in New Zealand's mandated National Standards; that all learners should master identified skills and learning stages at the same time.

Assessment as a White Space

Determining Self: Self-Knowledge

The Power Lenses Learning Model described earlier, was initiated in 2003. Throughout 2004 and 2005, staff debated the issue of assessment of learning in the self-learning lens. In the Education Review Office report for Clover Park Middle School in February, 2003, the following comment was made as a suggested "Area for Improvement."

> The teachers have not yet collected data on all aspects of the cultural competence of students. This review observed high levels of achievement in cultural performance that is tracked under the performance arts. However, similarly high levels of achievement in areas of manaakitanga, group work and co-operation were not acknowledged in the database. The managers are not yet optimising the potential of the essential skills of the New Zealand Curriculum Framework to monitor cultural competence. The collection of more data on cultural literacy would enable a closer fit between student achievement reporting and the kaupapa of the school. (Education Review Office, 2003, p. 9)

Stung by this comment, which we felt had not recognized the work we were already implementing, in the Plan of Action required by the Education Review Office to explain how we intended to address issues raised in the report, the Board of Trustees retaliated:

> Māori and Pacific staff are not convinced that the essential skills, developed for the Framework from a Eurocentric perspective, are the best tool with which to monitor cultural competence, and therefore are not sure we wish to "optimise their potential." The school will continue to explore relevant assessment practices, in consultation with community elders, to measure and feedback to students their achievement and progress in their cultural knowledge and skills.

In our follow-up discussions regarding the ERO comment, the first question we asked ourselves was why should we "measure" cultural skills and competencies? Surely this was an area where teachers and families, experienced in their respective cultures, would be the best judges? To establish any measure would surely be perpetuating the Eurocentric model? Were there Māori, Samoan, Tongan or Cook Islands Māori ways of knowing our children were developing these competencies and "self-knowledge" that didn't require us to quantify them? Why wouldn't we just see this development through observation? Wasn't that enough? Why "write it down"? That was one school of thought.

The other side of the argument asked, if we are as serious as we say we are about the self-learning lens and about self-knowledge being legitimate, high stakes learning, valid in its own right, and of equal status with school or academic learning, are we devaluing it ourselves by not being able to describe it? The two sides of the discussion are evident in these staff comments (first names only used according to staff preference):

> As soon as you do anything different—up goes the anti and up goes the requirement of having to prove it. Why do we have to prove stuff all the time? We are proving it when they go out to other schools and they are more confident, and we are proving it when they come back as ex-students who show that they can't leave, that they have that connection still. We are proving it by the fact that they are coming to school every day. I mean, we've got kids who are coming to school every day and not going home every day. We've got kids from pretty significant, traumatic backgrounds who are at school every day. Do we buy into the requirement of having to justify, or do we actually start saying we don't need to justify—we know what we are doing is right? (Haley)

> Ann has asked an interesting question because I think for all of us, the dream would be that Te Whānau o Tupuranga and Clover Park Middle School are not unique but rather the norm, so how do we achieve that? That's about promoting ourselves. In some ways we do need to qualify achievement and we do need to quantify success, because those are going to be the hooks for the rest of the education community. (William)

This debate highlights what Wilkie (2010) refers to as the "exclusion and rendering invisible of Māori worldviews through the dominant Pākehā discourse of success and failure" (p. 215). In a personal communication to Wilkie elder, Dick Grace, explained a Māori viewpoint that is relevant to our thinking throughout the five years' action research to develop the self-learning tool:

> [In] tikanga Māori every individual is unique and they have their own time in which to know. ... A Māori perspective on this difference is the equality of mana, that applies to poutama; if a person is on Level 1 of knowing in a certain area and another is on Level 6 that person on level 6 has no greater mana than the one on Level 1, that mana is equal, they both have that special power which is the same. (Wilkie, 2010, p. 216)

This respect for every person's mana (prestige, authority, power) and dignity; the "time to know;" the necessity for face to face interaction in any assessment; the tuakana-teina relationship where those with knowledge have a responsibility to share with those who don't; were all concepts that had to underpin this development.

How Do We Know?

We searched for examples of measures of cultural identity from the psychological field but found these did not suit our purpose. We wanted indicators that informed our future teaching and learning, and we particularly wanted a measure that was relevant to Māori and Pasifika children and one they would understand themselves. Right from the start we felt we wanted to use Māori and Pasifika understandings and values so it was unlikely that a generic or existing measure would suffice. It was obvious to us that Māori and Pasifika ways of knowing must be supported by Māori and Pasifika ways of assessing.

As we discussed what we needed, through formal staff meetings and more often, informally in small groups, I asked questions of our Māori and Pasifika staff. How do you decide which boy you will ask to speak to welcome visitors in a formal pōwhiri? How do you choose the girls who will karanga (ceremonial call)? Who are the students who will assist in the ava (Samoan welcome) ceremony? Each time teachers were unable to answer the question. Playing devil's advocate, I would probe further and suggest other children who might be candidates for these important tasks. Would they be chosen? Again, every time, teachers told me that child would be unlikely to be chosen or asked to take on the role. These choices were not about which children were fluent in the language. Most times the children chosen then needed to embark on a process of training to be able to do the job.

Teachers became fascinated with these questions and kept adding new scenarios to discuss. All agreed they did not know what criteria they were using to allocate these responsibilities or other tasks that required cultural understanding. Often they thought it might be a child who had been brought up by their grandparents, or it might be someone they instinctively felt had an aptitude for the task, or a particular attitude, or someone whose Nanny could karanga for example, but they were at a loss to explain how they could sense this. Teachers commented they had never thought about their selections before. They also agreed there was tacit understanding and agreement among Māori and Pasifika staff about the students selected. All seemed to agree most of the time that the child selected, possibly just by one teacher, was the "right" one for the role. Barnhardt (2002) describes this conflict of knowledge systems:

> The complexities that come into play when two fundamentally different worldviews converge present a formidable challenge. The specialization, standardization, compartmentalization, and systematization that are inherent features of most Western bureaucratic forms of organization often are in direct conflict with social structures and practices in Indigenous societies, which tend toward collective decision-making, extended kinship structures, ascribed authority vested in elders, flexible notions of time, and traditions of informality in everyday affairs. (cited in Barnhardt & Kawagley, 2005, p. 13)

Cultural Standards

We searched for work being done elsewhere in cultural knowledges and competencies. Alaska Native educators had developed "cultural standards" based on the belief that a "firm grounding in the heritage language and culture indigenous to a particular place is a fundamental prerequisite for the development of culturally-healthy students and communities associated with that place" (Alaska Native Educators, 1998). These standards were adopted by the Alaska State Board of Education and Early Development in the same year (Alaska State Board of Education & Early Development, 2006). Standards covered five areas: for students, educators, curriculum, schools, and communities. These standards have these five broad goals that culturally knowledgeable students:

1. are well grounded in the cultural heritage and traditions of their community.
2. are able to build on the knowledge and skills of the local cultural community as a foundation from which to achieve personal and academic success throughout life.
3. are able to actively participate in various cultural environments.
4. are able to engage effectively in learning activities that are based on traditional ways of knowing and learning.
5. can demonstrate an awareness and appreciation of the relationships and processes of interaction of all elements in the world around them. (pp. 28–29)

Each of these goals is further broken down into specific indicators. The indicators for students who meet the first cultural standard, for example, are shown in Table 7.1:

Table 7.1. Alaska Cultural Standards Indicators

Standard	Specific Indicators Students who meet this cultural standard are able to:
Culturally knowledgeable students are well grounded in the cultural heritage and traditions of their community.	Assume responsibility for their role in relation to the well-being of the cultural community and their life-long obligations as a community member. Recount their own genealogy and family history. Acquire and pass on the traditions of their community through oral and written history. Practice their traditional responsibilities to the surrounding environment. Reflect through their own actions the critical role that the local heritage language plays in fostering a sense of who they are and how they understand the world around them. Live a life in accordance with the cultural values and traditions of the local community and integrate them into their everyday behavior. Determine the place of their cultural community in the regional, state, national and international political and economic systems.

Source: Alaska State Board of Education & Early Development (2006, p. 28).

Would these standards suit our situation? Was any research being done in New Zealand and the Pacific that might help? We looked at Durie's (1998) four key "markers" for Māori cultural identity: identification as Māori, cultural knowledge and understanding, access to and participation in Māori society, and communication (p. 58).

Recurring themes in the work of Pasifika researchers on cultural identities included social structures, language, ceremonies and rituals, access, cultural performance, and knowledge of genealogy (Balme, 1998; Hunkin-Tuiletufuga, 2001; Mailei, 1999; Mitaera, 1999; Mulitalo-Lauta, 2001).

As a staff we had considered all of this research throughout 2003. We had now moved far beyond being somewhat offended by the ERO report comment. We felt that our "self-learning" self-knowledge learning, was not only about cultural identity. There were other "selves" to take into account and we wanted to describe these as well. We decided that the six relationships that were central to our learning model and therefore central to all our three "lenses" should be the basis of our assessment. These were the student's relationship to:

1. *self* (cultural identity, who am I, where do I "fit"),
2. *their learning* (relevance to students' backgrounds and experiences),

3. *the teacher* (mutual respect, trust, high expectations, support—whānau)
4. *other students* (positive peer influence & support—whānau),
5. *the wider world* (critical, emancipatory, anti-racist, tolerant, against prejudice), and
6. a reciprocal relationship between *home and school* (a mutually beneficial, authentic partnership—whānau).

However two of these: the teacher-student and home-school relationships, included adults. While both are crucial, the adult component in each of those relationships could make it difficult for the student to assume any influence over the quality of the interaction. We felt that the other four relationships encapsulated the self-learning we expected through the self-lens. Our goal was to find ways of showing that students were developing a secure identity and positive relationships.

In 2004, teachers from each of the four ethnic groups, Māori, Samoan, Cook Islands Māori, and Tongan, met separately over several months to consider indicators they felt could show cultural identity. There was consensus that, after considering all of the research, Durie's (1998) four key areas of identification, cultural knowledge and understanding, access to and participation in the cultural society and communication, were common threads through everything we had read, and more importantly were felt by the teachers from each ethnic group to be suitable.

We were fortunate to have teachers on the staff, who were very knowledgeable in their cultures. Most were experienced teachers who were fully involved as leaders in the community and in their cultural worlds. This was a critical point. In developing indicators to describe cultural identities, Western academic theory and research cannot be as relevant or valid as the cultural knowledge of the experts in the specific culture. Among our Māori staff at the time, we had several teachers who were fluent in the language, extremely knowledgeable in tikanga Māori and had longstanding connections to te ao Māori as well as the local community.

In Clover Park, the fact that there were three different cultures meant we needed experts from each. This depth of knowledge and expertise was an invaluable resource in developing the indicators for each of the different Pasifika cultural identities. The discussion of experiences by this group of staff, in collaboration with Māori staff, also caused them to bring up issues I had not considered. If this tool was to be useful teachers felt it had to be relevant to young people and had to relate to their lives. Our students might have little access to their home marae, but how they interacted on our school marae might be a more relevant indicator of their learning. The "relationship with the wider world" for Samoan students in Samoa would be different from that for our students living in New Zealand, many of whom were born here. It might also include their relationship to Māori as tangata whenua in New Zealand. Teachers wanted these issues to be included in the indicators. Our aim was to describe our students' growth in these areas at school, for their own self-knowledge, and so we could evaluate our practice and be aware of areas we needed to strengthen or develop.

The teacher groups met to compare their initial thoughts until finally each ethnic group had a list of indicators they thought would allow them to determine students' self-development in each of their specific cultural identities. These are listed in Tables 7.2–7.7:

Māori Identity Indicators

Table 7.2. Māori Identity Indicators

Category	Indicators
Identification	Self-identifies as Māori
	Has positive attitudes towards being Māori
	Understands roles and responsibilities within whānau
	Understands status as tangata whenua (indigenous, "people of the land")
Knowledge and understanding	Knows own whakapapa (genealogy)
	Seeks understanding of tikanga (custom)—and follows this
	Can explain tikanga to others
	Practices values—manaakitanga (hospitality), tautoko (support), whanaungatanga, aroha tētahi ki tētahi (looking after each other)
Access and participation	Participates in kapa haka
	Participates in marae activities—looks after the marae and manuhiri (visitors)
	Has links to own marae—is involved in whānau activities
	Encourages others to participate, leads by example
Communication	Proactive about learning and using te reo Māori
	Takes on speaking roles
	Teaches teina (younger students) kapa haka
	Leads in kapa haka
	Explains Kaupapa (school philosophy) to manuhiri

Source: Kia Aroha College

Samoan Identity Indicators

Table 7.3. Samoan Identity Indicators

Category	Indicators
Identification	Self-identifies as Samoan
	Has positive attitudes towards being Samoan
	Understands roles and responsibilities within a aiga (family)
	Understands the relationship with tangata whenua (Māori) and other cultures.
	Is able to identify negative stereotypes and racism and be a staunch advocate for fa'asamoa (the Samoan way)
Knowledge and understanding	Knows own family tree
	Seeks understanding of fa'asamoa—and follows this
	Can explain le aganu'u ma tu Fa'asamoa (culture and Samoan way of life) to others
	Practices Samoan cultural values
Access and participation	Participates in Samoan performing arts in any given situation
	Practices the fa'asamoa and aganu'u in appropriate situations
	Has regular links to Samoa—and involves in aiga and lotu (church) activities
	Encourages others to participate and is a role model
Communication	Proactive about learning and using gagana Samoa (Samoan language)
	Has ability to use appropriate language for appropriate situations
	Is competent in reading and writing in gagana Samoa
	Is comfortable in talking to audiences in different contexts
	Shows an ability to lead

Source: Kia Aroha College

Tongan Identity Indicators

Table 7.4. Tongan Identity Indicators

Category	Indicators
Identification	Self-identifies as Tongan
	Has positive attitudes towards being Tongan in Aotearoa/New Zealand
	Understands roles and responsibilities within the family (family)
	Understands and acknowledges Māori as tangata whenua
	Acknowledges their Tongan heritage

Category	Indicators
Knowledge and Understanding	Knows own Ha'a (Clan/Tribe)
	Seeks understanding of Anga Faka Tonga (Tongan customs) and uses values and morals that are relevant to their lives
	Can explain Anga Faka Tonga to their friends, educators, visitors and community
	Practices Values: caring, respect, honesty, friendship, patience, tolerance, acceptance
	Participates in Faiva Faka Tonga (Tongan cultural dance)
	Participates in Fono activities—looks after the fale fono and kau'hi (classroom, environment)
Access and Participation	Has links to own church and Tongan community—is involved with famili/community/church activities
	Encourages others to participate and leads by example—role modelling
Communication	Proactive about learning and using Tongan as a medium of learning
	Takes on speaking roles
	Converses with other students in Tongan

Source: Kia Aroha College.

Cook Islands Māori Identity Indicators

Table 7.5. Cook Islands Māori Indicators

Category	Indicators
Identification	Identifies as Cook Islands Māori
	Has positives attitudes towards being Cook Islands Māori
	Understands roles and responsibilities within anau (family)
Knowledge and Understanding	Knows own akapapaanga (genealogy)
	Seeks understanding of akonoanga (protocols)
	Is able to explain akonoanga to others
	Practices values aroa, tauturu (love, support)
	Understands takinga meitaki (caring)
	Understands importance of taokotaianga (unity)
Access and Participation	Participates in kaparima and/or ura pau (action song and/or drum dance)
	Performs as a rangatira (leader)
Communication	Proactive about learning and is a fluent speaker of Cook Islands Māori language and the different dialects
	Takes on speaking roles

Source: Kia Aroha College.

Generic Identity Indicators

The indicators above reflected the strengths of the four main ethnic groups in the school. However some students didn't belong to any of these groups. Having developed four other sets of markers staff felt that the broad categories would remain constant. They then went on to develop generic indicators that we could use to assess those students who were not Māori, Samoan, Tongan or Cook Island Māori:

Table 7.6. Generic Identity Indicators

Category	Indicators
Identification	Self-identifies as a member of his/her own culture
	Has positive attitudes towards own culture
	Understands roles and responsibilities within own cultural norms
	Understands status of Māori as tangata whenua in NZ
Knowledge and Understanding	Knows own genealogy
	Seeks understanding of own cultural beliefs/customs/norms and follows these
	Can explain these values to others
	Practices these values
	Participates in own cultural events
Access and Participation	Participates in own cultural activities
	Has links to own culture in New Zealand
	Encourages others to participate, leads by example
Communication	Proactive about learning and using own language
	Takes on speaking roles
	Converses with others in own language
	Explains own culture to others

Source: Kia Aroha College.

Having decided on the markers for the specific cultural identities we turned our attention to the other four relationships we had chosen. The indicators for these would be generic across all the four cultures in the school. Again we examined the literature and existing research.

Relationship with Learning Indicators

Otero and Chambers-Otero (2002) introduce four levels of relationship, each one adding more power to the learner, and believe that it is necessary to move beyond the simplistic evaluation of relationships as good or bad. They suggest that all learning progresses through four levels of relationship. We are always in a relationship but the quality of that relationship and therefore the quality of learning varies considerably. As our Learning Model is based on these relationships, we felt the continuum provided in the four phases of relationship was an appropriate framework. These four phases are summarized in our self-learning "Relationship with Learning" indicators:

Table 7.7. Relationship with Learning Indicators

Category	Indicators
Isolated Learners "Facts for Forgetting"	All content obtained by listening or reading
	Information downloaded, copied, cut and pasted
	Learning is incidental or on the surface
Engaged learners "Concepts for Analyzing"	Information is absorbed and understood
	Links are made to other learning
	Information makes sense because it is relevant
	Can see the potential use of the information to their lives
Interactive/ Introspective Learners "Ethics for Discussing"	Has started to value learning to him/herself personally
	Understands learning is integrated into own life and lives of others
	Learning with, rather than from, teacher—teaches others too
	Starting to self-govern own learning
	Becoming more creative and authentic
	Beginning to decide what really matters to him/her
Global Self-Regulated Learners "Options for positive action"	Shares learning with others in meaningful, productive ways that enhance the functioning of the learner, others, and the whānau
	Thinks critically, seeks different perspectives, can challenge appropriately
	The learner is now part of a larger structure of personal freedom—aware, adaptable, interdependent

Source: Otero and Chambers-Otero (2002).

Relationship with Peers

Cultural context plays a pivotal role in the development of peer relationships. If we wanted to describe our students' development in their relationships with each other we had to take their cultural context into account. Research on peer relationships has traditionally focused on Western cultures, however, here has been a steady increase in the number of studies focused on peer relationships in different cultures. The findings have illustrated the wide variety of peer experiences across cultures.

One of the cultural dimensions that has been extensively explored is collectivism versus individualism or interdependent versus independent orientations (Chen, French, & Schneider, 2006). In Western cultures individual needs and characteristics, personal freedom and independence, and self-realisation are highly emphasized. People are encouraged to become autonomous, self-reliant, and emotionally detached from their groups (Triandis, 1995). In collectivistic societies however, the interests of the individual are considered subordinated to those of the collective. The expression of individuals' needs or striving for personal autonomy, especially when it threatens the group functioning, is often viewed as unacceptable. Cultures with collectivistic values typically emphasize interdependent ties among individuals, group loyalty, limited personal privacy, and conformity to collective standards (Triandis, 1995). These values are of considerable relevance to social interactions and relationships in the peer context.

Moreover, children are not passive recipients of cultural influence, but instead, are active participants in adopting and modifying existing conventions and values, and more importantly, in constructing their own norms and cultures in peer interactions (Corsaro & Nelson, 2003; Wenger, 1998). Cultural beliefs and values are likely reflected at each level of children's peer relationships, including interactions, friendships, social networks, and acceptance and rejection within the larger peer group.

The peer relationship continuum (Table 7.8) had to cover a wide range of characteristics. Students could start at any point on the continuum, for example, most children do not bully others, act dishonestly or spread rumors, but some do, and this behavior is a symptom of other issues which, once identified, can be supported to change. The continuum needed to cover the full range of potential behaviors.

Peer Relationships Indicators

Table 7.8. Peer Relationship Indicators

Category	Indicators
Peer Relationship Continuum	Interaction with peers mainly involves teasing, bullying or making trouble
	Isn't honest with others—twists truth to suit own ends
	Is OK with starting rumours, spreading gossip, setting others up
	Acts staunch—tries to intimidate others

Category	Indicators
	Uses peer pressure negatively—or gives in to pressure from others
	Little understanding of whānau or responsibilities to the group—everything is about self—operates as an individual
	Mostly respectful to peers, but can forget at times
	Tries to be honest with others—most of the time
	Sometimes gets involved in other people's dramas
	Seeks help or advice with conflict
	Tries not to give in to peer pressure—not always successful
	Understands he/she is part of a whānau but makes minimal contribution
	Shows respect for peers even if they are not his/her friends
	Honest with peers—works hard at not being two-faced
	Never gets involved in others' business—never "backstabs" or gossips
	If there is conflict with a peer, tries to talk it out or seeks adult help
	OK with self as is—doesn't feel the need to change to impress
	Understands whanaungatanga and actively contributes to the collective
	Always respectful to peers and encourages others to do the same
	Always honest—can be trusted absolutely
	Never nosey and will actually report rumors etc to adults
	Has the skills to resolve his/her own conflicts
	Never bows to peer pressure and encourages others to do same
	Understands whanaungatanga and teaches it to others

Source: Kia Aroha College.

Relationship with the Wider World

Self-acceptance is a prerequisite to the acceptance and valuing of others. Banks (2004) believes teachers should be aware of and sensitive to the stages of cultural development that all of their students—including mainstream students, students of color, and other marginalized groups of students—may be experiencing, and should facilitate their identity development.

Banks believes that students need to reach Stage 3 of his typology, before we can expect them to embrace other cultural groups or attain thoughtful and clarified national or global identifications. The typology is a framework for thinking about and facilitating the identity development of students who approximate one of the stages. It is not intended to be a strictly linear process. As a staff we had closely examined this typology, before the work on developing our self-learning lens tool began. We had placed ourselves on the continuum in a staff workshop and identified stages we felt individual students had reached, and we felt Banks' typology was a very useful guide. We decided to include Banks' stages in our self-lens tool to determine students' readiness to engage positively with their own specific cultural identity and as indicators of our students' social interactions beyond their chosen cultural groups. The continuum we decided to use (Table 7.9) comes from Stage 1 to Stage 3 of the Banks' typology. These indicators show students' interaction with culture—initially their relationship with their own culture, and then as that becomes positive, their readiness to understand and respect the cultural identities of others. This is a different measure from the attributes specific to their Māori identity (Table 7.1) or Tongan identity (Table 7.3).

Cultural Identity Indicators

Table 7.9. General Cultural Identity Indicators

Category	Indicators
Cultural Identity	Low self-esteem
	Takes on negative stereotypes about own culture—believes them
	Rejects own culture
	Newly discovered awareness of own culture
	Believes now that their ethnic group is superior to others—interacts exclusively within this cultural group
	May not be sure about this—trying to convince themselves
	Is able to clarify their own personal attitudes towards their culture
	Now has genuine pride in their own culture—not contrived
	Genuinely bicultural—healthy sense of cultural identity
	Participates successfully in their own cultural community as well as in another cultural community
	Strong desire to function effectively in two cultures

Source: Banks (2004).

Using the Indicators

The action research now became technical. Having established indicators we were all happy with, how were we actually going to "score" this assessment so that the data were useful to us in showing trends and individual progress? Just ticking items on a checklist was not going to give us this analysis.

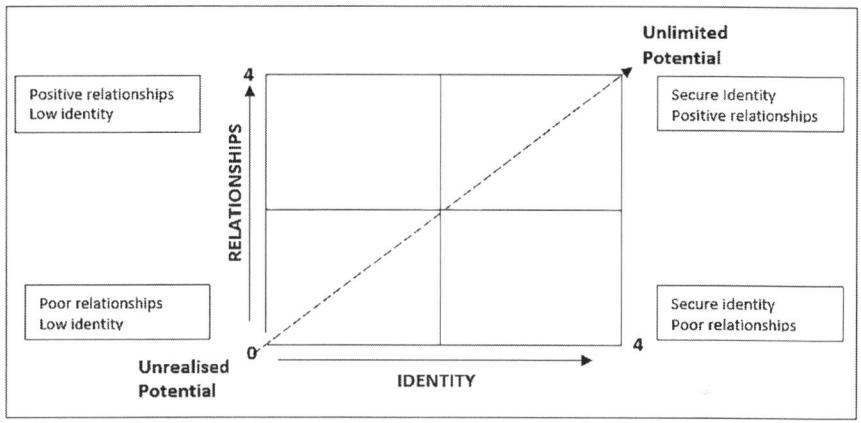

Figure 7.1. Suggested Self-Learning Lens Diagram
Source: Kia Aroha College

Our school's student management and assessment system[3] was a database we had been actively involved in developing with the programmer over many years. By 2006 it was a widely used product in many schools but we had a close relationship with the firm and our staff often helped demonstrate the product to new customers. We knew the program's capabilities and we contracted the software developer to turn our lists of indicators into an assessment tool that would be robust and could then be tracked over time and used to show trends and patterns. We took a version of this sketch (Figure 7.1) to the developer as a starting point and continued to work on this throughout 2005 and the first half of 2006.

The following decisions became incorporated into the assessment as our discussions progressed:

1. Three of the sets of indicators: the relationships with learning, the relationship with peers and the general identity/wider world relationship were clearly understood as continua. We realized that these were not strictly linear developments but there were recognisable stages and levels that we could identify. Once a certain indicator was chosen, the tool would assume that the indicators prior to the selected indicator in the continuum were also achieved.
2. The specific Māori, Samoan, Tongan and Cook Islands Māori indicators were not a continuum at all and depended very much on participation and involvement. A family might have access to their marae, but no active involvement in learning te reo Māori for example. This meant that these indicators could be selected randomly and each one would be scored separately.

3. We decided to use a 1–4 scale on each axis. The horizontal axis would show identity development, using the general and specific cultural identity markers. The vertical axis would show relationship development, using the learning and peer relationship indicators. A formula, developed by the computer programmer, would convert the indicator scores to a result on a 1–4 scale, and plot the student's outcome in each of the sets of indicators on the matrix.

Key Competencies

In light of the developments arising at the time from work in the *New Zealand Curriculum* on key competencies, staff considered whether the elements we had selected for the red, self-learning lens tool might also relate to some of the key competencies in the national curriculum. Although this was not the primary purpose of this tool, we felt there was some alignment as Table 7.10 shows. However, although there was certainly alignment, the deeper question was did we really want to make this link?

Macfarlane, Glynn, Grace, Penetito, and Bateman (2008) critiqued the key competencies to align them with a Māori cultural worldview. They felt that Māori knowledge, values, beliefs, and ako (learning and teaching), could inform and critique not only the five key competencies, but could also enrich the development of the national curriculum itself. They concluded:

> While there was some commonality in meaning between particular key competencies and particular Māori constructs there is more evidence of where the Māori constructs did not "match", because they were coming from quite different knowledge and value bases, and their meaning within a Māori worldview was both wider and deeper than the meaning within the majority European cultural worldview. (p. 123)

Table 7.10. Alignment of Self-learning Lens Indicators with New Zealand Curriculum Key Competencies

Indicators	Key Competencies
The relationship to learning indicators	Thinking
The peer relationship indicators	Relating to others
The specific Māori, Samoan, Tongan, Cook Islands Māori identity indicators	Managing self
The general cultural identity indicators	Participating and contributing

Source: Kia Aroha College.

In their discussion of "managing self" Macfarlane et al. contrast the western context of individualism and individual achievement with the Māori constructs of whanaungatanga and rangatiratanga which require individuals to fulfil their responsibilities to work for the well-being of the group (p. 118). Te Whānau o Tupuranga and Clover Park Middle School staff developing the self-lens assessment tool indicators and exploring possible links to the "managing self" key competency in 2004 had clearly made the same comparisons. Macfarlane et al. also point out that continuing colonizing practices with the New Zealand education system marginalize and belittle Māori language, thinking and analytical skills which are seldom evidenced in the curriculum and pedagogical practices imposed in our schools (pp. 105–106). Again, this thinking is also evident in our staff conversations as this comment shows:

> The fact that we've spoken at length about where mainstream schools are at is the same process that our people have had to undertake in terms of imperialism and colonisation. There is no such word as post-colonialism for Māori. Freire talks about the oppressed freeing the oppressors, and we have that really strongly on-site. (Judith)

The key competencies debate resulted in the decision to retain the capability in the computer program to produce key competencies results and to determine, with use, if this information was relevant. In practice it hasn't proven to be as relevant as the self-learning indicators, but the capacity to make this link provides evidence that a critical, culturally responsive assessment can be aligned with mandated or national curriculum requirements, while still retaining its legitimacy and validity as cultural knowledge in its own right.

After ongoing staff discussion and then professional development with the indicators and the computer database we were ready to trial the self-lens tool at the beginning of 2007 with an assessment school-wide to establish baseline data for the students who were in Years 8–13 in 2007. These initial assessments were made through teacher observation, using teachers' cultural competence in the respective cultures represented in the school as the arbiter for cultural skills and strengths. Subsequent assessments have been made in partnership with students themselves and with whānau. The results of these assessments are shown in the following sections.

Self-Learning Lens: Progress Over Time

Using the indicators, we can show progress in the self-learning lens, for the whole school, by gender, by year level, or for specific groups. We can also show an individual student's progress over time. Figure 7.2 shows one student's assessments from 2010 (Year 8) to 2015 (Year 13). This graph is included in our students' formal written reports to parents and is discussed with them at parent/student conferences.

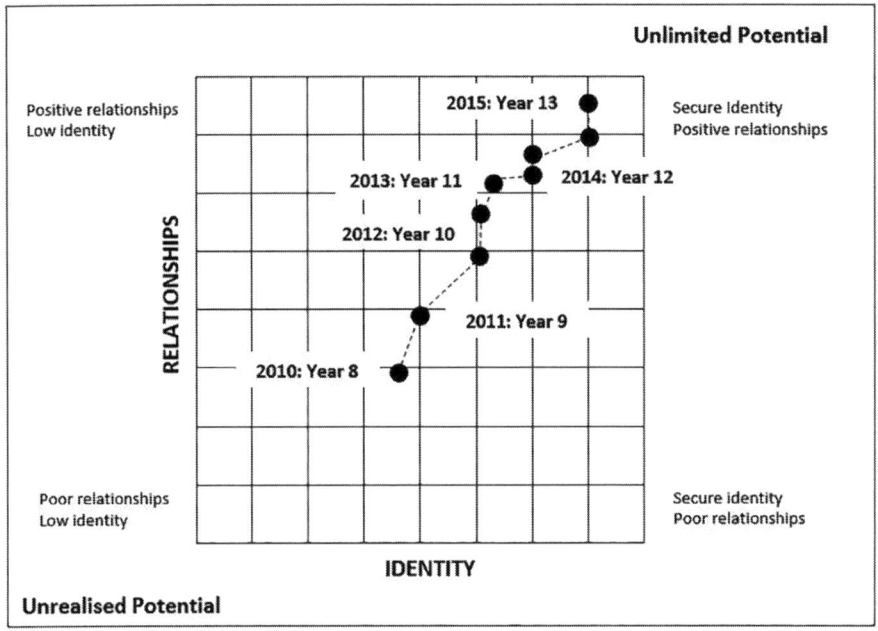

Figure 7.2. One Student's Self-Lens Assessment over Six Years 2010–2015
Source: Kia Aroha College.

Putting Self and School Lenses Together

Combining Results

As well as showing specific cultural learning development for groups and individuals., we can now put all our different assessments together to show dramatically that progress in cultural identity and relationships shift *first*, and other learning follows. The following examples, again chosen over time to show the consistency of these data, demonstrate the detail that is possible when self-lens assessments are plotted alongside school reading, writing, and numeracy data.

Figure 7.3 shows the results over three years for one student who was excluded from his previous school in Year 7. After several failed attempts to enrol him in other schools closer to his home, he was brought to Te Whānau o Tupuranga by the Ministry of Education. The student and his whānau were angry about their experience and resistant to the Ministry's efforts to find a new school. He had not been attending school for several months and Ministry officials admitted they had found the process of re-enrolment intimidating.

In 2007 the student was reading at a 10 year level and was working at almost four years below his chronological age in English and mathematics. He was unaware of his Māori identity, and isolated himself from other students. Between March 2007 and May 2008 however, there was a dramatic increase in his self-lens identity scores—a gain of over 40%. Up until this time, his other learning had very slowly improved. Through 2008, his self-lens results remained steady and increased again in 2009. In August 2009, at the age of 15 years, this student was working at or above his chronological age across the curriculum. He was a recognized leader in the middle school whānau and his parents were extremely supportive of him and the school. In Year 10 he had seven NCEA Maths credits and continued to achieve further credits in 2009. Teachers commented in his reports on his ability to critically analyze what he was reading and on his understanding of what that meant to him and to Māori generally—and to suggest ideas as how that should be changed.

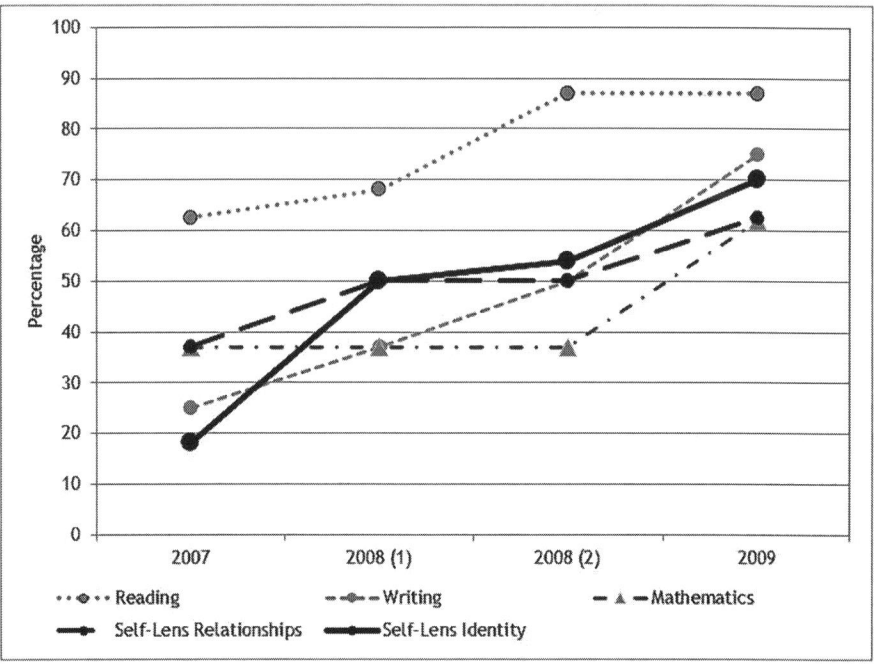

Figure 7.3. Self and School Lens Results: One Māori Student, 2007–2009
Source: Kia Aroha College.

In Figure 7.4 a similar pattern is seen for a Cook Islands Māori student, whose early years were plagued by chronic absence and disengagement from school. With a change of home circumstances and improved attendance he began to participate in school activities and to learn about his identity. This is seen in the significant changes in his self-learning results in 2013. In 2015, he was a member of a group invited to speak to education leaders on the question, "What are the biggest issues in leadership in education in Aotearoa New Zealand in 2015 for you?" He wrote:

> I believe that the biggest issue for me in leadership in education is that our cultural heritage is barely being acknowledged or recognized. Personally, I would be greatly reassured if culture was being acknowledged at all. However very few, by very few I mean next to no schools, are offering this.
>
> … I also believe that leaders in education should be encouraged and be courageous to take the abstract pathway. I personally do not want to take the already paved pathway. Without even realizing it, when we walk that pathway we are wearing a mask that bounds our identity.

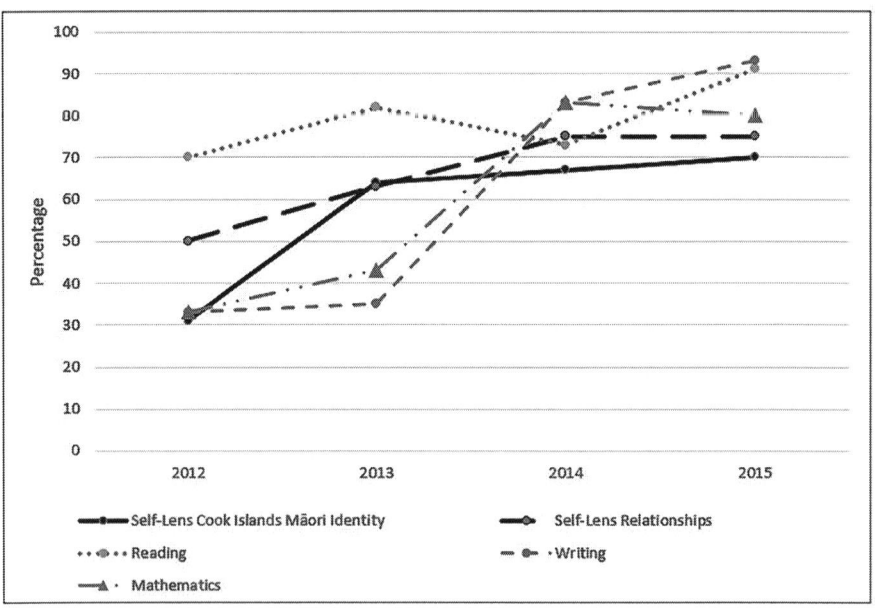

Figure 7.4. Self and School Lens Results: One Cook Islands Māori Student, 2012–2015
Source: Kia Aroha College.

Both these examples show that when the self-lens identity measures improve other learning gains are made. This is a common pattern. In some cases however, the importance of the self-lens results is that they can alert staff to abilities they may not have noticed at all without this tool. Both also show that our narrow focus on reading and literacy can hide other learning needs. For both these students their reading level was higher than their other results to begin with, however simply improving literacy outcomes does not necessarily lead to greater engagement in learning.

There has been dramatic progress in both relationships and identity development and this is evident in the leadership roles this student is both seeking and taking on. The self-lens assessment tool provides the explanation for this growth and change.

As well as the improvement in cultural identity, relationships, and self-belief, which obviously influence all aspects of a young person's learning, a key factor in these shifts in achievement is the power of the self-lens assessment outcomes to change teachers' assumptions about a student's capability. Teachers have also developed graded texts for assessment of reading levels in Samoan and Tongan languages. These results, placed alongside high scores from the Samoan identity indicators, completely change teachers' perspectives for a Samoan child who might have very low English reading results. Without the information the self-lens assessment tool provides, teachers could make decisions about such a student's ability in English, based on various "English for Speakers of other Languages" (ESOL) assessments. With the information about Samoan identity and language however, teachers see that these skills are transferrable to reading and writing in English. This is authentic culturally responsive pedagogy.

Conversely, teachers can examine all of their assessments for a student who is consistently disengaged from learning, often with associated behavioral needs, and find that has been little improvement in the student's self-lens assessment. This is particularly obvious in students who enter Kia Aroha College at a more senior year level, with long term, embedded, disengagement from school and little previous experience or knowledge of their own cultural identity. Again such information is valuable for teachers who can identify inconsistencies and plan specifically for that student's needs. A Cook Islands, teacher explains the value of this learning for Cook Islands students:

> It's not so much about the child coming into the school with the knowledge of their culture. Some of our children come into here without culture, without anything. We have reversed the process here for them so that they do appreciate where they come from and seek some form of understanding of their own identity, and build on it.
>
> I believe that the majority of our Cook Islands students do not have a clue about their culture. If anything, they live as White—that's the culture they've been brought up in. Most of them were born in New Zealand with no understanding of Cook Island values and things like that. Above anything else, our school offers that opportunity

for them to have a window and to see that—not only see it, but also live it, and I think that's the important thing is that we've created that kind of environment in our school so that the children can exercise what they are learning as well—so become holistic. (Holiday)

Following a presentation of this research at the Teacher Excellence Conference (TEN) in Oakland, CA, in August 2015 (Milne, 2015), co-founder of TEN, Dr Jeff Duncan-Andrade, commented, in a personal email, on the ability to plot Western academic learning with cultural learning using this assessment tool:

> Kia Aroha College has unlocked one of the most pressing issues in the field of education by developing a process for identifying, assessing, and measuring change over time on the metrics that research has shown for decades to be directly correlated with academic outcomes. That is to say, Kia Aroha has developed the tools to measure critical markers of student development such as cultural identity, relationships, self-efficacy, and resilience. Furthermore, they have been able to clearly link growth in these areas to subsequent growth on traditional academic measurements such as literacy and maths. (J. Duncan-Andrade, personal communication, January 13, 2016)

The Purpose of the Self-Lens

The examples provided here show that the self-lens assessment tool is doing what it was designed to do. It was never intended to stand alongside standard psychological assessments of identity and doesn't pretend to. The indicators developed by staff have stood almost ten years of trialing and application. In practice they provide rich information we wouldn't see if we persisted in assessing solely for literacy and numeracy against national benchmarks and standards. The self-lens assessment tool identifies and describes for Kia Aroha College what "as" Māori, Samoan, Tongan, Cook Islands Māori look like in the school.

It is important to re-emphasize that self-lens learning and achievement is seen by the school as valid, high status learning in its own right. Although the examples provided illustrate how all learning is related, and how gains in identity and relationships results do in fact lead to related shifts in other learning, this is not the primary purpose of the self-lens. The self-lens exists to enable the school to legitimate and validate Māori and Pasifika knowledges and values in their own right, and to continue to develop this knowledge in our learners. Self-lens learning is a valid "end point" in itself. Māori and Pasifika knowledges and values should never be seen as peripheral, or less important learning. Secure self-knowledge and identity might be a prerequisite for self-esteem and self-efficacy. Self-efficacy in turn might lead to higher engagement in learning in general, which could well include improved English literacy and numeracy outcomes. Self-lens learning however, is intentionally counter-hegemonic. To treat self-lens learning as merely a stepping stone towards improved literacy and numeracy is to make a deliberate choice that perpetuates Western academic hegemony and relegates Māori and Pasifika learners to the margins in our education system.

Learning in the Self-Lens

The development of cultural identity in school cannot be left to chance. Teacher planning deliberately requires, not only a cultural, critical consciousness in the school lens, but also specific planning for self-lens learning. Teachers plan collaboratively online using a template which asks them in every plan to identify which aspects of their plan are designed to support cultural identity, how this topic is critical, how it will develop students' conscientization about social justice, and how it supports the development of the school's graduate profile. All of these aspects are just as important in the teachers' discussions and thinking as their selection of standards or expected curriculum outcomes.

The self and school lenses obviously continuously and seamlessly overlap. Within a Year 13, Business Studies Young Enterprise plan for Te Whānau o Tupuranga, perhaps not the most likely place you would expect to develop cultural identity, the teacher included intrinsic Māori dimensions of oranga (wellbeing), wairuatanga (spirituality) and whanaungatanga (relationships) in the plan, and aligned Māori values of manaakitanga (duty of care) aroha (authentic caring) and mahi-tahi (working together) with students' personal values and their fledgling company's philosophy of behavior and operation.

Tongan, Samoan, and Māori students have successfully used their learning from their critical school lens learning in speech contests at regional and national level with speeches that included topics such as White spaces in information technology, the loss of language, global leadership, and hegemony.

The Place of Kapa Haka/Performing Arts in Self-Lens Learning

As well as intentional planning for the self-lens aspects in their regular program students are continually involved in Māori and Pasifika Performing Arts at an advanced level. Unlike most schools where these activities are understood as extracurricular, Kia Aroha College considers kapa haka or Pasifika performance art to be a core curriculum in itself. School teams enter prestigious competitions that require months of intensive preparation and hard work. Again, the school and self-lenses overlap with students able to achieve NCEA credits for their cultural performance, and the learning that leads up to this. However, the benefits of kapa haka and performing arts go far beyond an academic learning exercise.

Many schools in New Zealand participate in kapa haka. For many Māori students participation in these groups is what keeps them in school and keeps them connected. Cavanagh (in Macfarlane, Glynn, Cavanagh, & Bateman, 2007), asked the question of one senior student, "What it is like to be a Māori student in senior school?" She answered, "Most of the time the lights are turned off. The light comes on Tuesday afternoon at kapahaka" (p. 74). However, for many schools this is the only effort they make towards cultural responsiveness, bringing out the kapa haka group at school events to make a superficial, token gesture towards tikanga Māori. As May (2002) observes, "In short, a kapahaka (Māori cultural group) group, though not unimportant or inconsequential in itself, does not a multicultural programme make" (p. 11).

For many other schools participation and high level involvement in kapa haka doesn't transfer to any changes in classroom practice and the two spheres of learning can remain compartmentalized if teachers do not have the knowledge or experience to notice the positive benefits of this engagement and act upon it. Other schools ban involvement in kapa haka altogether, feeling that the time and energy students devote to it detracts from their academic workload. Interestingly, many of these schools participate aggressively in inter-college sports, music and other performing arts competitions without any similar concerns. Whitinui (2004) explains the importance of kapa haka from a Māori perspective:

> Kapa Haka allows Māori students to reveal the potential of self, culture and identity through the art of performing. It also possesses the ability to link the performance to appreciating individual uniqueness (difference) while helping students to come to know the value of human potential (Hindle, 2002). Kapa Haka instils levels of creativity through the expression of body movements and actions, the expression of words, the connections between the living and those who have past, principles reflecting life and knowing, as well as, how Māori now live today. It is in every dimension of the life itself and in how Māori as a people connect their destiny, philosophies and purpose for being. (p. 92)

Kia Aroha College staff agree. This excerpt from Te Whānau o Tupuranga's kapa haka philosophy describes the impact of this high level performance on all aspects of student learning:

> Kaiako (teachers) have always maintained that it is the journey students embark on, in preparation for a performance, the skills they develop, whanaungatanga and leadership opportunities that have more of an impact on student achievement, as opposed to the actual performance itself. We have found that Kapa Haka improves attendance, as well as students' general attitude towards school. It encourages parent participation, which flows on to other aspects of school life. Kapa Haka also modifies behavior, gives our students a sense of pride and history to build their own achievements on, while offering opportunities for collaborative and group learning situations. Kapa Haka is a unique medium for learning and developing relationships, between students, between kaiako and students, between whānau and kaiako, as well as introducing and developing a range of leadership skills.

Kapa haka is also a powerful platform for critical pedagogy and action. Senior students and former students compose and choreograph items with a strong message. This is a longstanding tradition in Te Whānau o Tupuranga where haka and waiata have been used consistently as forms of protest to the Ministry of Education and to government officials during the struggle to establish the school. Other items have been used to get across messages about the environment, or about health or social justice issues that affect Māori. This repertoire includes a haka of protest, *Taniwha Wāwāhi Mā*, about the White spaces in our education system, an action song, *Te Ara Tino Rangatiratanga*, about the pathway to self-determination.

In Te Whānau o Tupuranga the ongoing involvement in practice for kapa haka enables students regularly to experience living and sleeping on the school marae, which enables them to learn to perform the roles of providing hospitality and caring for people and to establish and maintain respectful relationships. The school's facilities attract adult national-level competitive kapa haka groups, who "live-in" at the school marae for their practices. This encourages our students to set their sights even higher. Teachers often describe our students' interest in kapa haka as an "obsession." It is certainly a passion for many students. Videos of adult national competitive groups are saved or frequently accessed via social media and our young people analyze each performer's every move and style. Many aspire to, and have achieved, membership of these well-known groups after leaving school. There is no doubt that kapa haka is a powerful liberating force in the shaping of our young people's cultural identity and self-knowledge.

Akom (2009), in the U.S.A., makes similar observations about hip hop and introduces a Critical Hip Hop Pedagogy (CCHP) "that can respond to issues of racism and other axes of social difference that Black people/people of color face in urban and suburban schools and communities" (p. 54). He argues that the "use of hip hop as a liberatory practice is rooted in the long history of the Black freedom struggle and the quest for self-determination for oppressed communities around the world" (p. 53).

> CHHP simultaneously (1) foregrounds race and racism and their intersectionality with other forms of oppression; (2) challenges traditional paradigms, texts, and theories used to explain the experiences of students of color; (3) centralizes experiential knowledge of students of color; (4) emphasizes the commitment to social justice; and finally (5) encourages a transdisciplinary approach. (p. 63)

Each of the ethnic groups in Kia Aroha College participates in their form of performing arts. Whether it is as dancers, singers, or drummers, students aspire to reach the pinnacle of success. For many students this is their very first experience of advanced achievement and this is a valuable lesson in what success feels and looks like—and the sustained hard work that is required to get there. For Kia Aroha College there is no "down side" to the involvement in these cultural activities. Performing arts is the medium that continually attracts older role models, former students, who maintain their connection with current students by acting as tutors and composers. This important group is known in the school as our "young elders," a description that acknowledges their status as kaitiaki or keepers of our knowledge and recognizes their experience. These young role models, now successful in their chosen careers, consistently reinforce powerful messages about identity and excellence.

Self-lens learning can't occur if students are not given opportunities for growth, to make mistakes and to learn about "being" Māori, Samoan, Tongan, Cook Islands Māori, or whatever their ethnicity is. Many opportunities are provided for all cultural groups to learn about leadership, to learn about custom, to observe appropriate ritual and ceremony and to fulfil cultural obligations. Far from being an add-on or token gesture, these opportunities are embedded within school policy and practice. All visitors to the school are given official pōwhiri (Māori ceremonial welcome). This might be a small affair or could involve all students and staff. Pōwhiri may happen on the marae or in the school Performing Arts Centre, or in a classroom. Appropriate Pasifika ceremonies are also observed, with "ava" ceremonies for Samoan visitors for example. Parents participate in many of these events, bringing food and fitting into cultural roles and expectations. Students travel to tangi and attend funerals when these are connected to school whānau. Underpinning all of these practices are the principles of whānau and whanaungatanga, as an authentic context for cultural norms to develop as a part of every day school life.

Determining Success: Whose Knowledge Is of Most Worth?

Tomlins-Jahnke (2008) states, "indigenous education outcomes are inevitably compared with, and measured against national and international norms, benchmarking tests and surveys embedded in western hegemonic values and ideals." Apple (2004) asks the questions, "What knowledge is of most worth?" and "Whose knowledge is of most worth?" (p. xix). He reminds us that not only do our educational institutions function to distribute ideological values and knowledge, "they also ultimately help produce the type of knowledge that is needed to maintain the dominant economic, political, and cultural arrangements that now exist." This "technical knowledge" legitimates the existing distribution of economic and cultural power (p. xxii).

Similar questions are posed by McLaren (2003) who explains that "critical pedagogy asks how and why knowledge gets constructed the way it does, and how and why some constructions of reality are legitimated and celebrated by the dominant culture while others clearly are not" (p. 72). McLaren identifies three types of knowledge constructed in schools: technical knowledge that can be measured and quantified, practical knowledge, that is useful in our daily lives, such as functional literacy and numeracy, and social interaction, and emancipatory knowledge. Emancipatory knowledge "creates the foundation for social justice, equality and empowerment" (p. 73) and is the goal of the critical educator and critical pedagogy.

It is technical knowledge however, that is considered the primary goal of our education system. Apple (2004) explains the connections between this technical, high status, knowledge and the economy. Technical knowledge is required to keep the economy running effectively and to maximize opportunities for expansion. However the widespread distribution of this knowledge is not required by everyone. As long as this knowledge is continually and efficiently produced, then schools are seen as doing their job well. "Thus, certain low levels of achievement on the part of 'minority' group students, children of the poor and so on, can be tolerated," because this is less important to the economy than the production of the knowledge itself. High status, technical, knowledge is also discrete knowledge with an identifiable and stable content that can be taught and tested. This makes stratifying individuals according to academic criteria easier (pp. 34–36). Duncan-Andrade & Morrell (2008) liken this sorting process to a "rigged game of Monopoly," where everyone supposedly starts at the same place with the same amount of Monopoly money:

> Like Monopoly the rhetoric of school-based meritocracy suggests that everyone starts at "Go" with equal chances to move around the board and capitalize on the opportunities that abound. … Whereas the outcomes in Monopoly are largely random, heavily influenced by the roll of the dice, educational outcomes are much more predictable. In the game of education, groups with high levels of social, political and economic capital move around the same game board as the rest of the population, supposedly competing under the same set of rules, but they afford themselves a supplemental bankroll that guarantees an unfair competition, one that for centuries has produced the same unequal outcomes in schools and in the larger society. (p. 3)

If schools are producing the outcomes they are in fact designed to do, and we continue to stratify and sort young people according technical knowledge this exclusive and primary status, the realities and outcomes for Māori and Pasifika students in New Zealand schools will not change, no matter how many school reform initiatives, strategic priorities, new curriculum documents, or national standards we develop. Duncan-Andrade and Morrell (2008) state, "We can cite a litany of research data and evidentiary claims to support the arguments that school is a rigged game, but what would be the point? How long must we argue over common sense?" (p. 5).

This chapter asked about the Māori, Samoan, Tongan, Cook Island Māori ways of knowing that young people were developing strength in their own cultural identity, and how we could know this was developing. The development of the self-lens tool, described in this chapter, and the knowledge it gives the school about these previously undervalued, but crucially important skills, have been Kia Aroha College's response to these questions. This is knowledge that will never be determined by assessments of literacy, numeracy, national standards or senior school qualifications outcomes. However, it is knowledge which, coupled with the critical scholarship in the school learning lens, changes both the learning and the assessment White spaces to make them relevant and authentic places for Māori and Pasifika learners.

Notes

1. Māori societal structures: whānau—extended family; hapū—subtribe, made up of one of more whānau; iwi—tribe, made up of several hapū—all connected through descent from a common ancestor or ancestors.

2. The stepped pattern of woven panels and mats, symbolizing growth, genealogies, and also the various levels of learning and intellectual achievement. The poutama pattern is featured throughout Kia Aroha College in paving, and in the school marae.
3. This programme is called eTAP (electronic Teaching, Assessment, & Planning), and has been developed by ESD (Educational Software & Devices), based in Manukau, Auckland, NZ.

References

Akom, A. (2009). Critical Hip Hop Pedagogy as a Form of Liberatory Praxis. *Equity & Excellence in Education, 42*(1), 52–66. http://doi.org/10.1080/10665680802612519

Alaska Native Educators. (1998). *Alaska standards for culturally-responsive schools.* Anchorage: Alaska Native Knowledge Network. Retrieved from http://www.ankn.uaf.edu/Publications/culturalstandards.pdf

Alaska State Board of Education & Early Development. (2006). *Content and performance standards for Alaska students.* Anchorage, Alaska. Retrieved from https://education.alaska.gov/akstandards/standards/standards.pdf

Aluli-Meyer, M. (2001). Our own liberation: Reflections on Hawaiian epistemology. *The Contemporary Pacific, 13*(1), 124–148. http://doi.org/10.1353/cp.2001.0024

Apple, M. W. (2004). *Ideology and curriculum* (3rd ed.). New York, NY and London: Routledge Falmer.

Balme, C. (1998). Hula and haka: Performance, metonymy and identity formation in colonial Hawai'i and New Zealand. *Humanities Research Journal Series, 3,* 24–41.

Banks, J. (2004). Teaching for social justice, diversity, and citizenship in a global world. *The Educational Forum, 68*(4), 296–305. http://doi.org/10.1080/00131720408984645

Barnhardt, R. (2002). Domestication of the Ivory Tower: Institutional adaptation to cultural distance. *Anthropology and Education Quarterly, 33*(2), 238–249.

Barnhardt, R., & Kawagley, A. (2005). Indigenous knowledge systems and Alaska Native ways of knowing. *Anthropology and Education Quarterly, 36*(1), 8–23.

Chen, X., French, D., & Schneider, B. (Eds.). (2006). *Peer relationships in cultural context* (Cambridge). New York, NY: Cambridge University Press.

Corsaro, W. A., & Nelson, E. (2003). Children's collective activities and peer culture in early literacy in American and Italian preschools. *Sociology of Education, 76*(3), 209–227. Retrieved from http://doi.org/10.2307/3108466

Duncan-Andrade, J., & Morrell, E. (2008). *The art of critical pedagogy : possibilities for moving from theory to practice in urban schools.* New York: Peter Lang.

Durie, M. (1998). *Te Mana Te Kawanatanga: The politics of Māori self-determination.* Auckland: Oxford University Press.

Education Review Office. (2003). *Clover Park Middle School Education Review Report.* New Zealand Education Review Office.

Hunkin-Tuiletufuga, G. (2001). Pasefika languages and Pasefika identities: Contemporary and future challenges. In C. Macpherson, P. Spoonley, & M. Anae (Eds.), *Tangata o te*

Moana Nui: The evolving identities of Pacific Peoples in Aotearoa/New Zealand (pp. 196–211). Palmerston North: Dunmore.

Macfarlane, A., Glynn, T., Cavanagh, T., & Bateman, S. (2007). Creating culturally-safe schools for Māori students. *The Australian Journal of Indigenous Education, 36*, 65–76.

Macfarlane, A., Glynn, T., Grace, W., Penetito, W., & Bateman, S. (2008). Indigenous epistemology in a national curriculum framework? *Ethnicities, 8*(1), 102–126. http://doi.org/10.1177/1468796807087021

Mailei, F. (1999). Identity as a concept: A New Zealand-born Samoan's perspective. In *Pacific Vision Conference proceedings*. Auckland: Pacific Vision Conference.

May, S. (2002). Accommodating multiculturalism and biculturalism in Aotearoa New Zealand: Implication for language education. *Waikato Journal of Education, 8*, 5–26. Retrieved from http://researchcommons.waikato.ac.nz/handle/10289/6256

McLaren, P. (2003). Critical pedagogy: A look at the major concepts. In A. Darder, M. Baltodano, & R. Torres (Eds.), *The critical pedagogy reader* (pp. 69–96). New York, NY: Routledge.

Milne, A. (2015). *Colouring in the White spaces: A critical pedagogy of Whānau*. Oakland, CA: Keynote presentation: Teachers Teaching Teachers: The TEN Community Responsive Teaching Conference.

Mitaera, J. (1999). Pacific vision—Navigating the currents of the new millennium. In *Pacific Vision Conference proceedings*. Auckland: Pacific Vision Conference.

Mulitalo-Lauta, P. (2001). Pacific Peoples' identities and social services in New Zealand: Creating new options. In C. Macpherson, P. Spoonley, & M. Anae (Eds.), *Tangata o Te Moana Nui: The evolving identities of Pacific Peoples in Aotearoa/New Zealand* (pp. 247–262). Palmerston North: Dunmore.

Otero, G., & Chambers-Otero, S. (2002). *RelationaLearning: Toward a human ecology in 21st century schools*. Retrieved from http://relationallearning.com/wp-content/uploads/2013/09/RL-Position-Paper-PDF1.pdf

Penetito, W. (2001, October). *If we only knew. Contextualising Māori knowledge*. Keynote Address to the New Zealand Council for Educational Research Early Childhood Education Conference, Wellington.

Tomlins-Jahnke, H. (2008). The place of cultural standards in Indigenous education. *MAI Review*, (1). Retrieved from http://www.review.mai.ac.nz/

Triandis, H. C. (1995). *Individualism and collectivism*. San Francisco, CA: Westview Press.

Wenger, E. (1998). *Communities of practice: Learning, meaning and identity*. Cambridge: Cambridge University Press.

Whitinui, P. (2004). The indigenous factor: The role of Kapa Haka as a culturally responsive learning intervention. *Waikato Journal of Education, 10*, 85–97.

Wilkie, M. A. (2010). *Te Taumata—Te Timata: The pinnacle—The First step* (Unpublished PhD thesis). Victoria University of Wellington.

· 8 ·

COLORING IN THE WIDER LEARNING SPACES

The Global-Learning Lens

The previous chapters have detailed the school's practice and outcomes in the school-learning and self-learning lenses. The development of a secure cultural identity, which allows young people to live and learn as who they are has been a fundamental premise. Developing a strong cultural identity however, does not ignore the complex, multiple, shared, and fluid identities our young people navigate both in and beyond school—and that is the purpose of the third lens, the global-learning lens. Knowing who they are in terms of their cultural identity is not to sentence young people to be forever trapped in a traditional cultural time warp. In fact, in order to effectively integrate all those other identities, the school's philosophy believes young people must firstly have a strong sense of self, and cultural identity is seen as the thread that acts as their compass, and weaves through all of the other pathways our young people walk. The global lens therefore is designed to connect students' self and school-learning to the many worlds beyond school—from immediately outside the school gates, to international and future spaces. This chapter examines one aspect of the global-learning lens: solidarity with social justice programs internationally, and the commonalities in Kia Aroha College's philosophy and practice and these initiatives.

Solidarity in the White Space

Durie (2001) proposed three goals for Māori education policies: that they should aim to equip Māori children and rangatahi (youth) to be citizens of world, to live as Māori, and to enjoy a high standard of living. As noted earlier, Durie's goals have been incorporated into the Māori Education Strategy, *Ka Hikitia* (Ministry of Education, 2013) which identifies, as a broad student outcome, that all Māori students will, "gain the skills, knowledge and qualifications they need to achieve success in te ao Māori, New Zealand and the wider world" (p. 2). In the Ministry of Education's *Statement of Intent 2014–2018* (Ministry of Education, 2014) this is interpreted as all New Zealanders becoming, "productive, valued and competitive in the world" (p. 8). These neoliberal, market-influenced goals have nothing to do with connecting Māori and Pasifika youth to the world in ways that empower them to see how their struggle, their histories, and realities connect with the experiences of other indigenous and minoritized communities internationally.

Sitting-in for Justice

The Clover Park Middle School Board of Trustees was once accused, by a senior Ministry of Education official that simply keeping the first group of senior students on our campus in spite of the Minister of Education's specific instructions they should be enrolled in other schools was tantamount to staging a "sit-in." The Board agreed, and continued sitting. During a study fellowship in 2009 I had the privilege of comparing the action taken by the Kia Aroha College community, with similar protest action taken in three communities in the United States of America (Milne, 2009, 2013). Some of these conflicts subsequently were studied by students at Kia Aroha College, all of the educators who had lead roles in these initiatives have visited Kia Aroha College, and our staff have an ongoing connection with them.

The protest for educational equity and social justice may have different contexts, different ethnic communities, and different schooling systems and regulations to negotiate, but the following three examples resonate with the struggle and the solutions the Kia Aroha College community has developed in Otara, New Zealand. Together they provide a powerful example of "audacious hope" (Duncan-Andrade, 2009) and a model that challenges and resists the White spaces in our schools.

Marching for Justice

I first encountered *The Definite Dozen* (Duncan-Andrade, 2010, p. 180) on the wall in Dr. Jeff Duncan-Andrade's and Dr. Wayne Yang's classroom at East Oakland Community High School in 2007. Students in this class were not able to participate in the program until they had committed the set of 12 principles to memory and their rendition had been approved by their classmates. Every lesson ended with the whole class saying *The Definite Dozen* in unison. At the end of our visit one of the gifts presented to us by the young people in the class was a framed copy of *The Definite Dozen* which I brought back to our students, and which is now displayed in our school Wharenui. Staff subsequently translated this into Māori, and composed a waiata based on these principles.

The East Oakland Community High School (EOC) opened in 2004, part of a wider community school reform movement, initiated by a group of mothers from the "flatlands" of Oakland who saw that their children, in large, overcrowded, poorly resourced schools were receiving a vastly different education from children in the affluent hills suburbs where schools were smaller.

The group of students I visited was part of the "Step to College" (STC) program, initiated by San Francisco State University's (SFSU) College of Education "as a response to the disturbingly low levels of academic engagement, achievement, graduation, and college eligibility among poor and working class youth of color" (Hidalgo & Duncan-Andrade, 2009). The STC program partnered a university professor with a local high school, allowing students to cross-enroll each semester in a high school class and a university seminar class. By exposing these young people to the rigor and culture of university courses the STC program hoped to prepare them for college success.

By 2007–2008 the Oakland Unified School District, under state control since its bankruptcy in 2003, had opened 49 new small schools and closed three "because of low enrolment and other problems" (Vasudeva, Darling-Hammond, Newton, & Montgomery, 2009, p. 5). One of those three was East Oakland Community High School. The closure meant that the STC class, embarked on such a transformational trajectory to college, were ousted from their successful environment, unable to complete their important senior year, and their junior year was disrupted by the threat of closure hanging over their heads:

> "We've finally created the conditions for which students are actually invested in school ... They're investing because they actually have hope. They have faith that

these adults will not let them down," Yang says. "I appreciate the challenge the district is throwing at us. ... Whether or not we believe in test scores, it's still telling. We believe those test scores should go up. They'll never be comparable to the population for which the tests were designed to measure, but our students will get into college and that's the difference." (Yang, in Maharaj, 2007)

The decision to close EOC devastated students, staff and the community and they took action On February 28, 2007, the community, students and staff of East Oakland Community High School *marched for justice* over eight miles to the Oakland Unified School District administrator/trustee meeting to protest, in vain, the decision to close their school. Parents were then left with difficult decisions about their children's education choices. Paperson (2010) explains that, in "the EOC ghostlife" some parents chose to leave the district, enrolling their children in other schools, and some chose not to send them to school at all. Some chose to enroll in a charter school and to travel each morning to class in a converted house on the opposite side of the city, so they could continue the program they had before closure. Paperson (2010) states:

> It is difficult to express without understatement, the risk taken by these students and their parents, the trust they had to muster in the volunteer adults staffing the program, and their total distrust of the Oakland school district. The state administrator saw these actions as irrational. Denouncing of colonial education, in both its aspects of dispossession and false generosity, appears completely irrational within the colonial epistemology. (p. 26)

The experience of this cohort of students from EOC was to be the catalyst for the establishment of the *Roses in Concrete Community School*, which opened in East Oakland in August 2015 (see later section in this chapter).

Starving for Justice

In Little Village, Lawndale, in Chicago, 19 people, including one 71 year old grandmother one high school student and one college student, both under the age of 20, *starved for justice*, staging a 19 day hunger strike in protest, when funding they were promised to build a high school in their community was spent on four other schools instead (Cortez, 2008, p. 17). Rather than an act of desperation or outrage, Stovall (2007) describes the hunger strike as "an intensely planned strategy to alert Chicago Public Schools to the community's power to resist and demand quality education" (p. 684).

Cortez says, "Their act was a show of force by brave ordinary mothers who confronted a patronage political platform dominated by men in the name of community empowerment and democratic principles" (p. 17). Cortez comments that Camp Cèsar Chávez, as the site of the hunger strike was named, "truly was a special place that embodied a force of hope by a wide range of people" (p. 54). Finally, almost four years after the end of the hunger strike, the Little Village Lawndale High School Campus opened its doors to four hundred students in the fall of 2005. The campus comprises four independent, autonomous, small schools: Multicultural Arts High School, World Language High School, Social Justice High School, and Infinity: Math, Science, and Technology High School. The Social Justice High School arose from the desire of the community and the activists involved, that the children who graduated from the new high school never forget the physical, spiritual, and communal struggle it took to achieve justice.

Reminiscent of the process described in Chapter 5 to develop a relevant learning environment in Kia Aroha College's design, the Little Village Lawndale High School Campus incorporated traditional signs and symbols that are reflective of its communities and are permanent reminders of the struggle to build the school. The design incorporates a numerological representation of the hunger strike and the Aztec story of the five worlds, which speaks of the elements of fire, air, water, and earth. In the school building design each element is represented by a color shown in the bricks in each of the schools. The bricks in the multicultural arts school are green, representing the earth. The bricks in the School of Social Justice are red, representing the world of fire (also representing the color of change). Bricks in the mathematics, science, and technology building are blue, representing water. The world language school has purple bricks, representative of the air. Stovall (2007) describes the feature in the center of the four schools:

> The fifth world is represented in a 60-foot sundial structure in the middle of the building. To commemorate the hunger strike, points are marked in the interior of the cone. From 13 May to 1 June (the original 19 days of the strike) the sun (by way of a skylight) hits a dot marked on the interior of the cone on each of the 19 days. On 1 June, the dot reaches the center of the cone and is reflected as a beam of light on a compass on the floor of the dial. (p. 687)

The sundial is used as collective meeting space for all four schools. Schools use the space for project displays, art projects, student meetings, and community forum. The main entrance to the four schools features bays between classrooms skewed at 19 degrees to represent the 19 days of the strike. Fourteen trees have been placed at the south end of the school to represent the 14 hunger-strikers who lasted the duration of the 19 days. A patch of tall grass rests on the north end of the campus, acknowledging the original site of Camp César Chávez.

Visiting Little Village Lawndale Social Justice High School in 2007, standing beneath the sundial, and hearing the story of the hunger strike was a powerful experience. As well as the architectural design features, the environment was rich with student murals, mosaics, and the central space windows when we visited hosted a display of silhouettes of civil rights leaders and images for social justice.

Running for Justice

In Tucson, Arizona, I met passionate, articulate, confident, young people engaged in the Tuscon Unified School District's Mexican-American Studies program. I visited high schools, a middle school, two elementary schools and a parent education class. I spent time with graduates from different cohorts of the Social Justice Education Project (Romero et al., 2010), then undergraduates at the University of Arizona and working as student-workers and mentors in the program's schools. The experience made a lasting positive impression.

It could be expected that, with the academic achievement of the students involved in this program, together with the strong committed support of families, the advocacy of eminent educators and universities, and the caliber of the young people whose learning I witnessed, that this program would receive the highest support and praise from education authorities. Unfortunately, as with all the other examples in this section, nothing could have been further from the truth. In fact, the opposition from Arizona education officials to the Ethnic Studies and Mexican-American Studies program was sustained and vitriolic.

On June 27, 2009, over 50 young people *ran for justice* over 190 kilometers in the extreme heat of the desert, from Tucson to Phoenix to protest the threat of closure of the program by state officials. It took them two days and they were joined by hundreds of supporters from the barrios and communities of Tucson, Eloy, Casa Blanca, Guadalupe and Phoenix, both as the run progressed, and on arrival in Phoenix where they marched to the State Capitol Building. It also involved the spiritual support from the Native-American Yoeme and Akimel O'odham Nations when runners passed through their territory (Rodriguez, 2009). The then Director of the Ethnic Studies program in Tucson, Augustine Romero, explained that the run was about healing and it was linked to indigenous traditional practice:

> The Run was used as a channel to carry out positive change in our communities, and in our State. The Run was not a march, a rally, or a race; but rather, an opportunity for our people to work united with all the rest of creation to bring about healing. In addition, the Run was a reflection of a historical Indigenous tradition that brings about change through prayer. It is believed that the energy that is projected from the momentum of the run, its runners and their intentions and their constant connection to the earth will be reciprocated in the form of a healing and ultimately a blessing. (Personal communication)

However, the run, along with further prolonged protest action the following year, was in vain and the ban on the Ethnic Studies program became law in Arizona in January 2011, and subsequently, the center of the nation's attention amid acrimonious controversy and conflict. Why was there such opposition to the program and why was it banned? Sleeter (2012) explains:

> I believe the core issue is fear of the knowledge Mexican-American students find precious and empowering. Ethnic studies names racism and helps students examine how racism works in their everyday lives, how it was constructed historically, and how it can be challenged. For students of color, ethnic studies draws on knowledge from within racially oppressed communities, and affirms what students know from everyday life, taking the concerns of students seriously and treating them as intellectuals.

This embedded racism, and fear of relinquishing or sharing power was best demonstrated to me when I asked a member of the New Zealand Ministry of Education why, in spite of the success of our program and philosophy, and in spite of the engagement of our youth, education officials remained so adamantly opposed? "Because," he said, "they are afraid you might be right." He went on to describe the implications of that for other schools, the greatest being that they would face major change.

Challenged Spaces

In comparison with the protest action taken in East Oakland, Little Village and Tucson, the sitting-in of the Kia Aroha College community may seem relatively innocuous, however, protest, in the form of simply going ahead and carrying out the community's wishes in the face of prolonged and bitter resistance from education authorities, was sustained by the school's community over three separate struggles spread over two decades. Whatever the type of action taken, and regardless of the outcome of their actions, each of the communities described in this section refused to accept the status quo for their children and went to extraordinary lengths, in the face of extreme opposition, to achieve an educational model that was relevant to their values and beliefs about learning, achievement, culture and identity.

While each of these contexts is different, across different ethnic groups, school systems, legislation and international borders, there are remarkable similarities across the solutions each of these four communities developed to challenge the system's White spaces. These fall into seven broad categories:

1. Race, ethnicity and cultural identity were central to their curriculum and practice. Each school or program worked successfully across different ethnic groups on the same sites or in the same classes.
2. The programs developed in each context were strongly supported and driven by parents and community, who often became strong advocates for the initiatives due to the engagement they saw in their children. Parents were prepared to take risks and to trust the programs. All programs were developed in underserved communities with youth who have been minoritized by their respective societies. The community was actively involved in the design of environments, the curriculum, and in discussing the historical significance of cultural leaders, artefacts, symbols and sites.
3. The programs were based in authentic caring, love, aroha, whānau, cariño, and compassion. Across all sites the young people were not seen as "other people's children" (Delpit, 2006) and the building of relationships of trust and care was crucial and genuine. There was a clear continuum across cohorts and generations and an expectation of reciprocity. Young people saw their connectivity to each other and to their past and future, and their responsibility to advocate for change that would better the collective.
4. All these programs were informed by critical theory and the work of Paulo Freire. They were based in critical pedagogy and critical race theory which see racism as a "given," and are driven by social justice goals for humanization, conscientization and transformation through critical praxis. The curriculum was based in the community and in the realities youth experience in education and in society. Examples of this

curriculum and delivery are the Critical Pedagogy of Whānau in Kia Aroha College, the barrio and Raza Studies pedagogies developed in Tucson, and the Youth Participatory Action Research (YPAR) work carried out in East Oakland.
5. Students were involved in the identification of issues and the production of knowledge through participatory action research. All four programs drew heavily on other knowledges—traditional cultural knowledge and practices, youth knowledge and culture, and community knowledge, that are usually considered irrelevant or peripheral to core or national curricula. Contexts for study were youth-centered. Students were highly engaged with new media literacies through the use of information and communications technology and digital resources, as well as learning advanced traditional literacies. All four programs had extremely high expectations for the achievement of academic standards and outcomes and the development of "Warrior-Scholars."
6. There was a high stakes end result that gave students a purpose for their learning. Students presented their research to well-informed and critical peers, to parents and families, to staff, administration, educators and academics outside the school, legislators, members of parliament, and city councils. They spoke at highly regarded conferences alongside adult academics and answered questions about their research.
7. Each community faced resistance and barriers over sustained time but did not allow these to dictate or change their direction. The programs were all intentionally counter-hegemonic.

Ukukura: Roses in Concrete Community School

When East Oakland High School suddenly closed in 2007, a cohort of students taught by Jeff Duncan-Andrade rallied around the idea of forming their own school where they could come back to the community and contribute to growing the next generation of change agents in Oakland, however they wanted to start this opportunity at a younger age. *Roses in Concrete Community School* is the realization of that thinking, and some of those early students now have their own children attending the school.

Roses in Concrete is a Kindergarten to 8th grade public charter school in Oakland, CA (USA). The school's special character emphasizes a bilingual/multilingual, critical and community responsive approach that centers on students' cultural identities. The school's name was inspired by the poem, *The*

Rose That Grew from Concrete, written by Tupac Shakur (1999). This vivid image captures the need to celebrate the tenacity and will of the rose that against-all-odds, finds a way to grow in the inhospitable and toxic environment of the concrete. Instead of designing a model that plucks out individual roses that find their way through cracks in the concrete, the school aims to break up the concrete so that entire rose gardens can blossom in our highest need neighborhoods. In short, the school believes that the point of education is not to escape poverty, but to end it.[1]

In 2015, I received a request from Dr Jeff Duncan-Andrade for Kia Aroha College to partner with Roses in Concrete Community School as "sister schools," a description neither of us liked. He asked could we provide a Māori word to better describe our partnership. I consulted te reo Māori exponents, to find that there was no word that exactly fitted our needs. Certainly we could have used a word such as whānau, or words about joining or partnering, but none were quite right. Finally, our advisers suggested the new word, *Ukukura*. Kura is the Māori word for school. The word, uku, denotes an ally, or a supporting tribe, in battle for example (Moorfield, 2011). The two words combined gave us the perfect description of two schools working closely together in solidarity as allies in the struggle for educational sovereignty and equity. Both schools proudly feature our Ukukura status on our respective websites.

I was privileged to be at Roses in Concrete Community School in August, 2015, during the week when the staff first took up their positions, and to be part of the ceremonies that honored the indigenous people of the area, and introduced teachers, carefully selected for their expertise in critical pedagogy and social justice, to the school and to each other. I was fortunate to be able to visit again, seven months later, to see classes in action. On my return home I wrote to congratulate Dr Duncan-Andrade and the staff, commenting in particular about the special "feeling" of being in the school, intangible, and difficult to name, but very obviously "there" in every aspect of the school:

> It's palpable, in the faces of your children, in the drumming and call and response to start the day, in the energy of your teachers, in the classrooms, in the thinking that is so evident behind all your decisions and careful planning—like meeting children on the footpath in the morning, so simple but so profoundly important. It's also there in the huge support from the volunteers and parents and community—like your board members and your former students, and it's there when things get real, when someone needs extensive support.

The seven categories identified as core components of the programs described earlier in this chapter are clearly evident as you walk around Roses in Concrete, and talk to educators, children, and community. A prominent wall display in the main entrance hall with the title "Mamas" features mothers of staff and community, and another photo display celebrates International Women's Day with images of educators, activists, and social justice leaders. I am honored to find that my image is included! The integration of our Ukukura relationship is obvious in the children's writing, in both English and Spanish, about Māori in New Zealand, and in the guitar a Kia Aroha College teacher gifted to the school, adorned with a Māori pattern and Māori proverb, used daily by the World Music teacher to teach and accompany Indigenous music and dance. In the main office, the original art work created by a former student of Kia Aroha College for the opening of Roses in Concrete is proudly displayed. I take all of these messages back to Kia Aroha College, where they are greatly appreciated.

In the vibrant displays in the junior classrooms, typical teacher charts and learning aids jostle for wall space with a series of posters stating, "Justice for …" and "Black Lives Matter." Another poster states "Migration is a Human Right" and another displays the principles of "In Lak'ech." All children are learning in English and Spanish. In a senior class we observe a circle, where the teacher asks for the students' opinions about the reintegration into the class of a peer who has not met their expectations. They are not convinced he is ready yet and give their reasons why. Returning to this Grade 4 (Year 5) class later that morning we interrupt the planned discussion on "internalized oppression." These walls too are crowded with messages, "We are the Difference" a display heading proclaims, above photos and posters—there's Che Guevara, Ella Baker, Cesar Chavez, Martin Luther King, and the Black Panther Party. In another wall space there is children's writing, one piece is headed, "What I learned about the Taino Indians." Again, this is what authentic, critical, culturally responsive pedagogy looks like in action. It is also, very definitely, a critical pedagogy of whānau.

The programs described in this section provide the counter-narrative to the rhetoric of school reform and the intense focus on technical knowledge and high stakes testing and standards. They demonstrate what is possible. They don't try to change the children, they aim to change the White spaces so that children can flourish and thrive in their own community.

In each case, there was synergy with the experiences of Kia Aroha College, so similar it might have been our story. In many ways it was. Kia Aroha College students interacted with East Oakland youth, contributing to their research about designing a school, and talking online about their study of restorative justice practices. Two students from East Oakland visited Kia Aroha College and struck up strong friendships, fitting instantly into our Samoan and Tongan learning environments. Kia Aroha College students and other youth from the programs described in this section met in Vancouver at an American Education Research Association Conference, and most recently have connected with youth in Los Angeles about learning in a cultural environment, school discipline, and Māori perspectives on restorative justice. Indigenous students in the final year of schooling in a remote school in Australia's outback are due to make their third biennial visit to Kia Aroha College in 2016.

Although these examples describe international connections, the "global" in this learning lens includes all of the places and communities our students interact with beyond school. This also means for example, participation in Māori, Samoan and Tongan community activities, hosting conferences and visitors on the school marae, speaking at functions, and developing political awareness of wider social issues. Driver (2015) explains the students' and Kia Aroha College's understanding of this wider "beyond school" learning and action:

> Significantly, activism was defined by these educators as a normalized, everyday activity, and not necessarily protest actions. A student is an activist when they are on the kapa haka stage, or taking part in manu korero (speech contests)—often with an overt political message. They are also activists in their academic learning. Students articulate their own ideas in their written English studies, for example, when exploring the history of colonization and its ramifications for social justice today, including their own lives. In the context of academic learning, addressing the root causes of current structural inequities (like disproportionate levels of poverty for Māori and Pasifika families) is viewed as necessary to counteract the reinforcement of negative stereotypes and the passivity of victimhood. By learning this and speaking to it, students are being activists. (p. 102)

Youth Spaces

The previous section has described schools in solidarity, schools where the community and staff were prepared to fight for educational sovereignty and social justice, schools that identified the barriers, and tackled them head-on. An important link between these solutions and principles that challenge the system's White space, can be found in the work of Akom, Cammarota, and Ginwright (2008), in their concept of "Youthtopias." This term describes, "the processes of creating systematic, formal and informal, traditional and non-traditional educational spaces that produce pedagogies of love, resistance, resiliency, hope and healing" (p. 125). Akom et al. see this as an alternative asset-based approach for confronting the challenges of teaching and learning for social justice in the twenty-first century.

> this understanding of the vital role that young people play, not just in the consumption of social capital, but in the production of social and cultural capital, is important precisely because it highlights the importance of critical consciousness, youth agency, and youth activism in the development of effective social networks and neighborhood change. ... More often than not, a Youthtopian framework facilitates a process that develops critical consciousness and builds the capacity for young people to respond and change oppressive conditions in their environment. In other words, Youthtopias are simultaneously individual and organizational processes that promote civic engagement among youth and elevate their critical consciousness and capacities for social justice and community activism. (Akom et al., 2008, p. 115)

Youthtopias merge the frameworks of critical race theory, youth participatory action research, and critical media studies. Akom et al. identify the five elements that distinguish Youthtopias from other theories and methods in critical youth studies and beyond, and form its basic core. They state that the essential features of Youthtopias are created when these five conditions are met:

1. An explicit commitment to understand how race intersects with other forms of social oppression such as class, gender, religion, nationality, sexuality, phenotype, accent, immigration status, and special needs,
2. Challenging traditional paradigms, texts, and theories used to explain the experiences of students of color,
3. Fore-grounding the experiential knowledge of students so that young people and adults are "co-constructing" the learning environment,
4. A commitment to developing critical consciousness,
5. A commitment to social justice.

The following story is one example of how Kia Aroha College's program intersects and interacts with the work young people engage with in the after-school program in Studio 274, described in Chapter 2, to provide these conditions.

"Now We Are Activists"

One morning a few years ago, we all arrived at school to find that we had been "poster-bombed" overnight. Luckily, I had some inside knowledge, but staff and students wandered around unsure as to what they should do.

Hundreds of copies of a clever photo-shopped poster had been placed everywhere, both inside and outside the buildings. A data projector beamed the poster through a hidden window on to the side of the main school entrance way. When teachers and students turned on their computers the poster was now the screensaver, when they lifted the lid on the photocopier, it was there too, and it kept appearing in unexpected places all day.

The "non-destructive" Graffiti-Bomb was the brainchild of the Adobe Youth Voices (AYV) group in Studio 274. AYV is a project that aims to empower youth in underserved communities around the globe with real-world experiences and 21st century tools to communicate their ideas, exhibit their potential, and take action in their communities. In 2009, 2011, and 2013, Studio 274 members attended the World AYV Summit at Stanford and Santa Clara Universities in the U.S.A.

The 2010 AYV group decided on the Graffiti-Bomb as a method of sending a powerful anti-smoking message to our school community. As everyone arrived at school the AYV crew unobtrusively filmed their reaction. The group's work resulted in a documentary, which showed the idea's development from its inception through to the final reactions and their evaluation. In a debrief in the afternoon the group reported they felt they had seen the benefit of making their message so visible, particularly in terms of the way it had people asking questions and discussing it. However, the group felt that simply highlighting the issue wasn't enough, their new question was, "What now?" How could they provide support for young people who smoke and wanted to stop? How could they explore the wider issue of the high incidence of smoking in Māori whānau? Who was responsible? In their evaluation email message to staff the group said:

> Thanks again. It's such a cool thing to have such a supporting school that the members can do this kind of thing without too much fear of reprisals. As one AYV group member said to our group yesterday, "Now, we are activists."

Note

1. From the Roses in Concrete Community School website, http://rosesinconcrete.org/ and personal knowledge.

References

Akom, A., Cammarota, J., & Ginwright, S. (2008). Youthtopias: Towards a New Paradigm of Critical Youth Studies. *Youth Media Reporter*, *2*(1), 108–129. Retrieved from http://cci.sfsu.edu/files/Youthtopias.pdf

Cortez, G. (2008). *Education, politics, and a hunger strike: A popular movement's struggle for education in Chicago's Little Village community* (Unpublished PhD dissertation). University of Illinois, Urbana-Champaign.

Delpit, L. (2006). *Other people's children: Cultural conflict in the classroom* (1st ed.). New York, NY: The New Press.

Driver, A. (2015). *Cultural leadership: The reciprocities of right relationship at Kia Aroha College.* (Unpublished Master's thesis) Auckland: Auckland University.

Duncan-Andrade, J. (2009). Note to educators: Hope required when growing roses in concrete. *Harvard Educational Review, 79*(2), 181–194.

Duncan-Andrade, J. (2010). *What a coach can teach a teacher: Lessons urban schools can learn from a successful sports program.* New York, NY: Peter Lang.

Durie, M. (2001). *A framework for considering Maori educational advancement.* Paper presented at the Hui Taumata Matauranga II (Māori Education Summit). Turangi, Taupo, New Zealand.

Hidalgo, N., & Duncan-Andrade, J. (2009). When stepping to college is stepping to consciousness: Critical pedagogy for transformational resistance in an urban high School classroom. In E. Murillo, E. Villenas, S. Galvan, R. Munoz, J. Martinez, & M. Machado-Casas (Eds.), *Handbook of Latinos and education: Theory, research, and practice.* New York, NY: Routledge.

Maharaj, Z. (2007, July 16). A dream deferred. *OhDang Webzine.* Retrieved from http://www.ohdangmag.com/archivehttp://www.ohdangmag.com/archive/features/a_dream_deferred.html

Milne, A. (2009). *Colouring in the White spaces: Cultural identity and learning in School.* ASB/APPA Travelling Fellowship Report.

Milne, A. (2013). *Colouring in the White spaces: Reclaiming cultural identity in Whitestream Schools* (Unpublished PhD thesis). University of Waikato. Retrieved from http://researchcommons.waikato.ac.nz/handle/10289/7868

Ministry of Education. (2013). *Ka Hikitia—Accelerating success 2013–2017.* Wellington: Ministry of Education. Retrieved from http://www.education.govt.nz/ministry-of-education/overall-strategies-and-policies/the-maori-education-strategy-ka-hikitia-accelerating-success-20132017/

Ministry of Education. (2014). *Statement of intent: 2014–2018.* Wellington: Ministry of Education.

Moorfield, J. (2011). *Te Aka Māori-English, English-Māori dictionary and index* (3rd ed.). Auckland: Longman/Pearson.

Paperson, L. (2010). The postcolonial ghetto: Seeing her shape and his hand. *Berkeley Review of Education, 1*(1). Retrieved from http://escholarship.org/uc/item/3q91f9gv

Rodriguez, R. (2009). *Perspectives: Running for our lives: Victory for ethnic studies.* Diverse: Issues in Higher Education. Retrieved from http://diverseeducation.com/article/12713/

Romero, A., Cammarota, J., Dominguez, K., Valdez, L., Ramirez, G., & Hernandez, L. (2010). The opportunity if not the right to see: The social justice education project. In J. Cammarota & M. Fine (EDs.), *Revolutionizing education: Youth participatory action research in motion.* (pp. 131–150). New York, NY: Routledge.

Shakur, T. (1999). *The rose that grew from concrete*. New York, NY: Pocket Books.
Sleeter, C. (2012). Ethnic studies and the struggle in Tucson. *Education Week, 31*(21).
Stovall, D. (2007). Towards a politics of interruption: High school design as politically relevant pedagogy. *International Journal of Qualitative Studies in Education, 20*(6), 681–691. http://doi.org/10.1080/09518390701630825
Vasudeva, A., Darling-Hammond, L., Newton, S., & Montgomery, K. (2009). *Oakland Unified School District new small schools initiative evaluation*. Stanford, CA: School Redesign Network at Stanford University.

· 9 ·

POWERFUL SPACES

Chapter 1 posed five questions that arose from the story of the Samoan girl at the principal's office door, as fundamental to critical, culturally responsive classroom pedagogy and practice:

1. Can a school create the conditions that empower a student to follow their cultural norms throughout the school day?
2. Why is this important?
3. How can a school ensure all students have this strength in their own cultural identity?
4. What are the specific cultural ways of knowing that young people are developing these skills?
5. How can schools recognize, and address, barriers that exist in their practice to the development of a student's secure cultural identity?

These questions about cultural identity are linked to resistance and the struggle to wrestle knowledge from the colonizer (Dei, 2011, p. 168). The questions are revisited in this chapter.

Self-Determining Spaces

In 2010 a group of senior students worked together to develop a set of critical messages, following the example of the *Definite Dozen* (Duncan-Andrade, 2010, p. 180), which was introduced in Chapter 8. *Te Ara Tino Rangatiratanga: The Pathway to Self-Determination* is the result of the senior students' thinking. Duncan-Andrade explains that the idea of a set of principles such as the *Definite Dozen* is not about the principles themselves, but about the importance of creating scaffolding tools for young people that they can draw on in other situations and in their future lives. *The Definite Dozen* creates a common language and a core set of values that take students through three stages: to enter your revolutionary state of mind, to discipline your revolutionary state of mind and to build a successful revolution (Duncan-Andrade, 2010, Appendix C).

Te Ara Tino Rangatiratanga provides the framework for this chapter to summarise the pedagogy and practice of Kia Aroha College. Like the *Definite Dozen*, "Te Ara" is many things: a rite of passage, a common language, a set of principles, or a creed to live by. In Te Whānau o Tupuranga it is the morning ritual, recited by all students, and it has also inspired the composition of waiata and haka. A similar set of principles, used in the same way, was also developed by senior Samoan, Tongan and Cook Island Māori students using their traditional values and in their languages. The English statements in *Te Ara Tino Rangatiratanga* reflect the essence of the Māori statements, but are not direct translations of the Māori text. The final statement is the whakataukī, which gave Te Whānau o Tupuranga its name. *Te Ara Tino Rangatiratanga* is the pathway we hope our young people will walk and therefore is therefore a fitting end to this story.

To develop *Te Ara Tino Rangatiratanga* students studied traditional Māori whakataukī, they looked at some of the sayings that students and staff had developed about Māori values. They incorporated statements from the *Definite Dozen* and beliefs from other indigenous people. Finally, having decided on what was important to them, students shaped the statements in a framework that follows Smith's (2004, p. 51) cycle of conscientization, resistance and transformative action. The *Definite Dozen* follows a three stage linear progression (although the elements of the three stages inevitably overlap). *Te Ara Tino Rangatiratanga* however, is an ongoing cycle of awareness and action that you enter at different places and where the stages may occur in any order, or at the same time.

Te Ara Tino Rangatiratanga acts as the central core and strength of the metaphorical "brown" spaces developed in the school to counter the pervasive hegemonic White spaces in our education system. *Te Ara Tino Rangatiratanga* is provided in its entirety first.

Te Ara Tino Rangatiratanga: The Pathway to Self-Determination

Oho ake: Conscientization (Becoming aware)

1. Ki te āwhina i ētahi atu, me arotahi ki au i te tuatahi (In order to help others, we need to help ourselves).
2. Ko au, ko koe. Ko koe, ko au (I am you. You are me).
3. Kia tū hei Māori tūturu (I can't experience success in anything else, until I experience success in being Māori).
4. Waiho mā te tangata kē koe e mihi (Let someone else acknowledge your virtues, be humble).

Tū Motuhake: Resistance (Saying "no more")

5. Ehara taku toa it e toa takitahi, engari he toa takitini (our unity is our strength).
6. Whakapono (Believe—we can make a change).
7. Mahia, akongia, i a rā, i ngā wā katoa (work and study every day, everywhere)
8. Papahueke (Never, ever, give up).

Te Hurihanga: (Transformation)

9. Whakanuia i te puna mātauranga (Acknowledge the knowledge, teach and be teachable).
10. Me whakawetewete i āu mahi (Be self-critical).
11. Whāia te iti kahurangi, ki te tūohu koe me he maunga teitei (Have the highest expectations of yourself).
12. Pai rawa atu i ngā mea katoa (Aim for the very best in all things).

Ka rūia te kākano, kei ngā rangatahi, kia tipu ai ngā hua, whangāia ki ngā tupuranga.

(We are the leaders of the future)

In the following sections of this chapter, each of the elements of *Te Ara Tino Rangatiratanga* is examined to summarize the practice of the school and to answer the five key questions.

Oho ake: Conscientization (Becoming aware)

In New Zealand, from the 1980s onwards, radical changes have occurred in respect of Māori education and schooling. This change developed out of Māori communities who were so concerned with the loss of Māori language, knowledge and culture that they took matters into their own hands and set up their own learning institutions, beginning with Kōhanga Reo (pre-school language nests) followed by Kura Kaupapa Māori (schools where students are totally immersed in Māori language and customs), and then followed by the establishment of three wānanga (Māori tribal universities). These occupy an important place in the New Zealand education landscape, though unfortunately still catering for a relatively small number of children in elementary/primary school and even fewer at secondary school levels. The establishment of schools like Kia Aroha College is a further model that has emerged as a consequence of the conscientization of a people and a community.

> The "real" revolution of the 1980's was a shift in mindset of large numbers of Māori people—a shift away from waiting for things to be done to them, to doing things for themselves; a shift away from an emphasis on reactive politics to and an emphasis on being more proactive; a shift from negative motivation to positive motivation. These shifts can be described as a move away from talking simplistically about "de-colonization," which puts the colonizer at the center of attention, to talking about "conscientization" or "consciousness-raising," which puts Māori at the center. These ways of thinking illustrate a reawakening of the Māori imagination that had been stifled and diminished by the colonization processes. (Smith, 2003, p. 2)

In the early 1990s, following the establishment of Te Whānau o Tupuranga as a Māori bilingual unit within Clover Park Middle School, we soon realized that simply changing the language of instruction did not, of itself, make the school a better fit for Māori learners. We began to explore the reasons why.

Schooling had been a negative experience for the majority of Māori families for generations. How could we reconnect parents and grandparents with their children's learning? We turned to the Māori concepts embodied in the first four principles of *Te Ara Tino Rangatiratanga*. These concepts signaled a return to authentic Māori values such as aroha, identity, whānau, humility, manaakitanga (caring for others) and reciprocity. As Smith (2003) explains, the changes we needed to make were shifts in thinking, being proactive, rather than reactive, and raising the community's awareness and consciousness—reawakening imaginations and countering hegemonic thinking. This process has been fundamental in the changes the school's community has fought for, and been successful in achieving, over the last 25 years.

Chapter 6 described the concept of whanaungatanga, and a critical pedagogy of whānau in practice; in school organization, in the school's curriculum design and learning model, in school policy and in the school's decisions about building design and facilities. This awareness is also very evident in the voices of students in research carried out by the New Zealand Families Commission in 2011. Huia O'Sullivan, a Māori engagement adviser, who spent almost two years observing and participating in the life of the school, writes, "In this school, teachers treat students as if they were their nieces or nephews and students regard teachers like their second mum or dad. A pedagogy of whānau creates a conducive learning environment in which students can succeed" (O'Sullivan and Action Inquiry Contributors, 2011).[1] Student voices in her research have been presented in the form of a poem. Students told her:

> We're about whānau
> Whether it's your whānau kura (school whānau)
> Or your whānau at home
> Your up-north whānau (tribal whānau)
> Or the whānau you never met
> When you're together, that's whānau
> That's the connection
> At Tupuranga, we're treated like people.
> This kura (school) is our haven; here, we feel safe
> I leave my house, walk down the road (to school)
> And I'm home again (p. 36)

The earlier verses of the poem refer specifically to the principles of *Te Ara Tino Rangatiratanga*, and to the Māori values at its core. The researcher returned to the school to seek the students' feedback on her treatment of their comments. The staff involved, myself included, had all thought it was great, however the student group was not happy. They informed the researcher that they would send her an addition—and did so. Their complaint was that the poem wasn't strong enough and didn't go far enough to explain what they felt about learning in Kia Aroha College, in Te Whānau o Tupuranga. Their additional comments were included as the final verse in the poem. This time, they approved.

> Looking to the future
> We will know who we are as Māori
> We will identify ourselves as Warrior Scholars
> We will be articulate thinkers speakers activists
> We will take ownership of our physical and spiritual wellbeing
> We will make decisions about what feels okay for us
> We will demonstrate a strong work ethic
> We will go on to achieve
> When we leave school
> Our future pathway will be clear
> We will have left our mark on Te Whānau o Tupuranga
> And the door will be open for our return
> At this place of learning
> Commitment to the kaupapa is everything
> Tūturu ki te kaupapa[2] (p. 38)

Can a school create the conditions that empower a student to follow their cultural norms throughout the school day? Why is this important?

This first section of Te Ara Tino Rangatiratanga; Oho Ake (Conscientization) has described the conditions that existed in the school that made it both acceptable and comfortable to empower the student to follow her cultural norms, why this was important, and how this confidence and cultural competence were of benefit. The answers lie in reclaiming Māori and Pasifika values and structures as the absolute foundation for decisions that determine pedagogy and practice and school organization, and that placed a central focus on developing an authentic whānau to enable whanaungatanga to flourish. These actions formed the basis of the more critical practice which develops in the second stage of the pathway to self-determination.

The expectations that are developed in this first stage of *Te Ara Tino Rangatiratanga*, through the school-learning lens are that students will have a confirmed future learning pathway, high academic achievement which includes NCEA Level 3 and university entrance requirements, will be role models, have a strong work ethic, be articulate speakers, have a respect for knowledge in all its forms and be conscientized to inequities and injustice in education and wider society. They will understand they have the absolute right to learn at school "as Māori" or as who they are, without compromising their cultural identity. They will also understand and model values such as whakaiti (humility) reciprocity and whānau. These Māori and Pasifika values are further developed through the second cycle of *Te Ara Tino Rangatiratanga*: Tū Motuhake (Resistance)

Tū Motuhake (Resistance)

The resistance of Te Whānau o Tupuranga, Clover Park Middle School and Kia Aroha College to dominant ideologies of school practice and reform has been one of trial and exploration over many years. It required commitment and hard work from the board of trustees, school leadership, staff, students, and families. Every new intake of students, every new staff member requires us to revisit and restate our position. The four principles in this stage of "Te Ara" have been essential to this process of making and then sustaining change. These principles advise us that our unity is our strength, to believe we can make a difference. They remind us that this is hard work, but to never, ever give up.

In this "resistance" cycle of *Te Ara Tino Rangatiratanga* we have fundamentally questioned and resisted the whole field of assessment and evaluation, and its limited focus on technical achievement and success determined by White knowledge and White ways of knowing. We have challenged our national pursuit of literacy and numeracy as the primary indicator of success in school and the sole aim of "solutions" to the inequity of outcomes for Māori and Pasifika learners.

This resistance led us to develop our own assessments, involving Māori and Pasifika staff steeped in their own cultural knowledge. The research, described in detail in Chapter 7, developed indicators based on Durie's (2006) four key "markers" for Māori cultural identity: identification as Māori, cultural knowledge and understanding, access to and participation in Māori society and communication—in Te Reo Māori (Māori language). Similar indicators were developed for our different Pasifika identities. Using these indicators, we can show progress in the self-learning/identity lens for the whole school, by gender, by year level or as individuals. With this information, we can then show very high Māori and Pasifika achievement that is based on cultural knowledge and competencies. We are very clear that learning in the self, identity lens is legitimate, high-status, end-point learning in its own right. The intent of the self-learning lens is to develop Māori and Pasifika knowledge. This is an intentional counter-hegemonic choice. We believe that a single goal of academic achievement, without knowledge "as Māori" demeans our Māori and Pasifika learners, who deserve better. The minute we define our students' success in those terms, we negate all the other learning we believe is equally important.

How can a school ensure all students have this strength in their own cultural identity?

What are the specific cultural ways of knowing that young people are developing these skills?

In terms of the central questions fundamental to critical, culturally responsive pedagogy, this section of *Te Ara Tino Rangatiratanga*: Tū Motuhake (Resistance) answers questions about the intentional contribution of the school to the development of a student's cultural knowledge and identity, and the school's goal to complement and support our young people's self and home or heritage learning, in partnership with whānau. The development of a tool to measure this growth, and the data gathered through the use of this measure mean that this development is never left to chance. The data give us very good information about how students are developing their cultural identity and how we can identity each student's strengths in their own cultural knowledge and in whanaungatanga (relationships). The specific indicators for each ethnic group, developed by those with experience and knowledge of these different cultures, ensure that we are using Māori, Samoan, Tongan, and Cook Island Māori norms to show that young people are developing these skills.

Te Hurihanga: (Transformation)

> Education either functions as an instrument which is used to facilitate integration of the younger generation into the logic of the present system and bring about conformity or it becomes the practice of freedom, the means by which men and women deal critically and creatively with reality and discover how to participate in the transformation of their world. (Freire, 1972)

The four principles in this third element of the cycle encourage our young people to have the highest expectations of themselves, to be prepared for learning in all its forms, to be self-reflective and to understand the responsibility to pass knowledge on to others. This section of *Te Ara Tino Rangatiratanga: Tu Hurihanga* is about action for social change and the further development of critical thinking. It prepares our young people for the worlds beyond school and home, with 21st century skills and knowledge, which gives them the toolkit they need in order to challenge injustice and seek equity for themselves, their families, their communities, and society. This toolkit includes advanced computer skills, information technology, and critical media literacy skills. It also develops hope and resilience

How can schools recognize, and address, barriers that exist in their practice to the development of a student's secure cultural identity?

The final two sections of this chapter address this question. The first section returns to the concept of hope. The restoration of genuine "audacious hope" (Duncan-Andrade, 2009), "radical hope" (Freire, 1998), "radical healing" and "healing justice" (Ginwright, 2009, 2010, 2015) are crucial to the reclamation of educational sovereignty and cultural identity of indigenous and minoritized learners in our schools. This is a key understanding for schools who seek to identify and address barriers in their own practice that prevent this development. The school's thinking and practice to change their disciplinary and behavior management to a hopeful and healing approach is explained as an example of what a school can do to understand and transform this space. The program described brings together the school, self, and global learning lenses and shows how they seamlessly overlap. The second and final section of the chapter begins with an explanation of the school's expectations for students and describes the school's goal to develop Warrior-Scholars. It then asks what did the three schools in the Kia Aroha College journey learn from their experience and the changes that they developed? What lessons learned might support other schools and communities explore the same issues and embark on a similar pathway, which they in turn will make their own?

Identity Found: Colored Spaces

Hopeful and Healing Spaces—Critical Hope and Radical Healing

Akom (2007) argues that all spaces are "politicized, racialized, and gendered, insofar as they are infused with questions of power and privilege. He uses the concept of "free spaces" as an important site for the development of theory and practice around youth activism, teacher development, and the transformation of public and private space in urban schools and communities. He defines free spaces as:

> Places that share some of the following characteristics: a sense of shared bonds, places to revive one's culture, places to rejuvenate our spirits, participatory and democratic spaces, places to civically engage—debate—dialogue, places to form social networks, places to educationally achieve, places to form democratic and revolutionary visions of social change, places to recover and enjoy group identity, places to cultivate self and community respect, cooperation and community uplift. (pp. 612–613)

Spaces that are transformative are free spaces in that they give youth of color choice and most importantly they give them hope. It would be easy to feel despair that the problems facing indigenous and ethnic minority youth, due to social conditions and circumstances far beyond their control, are too difficult, at least at the school and community level, to address. How can we possibly tackle the impact of colonization, assimilation and continued institutional racism, if this seems beyond the government's ability to even begin to change? Duncan-Andrade (2009) believes the answer lies in hope, and he categorizes this hope into two broad areas: false hope and critical hope. He cautions educators against the all too prevalent false hope of school reform, which he further classifies as "hokey hope," "mythical hope," and "hope deferred." These are the "enemies of hope." Given the prevalence of false hope in schools, the following definitions from Duncan-Andrade's (2009) work help us to clearly identify this type of hope.

Hokey hope places the responsibility on urban youth that if they just work hard and play by the rules they will succeed academically, but is "hokey" in that it ignores the "laundry list of inequities" (p. 182) they face daily in their lives and in school. Duncan-Andrade states, "It is a false hope informed by privilege and rooted in the optimism of the spectator who needs not suffer—a 'let them eat cake' utterance that reveals a fundamental incomprehension of suffering" (p. 182). Mythical hope, occurs where "individuals are used to construct a myth of meritocracy that simultaneously fetishizes them as objects of that myth." Hope deferred comes when we ask students to set distant and highly unlikely goals but then as educators are unwilling to help them meet those goals. Hope deferred justifies poor teaching and in the long term equates to hope denied.

The enemy of hopelessness and the opposite of false hope is critical hope, and again there are three elements: material, Socratic, and audacious hope. Unlike false hope, where each type can occur independently, all the elements of critical hope work together. Like Tupac Shakur's (1999) "roses that grow in concrete," educators committed to material hope don't pretend there are ideal conditions, but strive to help students achieve by finding the cracks in the concrete—quality teaching, resources and networks. Drawing on Socrates' statement that "the unexamined life is not worth living," Socratic hope treats the "righteous indignation" of youth to their socially toxic environments as a strength, and works in solidarity with them (pp. 187–188). Finally, critical hope is audacious—in two ways. It grows out of, then stands firmly in solidarity with, our students' communities, sharing their suffering, and it defies the marginalization of underserved youth:

> Audacious hope stares down the painful path, and despite the overwhelming odds against us making it down that path to change, we make the journey, again and again. There is no other choice. Acceptance of this fact allows us to find the courage and the commitment to cajole our students to join us on that journey. This makes us better people as it makes us better teachers, and it models for our students that the painful path is the hopeful path. (p. 191)

Freire (1998) calls this "'radical hope,' the knowledge that, although I know things can get worse, I also know I am able to intervene to improve them," and the understanding that, "my destiny is not a given, but something that needs to be constructed and for which I must assume responsibility." Freire describes the need to be aware of one's conditioning, so that once "conscious of such conditioning, I know I can go beyond it, which is the essential difference between conditioned and determined existence" (pp. 53–54).

The notion of radical, critical and audacious hope provides a foundation for practice in school classrooms to provide our young people with the tools they need to challenge the status quo and to change their worlds. In Kia Aroha College, audacious hope is sustained through a critical pedagogy of whānau and aroha. The restoration and building capacity for audacious, critical hope requires new pedagogies that focus on "radical healing" to transform White spaces into "right" or ethical spaces that understand education is a matter of life and death for marginalized and minoritized youth.

> Radical healing involves developing pedagogical spaces of resistance and resiliency that lead to improvements in teaching and learning for youth of color in the midst of structural inequity, as well as building the capacity of young people and adults to create the types of communities in which they want to live. (Akom, Duncan-Andrade, & Ginwright, 2011)

Ginwright (2010) defines the four "Cs" of radical healing as "Caring relationships, Consciousness, Community, and Culture" (p. 31). In Kia Aroha

College's pedagogy these concepts are closely linked to the restoration of indigenous knowledge, which is even more essential than ever for the future of indigenous communities, but which get left out of our conversations about 21st century and "futures" learning.

The importance of this understanding is described by Aluli-Meyer (2008) when she explains that, "To realize that all ideas, all histories, all laws, all facts, and all theories are simply interpretations, helps us see where to go from here. To understand this one idea has brought me to this point of liberation" (p. 230).

Breaking Free

Liberation, audacious hope, and radical healing all underpin Kia Aroha College's approach to support for young people who are disengaged from learning, and who have been failed by our education system. This approach is explained in detail in this section. The initiative this section explains could well have been described in terms of Kia Aroha College's self-learning lens (whanau, identity, cultural competence, "as Māori", or as Samoan"). It could have fitted equally into the school-learning lens in terms of the impact this troubled history has on a young person's learning. It definitely requires consideration of the worlds young people interact with beyond school—both positive and negative influences (youth culture, church, vocational pathways, technology, social media, gangs), and therefore is relevant to the global-learning lens. In fact, it features in this final chapter because it is a prime example of how the lenses interact and overlap to work together to bring about change, healing, and hope.

At the American Educational Research Association (AERA) Conference in Vancouver in April 2012, a group of Kia Aroha College senior students and staff, who were there to present a paper on their own research, listened to a presentation by Dr Patrick Camangian. He told a story to illustrate his own life, and the point where he realized that the system was doing "exactly what it wants us to do." He used the example of training an elephant to stay within a predetermined space. At first, the baby elephant is tethered with a rope to a stake and learns it can only move as far as the rope will allow. As it grows however, the rope is no longer needed and a piece of string, or nothing at all, would still keep the elephant confined. Its bonds are due to years of conditioning, which Camangian aligned with the conditioning of colonized, assimilated and marginalized people. His message was we need to break free from these bonds. In a conversation with Dr Camangian some days later one of our senior boys told him, "You were talking about me." He instantly recognized his own story, where he had been in institutionalized care from a young age and on a troubled pathway ever since. It was a powerful lesson, and one we discussed several times during our trip.

Back at school, we had been exploring a more cohesive approach to supporting young people with difficult histories and behaviors. Our philosophy of whānau means that we accept all students, regardless of their previous school history, and we rarely, almost never, stand down or suspend students. Young people are brought to us from the Ministry of Education, and various social agencies. Often, and understandably, families will enroll children without divulging their previous history as they have been refused enrollment from other schools. Kia Aroha College therefore has a significant number of students with major difficulties which are not adequately addressed by access to the usual supports, such as in-class interventions, in-school or external programs or differentiated learning. Although all of these have a place, and are used in the school, they did not address the range of needs of this group, nor did they ensure that interventions and support would be culturally responsive. Many other supports for youth and their families were already in place however, young people with a range of serious long-term concerns did not necessarily respond immediately to being immersed in a wrap-around whānau environment, and often had little knowledge of their cultural background.

Up until this point, although our interventions were supportive and effective in many ways, we felt our practice was still too ad hoc and reactive, when the behaviors and issues were complex. An incident would occur, or a teacher might make a comment about a student's anger. Support staff would source an anger management program, or bring in a counsellor. We would then often think of other students with similar behaviors and we would take the opportunity for them to join the group working on anger management. None of these interventions was very successful, and were over when the course or counselling was completed, with no ongoing follow up. Often too, they relied on external support from people who didn't have a relationship with our students which was completely opposite to the way we worked. In keeping with the school's philosophy it was important that we develop solutions and interventions based in whānau and strong relationships. We wanted to bring together the expertise of teachers and specialized support staff (social worker, youth health nurse, youth workers) with the young person and their family, to coordinate the support for each identified student.

We remembered the Vancouver story and the elephant, and we named our program, "Break Free." The Break Free program is a culturally responsive intervention which aims to develop new pathways for this significant group of students who present with a range of serious behaviors and histories which create major barriers to their engagement in learning. The program takes the leadership of the interventions out of the classroom, where often teachers do not have time for the significant follow up and liaison involved, and places it under the supervision of a coordinated team, overseen by the Whānau Center, to ensure the approach is culturally responsive to our youth and their whānau. The purpose of the program is to personalize the response and support to the specific needs of each student to enable them to break free from the current transcript they believe they have to follow or live up to, and develop a new story (restorying), by determining and agreeing on the way forward. The Māori concept of hui whakatika was a suitable framework for the program. Hui whakatika are underpinned by four quintessential concepts of traditional or pre-European Māori discipline. These are:

1. *reaching consensus* through a process of collaborative decision-making involving all parties;
2. *reconciliation:* reaching settlement that is acceptable to all parties rather than isolating and punishing;
3. *examining the wider reason* for the wrong with an implicit assumption that there was often wrong on both sides—not apportioning blame;
4. less concern with whether or not there had been a breach; more concern with the *restoration of harmony.* (Berryman & Bateman, 2008)

Berryman and Bateman (Berryman & Bateman, 2008) liken hui whakatika to the contemporary notions of restorative justice, becoming more widely used in schools. This practice also seeks to repair the harm done and to listen to those affected. However, they explain that what is different, "is that the initiation and legitimation of the hui whakatika process is able to be determined by and for Māori." Durie (2003) identifies three broad approaches which incorporate Māori cultural beliefs and values into counselling and healing: traditional, bicultural and Māori-centered. Māori-centered approaches have developed from Māori dissatisfaction with the "add-on" nature of bicultural therapies and their focus on the acquisition of particular skills (anger management is an example). The aim of Māori-centered healing is generally to strengthen cultural identity (p. 47). Durie comments that a Māori view of well-being is not of an isolated area of dysfunction, but is an indicator that the balance between emotions, social relationships, spirituality and the body have become distorted (p. 49).

Kia Aroha College is a relatively small school of 300 students. Through 2013 and 2014, a total of 151 students received wrap-around targeted support and intervention from the Break Free program for a wide range of significant needs. In the first few weeks of 2015, with roll growth of around 30 students, the school had identified 61 students who needed this support. That number grows throughout the year. We need to know this information, but this is very different from thinking in deficits. If you believe, as we do, that every child is a rangatira (leader) and every child has mana (prestige, authority), then our job is to understand that these behaviors and issues are symptoms, and instead of focusing on just fixing the symptoms, we have to own and expose the root causes of poverty, inequality, and inequity. For many of our young people, their greatest achievement is simply survival, and tragically, some of them don't manage that.

Break Free is a personalized program tailored to the specific needs of each young person. As described in Chapter 7, we believe that each young person is on a journey from unrealized to unlimited potential and, for the last ten years have structured our support around this belief. We don't use labels such as "special needs" or "at-risk" or "gifted and talented." We identify where each child is on this continuum and tailor our program to meet their needs. Our support process therefore uses the term "UP" (Unrealized/Unlimited Potential) as can be seen in the following Break Free process.

1. The young person is referred to the UP Team by a teacher, whānau, via other agencies or services, or may self-refer.
2. The UP Team discusses all the data and information available for this young person. Extra assessment is organized if necessary.
3. The UP Team decides on the area/s of special support required for this young person, and selects one of four potential areas: learning, social, behavior, or health, to take the lead and to coordinate other support as necessary. This process recognizes that almost all of the identified young people have multiple needs. Many are involved with multiple agencies, which don't liaise with each other, and which become overwhelming for the young person and their family. The selection of one primary area ensures that one person will coordinate the intervention so there is a clear line of accountability and responsibility.

4. The UP Team is comprised of two associate principals, the school social workers and the school's youth health nurse. One of the team members becomes the designated lead person, depending on the primary area of need, who will develop an individual action plan, in liaison with UP Team members, the young person, their family, and teachers. The action plan includes specific goals and indicators and a timeframe for reporting back to the UP Team.
5. Plans are shared with all involved, including whānau. Plans are implemented. The lead person has responsibility for regular reporting back to the UP Team's fortnightly meeting, against target indicators and milestones. Plans are regularly evaluated and amended as necessary. The process is open and within hui whakatika principles for collaborative decision-making, reconciliation rather than apportioning blame, examining the wider reasons, and the restoration of harmony to the young person, who is always at the center of all decisions and support.

Early in development of the Break Free program we worked with our student management database provider to computerize the process. We were aware that we had a great deal of information and knowledge about each young person that we rarely put together. Each of these pieces of information contributed to a potential solution. Each student's learning outcomes are entered on the database, which generates formal reports to parents. Behavior incidents are recorded by teachers on the database, as is attendance and truancy. The process to assess self-learning, cultural identity and relationships, was described in Chapter 6, and these data are also in the database. Families held other pieces of the puzzle, often shared with the social worker, but unknown by the teacher who is working all day with that particular student. While some of this information is confidential, other information could be shared, but we didn't have a way of doing this. A major step in the Break Free development was bring all of this information into one, easily accessible place.

When a young person enters the Break Free program, simply selecting their name on the school database, through the Break Free portal, synchronizes all of this disparate information. At a glance, learning strengths and weaknesses, cultural knowledge, relationships, behavior incidents and their outcomes, attendance, interaction with family, external agencies, are all drawn together. This means that action plans, incorporating goals developed with the young person, their family and their teachers, are based on information rather than guesswork or assumptions, and they are tailored to each student's specific needs. Typically, the action plan for each identified student might include goals for:

- greater awareness and understanding of their cultural identity
- improved relationships with others—peers, teachers, whanau
- greater family engagement and involvement
- increased engagement in learning
- increased participation in school activities
- improved motivation
- improved attendance
- increased literacy outcomes
- increased numeracy outcomes
- increased NCEA outcomes

They might also include very specific actions such as creating a work project which would allow a young person who has been sentenced to community service hours through the court system, to work off their sentence at school. These projects might include helping with catering for visitors on the school marae during weekends or gardening or cleaning projects. The school social worker helps these young people develop their court-required reports on their progress, and attends court and social service agency family group conferences with them, acting as an advocate for the young person, and often for their family. Actions might also include participating in kapa haka or Pasifika performing arts, connecting with elders, mentoring from older students, sports or music, or a traditional carving program. Each action plan is different. Teachers have access to the plan's goal on the online database, so can incorporate these when they plan their class program.

The Whānau Center

The Whānau Center team is integral to the Break Free program, and to the wider support needed by students and families. When the Whānau Center was first developed it had one social worker, and no other staff. Eight years later, the Center staff includes the senior social worker, who leads the team, a second part-time social worker, the full time youth health nurse and a whānau support worker. Very few of these services receive funding and the school seeks grants and other sources of funding, outside education sources, to provide these essential services. Both the senior social worker and youth health nurse, experienced practitioners in their respective fields, mentor social work and nursing students in their final year of study on practicum in the school. This helps to expand the resource. These Māori and Pasifika students-in-training experience a whānau-based practice, and our students benefit from having these role models who work under supervision in their support. The Whānau Center runs health and fitness programs, sources support for families in need, works with parents to help facilitate help and support when they are overwhelmed, take students to medical appointments, and accesses a myriad of services from helping teens develop positive relationships, to hosting a sore-throat clinic and regular testing, funded by the government's drive to eradicate rheumatic fever, a common and serious illness with a high incidence in Māori and Pasifika communities.

Kia Aroha College's mantra is "whatever it takes" to remove barriers that get in the way of our young people reaching their highest potential. The Whānau Center is the epitome of that philosophy, enabling us to provide services, as the Break Free program indicates, that utilize the people our students and families have strong relationships with, who they trust, and who they can relate to in terms of their cultural norms and languages.

Break Free Evaluation

An evaluation of the Break Free program was carried out at the end of 2014. Of the 151 students who had been supported over the previous two years, 63 students had exited the program having met their goals and no longer needing support, and 42 had left the school during this time. This is indicative of our highly transient school population and also included students who had graduated at senior level. A further 46 students remained in the program at different stages of their action plans.

A breakdown of these students' learning outcomes, using the Ministry of Education measures for literacy, numeracy, and senior (NCEA) qualifications, showed significant gains for 70% of this group. This is major progress for students, many of whom had made no shifts in terms of their learning in many years prior to their participation in Break Free. Even more significantly, using the self-lens learning assessment tool, we were able to plot the progress of this group over two years in three cohorts: Year 9 to Year 10, Year 10 to Year 11, and Year 12 to Year 13. Each of these groups made significant shifts in terms of their cultural identity, and all made gains in their relationships with school, and with peers, with this being most significant in the Year 12 and 13 group.

This resounding success spurred staff on to further refinements of the program's computer capacity, and to widen Break Free's scope to develop teacher professional development to support this school-wide approach. The improvements to the computerized system allow us to generate a wide range of graphs, including those shown in Chapter 7 (Figures 7.3–7.5) which overlay self-learning and school-learning on the same chart for every student.

Taurikura

Taurikura is the Māori word for to be at peace, undisturbed, free from distractions. The name implies a calm, positive classroom environment where rangatahi (youth) are able to move on to the next step/stage of their lives. Taurikura is the name chosen for the staff professional development program which supports young people to "Break Free." There are two parallel strands in the Taurikura program:

1. The introduction and development of the TEN (Teacher Excellence Network) tool (Duncan-Andrade, Tintiangco-Cubales, & Camangian, 2014)
2. The further development of the school-wide approach to positive behavior management which supports the Break Free program and embeds this into all teacher practice

The research underpinning TEN has developed from experienced practitioners teaching in urban school districts and social justice networks in the USA. Kia Aroha College has been a part of this development, and our own research and practice has contributed to it. TEN organizes the research on excellence in culturally responsive urban teaching into three key domains: relevance, responsibility, and relationships, and identifies 52 qualities of effective pedagogy. Teachers create a common language across all school stakeholders (staff, leadership, students, and families) by determining, through easily accessible surveys, the 12 qualities of teaching excellence that are priorities for Kia Aroha College. It was no surprise us to find that culture, community, critical thinking, authentic caring, high expectations and solidarity all rose to the top for our community (Table 9.1).

Table 9.1. Kia Aroha College TEN Priority Surveys Results, 2015

Relevance	Relationships	Responsibility
Connects lessons to students' cultures and community	Builds trusting relationships with students	Maintains an organized and vibrant classroom
Has clear goals and expectations for students	Authentically cares about students	Is self-reflective
Develops critical thinking skills	Provides high expectations and support	Uses effective teaching and learning strategies
Uses multiple ways to assess student learning	Motivates student learning	Shows solidarity with students and families

Source: Duncan-Andrade et al. (2014).

The results of these surveys have been used to inform conversations with staff about what drives effective teaching in the school. These conversations have identified key target areas for development and obvious points of disconnect between the different stakeholder groups. Survey responses from all stakeholders are used to develop a teacher feedback tool that is specific to our school community. This teacher online tool is used by families, students, and colleagues to provide educators feedback during the school year. Teachers can immediately identify their strengths and areas for improvement. Teachers can then use the feedback, the resources of TEN, and school-based professional development to target and individualize their professional learning and growth.

The Taurikura plan for teachers and support staff is supported by ongoing professional development and dialogue which is targeted to the specific needs of individual staff. The aim of the Taurikura program is to embed support and coaching in an environment of that is culturally responsive to teacher's cultures and values. Key elements of this support include honest feedback (using the TEN tool), and developing a common and positive language—a language of restoration towards positive relationship management and whanaungatanga, built on the belief that every child has mana, and every child is a rangatira. Taurikura professional development includes induction programs for all new staff, whānau, relief teachers, and engagement of whānau first, to allow for the co-construction of responses for children needing additional support.

Warrior-Scholars

This book opened with the valedictory speech of a graduating student, who was described as a "Warrior-Scholar." The ultimate goal of Kia Aroha College, in fact the sub-title in the school's letterhead and signage, is to develop Warrior-Scholars. Kincheloe and Hayes (2007) describe "the critical curriculum of self-study," as reading and appreciating the pain and the realities of "city kids" in urban classrooms, and developing relationships of trust with youth in these communities. This curriculum develops "warrior intellectuals" involved in critically grounded, engaged scholarship. They contrast these scholars with "chicken intellectuals" who, like chicken hawks, start and support wars but send other people to fight them, and who separate their academic work from the lived world (p. 29). Warrior intellectuals are not afraid to challenge the status quo and bring compassion, ethical behavior, social justice and critical insight, not just into their work in the classroom, but into their daily lives:

> They have been victimized by skill and drill, test-driven pedagogies and understand their limitations better than most people. They know that such rote based, indoctrinating forms of education breed passivity and contempt for learning. Top down, standards-driven modes of education suck the joy and soul right out of learning and spit them into the hegemonic latrine. (Kincheloe & Hayes, 2007, p. 34)

Duncan-Andrade and Morrell (2008) advocate for an approach that utilizes "critical counter-cultural communities of practice," which recognise the existence of a dominant set of institutional norms and practices and intentionally sets itself up to counter these (p. 11).

A critical counter-cultural community of practice intentionally targets the White spaces of alienation, intellectual disenfranchisement, despair, and academic failure and replaces them with "large quantities of community, critical consciousness, hope, and academic achievement." These communities of practice are continually renegotiated, joint enterprises that function through the mutual engagement of their members who share a common concern or passion and work together over time to produce a shared repertoire of communal resources (Wenger, 1998).

For Kia Aroha College staff, this definition of critical counter-cultural communities of practice seemed to be our description of a critical pedagogy of whānau, and it fitted perfectly with our already determined practice and direction. The elements of a Youth Participatory Action Research (YPAR) approach that moved our practice beyond the curriculum integration model

(Beane, 1997) we had adopted in 2001, were the intentional critiques of the White space norms in our system and the heightened focus on social justice. Both models begin with issues that are identified by students and are derived from problems and realities our youth encounter in school, in families, in communities, as well as national and international issues affecting indigenous and other minoritized youth. This ensures that the contexts for study are relevant, authentic, and culturally responsive to the lived experiences of our youth. As many of the issues our students identify are those experienced in their respective ethnic groups this approach also provides the opportunity to develop secure, decolonized, cultural identities that reflect the traditional as well as their fluid, negotiated, multiple, contemporary contexts.

These experiences, as the examples of students' work in Chapter 6 show, are transformative. Scorza, Mirra, and Morrell (2013) explain that these powerful experiences,

> are not inspired by standardized test preparation or through instruction in basic skills; instead, they arise from enriching learning spaces that push students to their intellectual limits and connect them to meaningful, authentic ways to express their ideas. (p. 16)

They argue that critical pedagogy should not be considered radical; in fact, it should be normalized as academic excellence.

> Critical pedagogy is more than a process through which educators engage urban youth in a culturally relevant learning manner. Effectively used, it is a framework that helps students connect to their own histories, develop legitimate uses of their voices and employ tools to navigate social and political barriers. It allows critical educators to situate various non-dominant narratives as legitimate forms of expression in a diverse set of cultural practices, languages and ideological frameworks (Giroux, 1999). It values students' identities and expands how we look at literacy by emphasizing problem-posing education in the learning environment to allow empowered students to challenge their social conditions. (Scorza et al., 2013, p. 31)

Graduate Profile: Redefining Success and Achievement

The complete *Kia Aroha College Graduate Profile* for Māori learners, which ties all of the stages of the *Te Ara Tino Rangatiratanga* cycle and the three lenses together, is provided in Table 9.2. Similar profiles have been developed for

Samoan, Tongan and Cook Islands Māori students. As the valedictory speech, which introduced this book, shows, the graduate profile is embedded in everything our young people set out to achieve.

Table 9.2. Graduate Profiles for Māori Learners

Year 9	Year 11	Year 13
Conscientizing	*Resisting*	*Transforming*
Critical thinkers	Critical questioners	Resisters
Make the right choices	Work everyday, everywhere	Self-determined
Strong work ethic	Strong work ethic	Self-driven
Understands marae protocols	Develops marae protocols	Excels in marae protocols
Relentless—understands persistence	Relentless—develops persistence	Relentless—never ever gives up
Self-identity	Respect for others	Ko au ko koe, ko koe ko au
Leadership skills	Positive role models	Manutaki
Many different achievements	NCEA Level 1	NCEA Level 3
	Working at NCEA Level 2	University Entrance
	Developing future pathways	Confirmed future learning pathways
Positive relationships	Secure cultural identity	Warrior-Scholars
Speaks confidently	Speakers for the whānau	Articulate, conscientized speakers for social justice
Understands unfairness	Advocates for social justice	Activists for social justice
Value cultural leaders	Cultural leaders	Strong cultural leaders
Live as Māori	Live persuasively as Māori	Live intentionally as Māori
Kia Mōhio	Kia Mārama	Kia Mātau
Consistent and focused	Uses intiative	Revolutionary
Participates in Kapa Haka	Contributes to Kapa Haka	Leads in Kapa Haka
Te Reo Tuāpapa	Te Reo Whakawhānui Whānau	Te Reo Panekiretanga

Source: Kia Aroha College.

Developing the graduate profile involved staff in weeks of discussion and debate. Initially staff were divided into groups and began by brainstorming what they thought a senior student, leaving at the end of Year 13, would "look like." Due to the designated-character of the school, we had a very good idea of why parents and whānau chose Kia Aroha College for their children. We had spent years developing our philosophy and our learning approach. If the graduate profile was to drive the development of our Warrior-Scholars it was important to get it right and to include all of our learning dimensions, particularly those from Māori, Samoan, Tongan, and other cultural worldviews. The graduate profile is intended to spell out exactly what success and achievement look like for our students, at three stages through their learning journey. We felt strongly that if all that schools focus on are literacy, numeracy, and university requirements then all their graduate profile should state is: "literate" "numerate" and "going to university." Every word on our graduate profile is an intentional goal, supported by a planned pathway, designed to develop our students' cultural and critical consciousness.

Our staff discussion initially focused on questions:—what did we want a graduating student to know, what sort of leaders would they be, and what academic outcomes were important? These were not just Western academic outcomes. What about advanced cultural knowledge, what cultural skills and competencies did they need to actively participate in the Māori world, as well as all the other worlds they would need to navigate? What did they need to develop in order to become critical agents of change? Why did they choose Kia Aroha College? How would our profile reflect those choices and that difference? Obviously, students are different and each will forge their own unique identity. Our profile needed to be broad enough to allow learners to find their own place and pace. Our Samoan and Tongan teachers followed the same process, with the whole staff working together on the generic aspects of the Year 13 profile, then splitting up to develop the unique cultural differences, and progressions.

Once we had consensus about the Year 13 graduate profile, we then worked backwards. If we wanted advanced fluency in Māori language at Year 13, where did we expect students to be by the end of Year 11, and the end of Year 9 after three years in the school? The graduate profile is a continuum with checkpoints when students graduate from Year 9, Year 11, and Year 13. Some aspects show a clear progression: "understands marae protocols, develops marae protocols, excels in marae protocols." Some caused heated debate and discussion before staff could agree on an attribute or its progression. Some become narrower and more focused as students get older; a variety of different achievements at Year 9 becomes specific qualifications achievements and university entrance requirements at Year 13. Others demonstrate deeper or wider skills, or a Māori perspective on learning as these examples show:

- Kia Mōhio (be knowledgeable)—Kia Mārama—(be clear/seek clarity)—Kia Mātau (excel, have a deeper knowledge or understanding)
- Te Reo Tuāpapa—Te Reo Whakawhānui—Te Reo Panekiretanga, shows a progression in speaking Māori language, from a foundation level, to developing further, to advanced fluency.
- Developing self-identity at Year 9 becomes "Ko au, ko koe. Ko koe, ko au" at Year 13. This Māori value, "I am you, and you are me" is similar to the Mayan concept of "In Lak'ech," which states, Tú eres mi otro yo (You are my other self), and aligns with other indigenous people's understanding of relationship with each other.
- Understanding unfairness at Year 9, becomes advocacy at Year 11, and taking action, as activists, at Year 13. Few schools will state activism as a measure of success and achievement, but it is certainly a skill we foster intentionally. A basic premise for this goal is often explained to our students as, you can't play, or change the game, if you don't know the rules.
- Even at Year 9 we expect youth to show leadership. This becomes understanding your responsibility to be a role model to others at Year 11. At the Year 13 level, leadership is explained through the Māori word, "manutaki," used in this context to describe the bird at the front of a flock of geese. This concept, and the concept of whānau, underpin why Kia Aroha College does not have a prefect system, and does not have a nominated "head" boy or girl as many schools do. All senior students are expected to be leaders. Driver (2015) found this idea embedded in the thinking of the senior students in his study of cultural leadership at Kia Aroha College. He observes, "A key concept employed by the Tupuranga students is that of manutaki and it illustrates nicely the diffused, shifting, and informal nature of student leadership." Students explained to him:

Tamati: This concept of manutaki, which is basically a flock of geese, you know they fly like this [Tamati demonstrates with his hands a v-formation] and they ... a triangle.

Cee: In a spear head.

Tamati: And the guy at the top takes the most force and whenever he gets tired he'll fall back, and someone else will come and take their place. And they keep on repeating that and repeating that—that's what we're expected to do, to be like a flock of geese. Where we're all leaders, not just ...

Cee: Not just one person.

> Significantly, the geese have a common destination and the birds who fly behind are followers, but not passive ones. Tamati observes that "even if you are at the back of the pack, it's still as vital to the thing. Like if that one person from the back drops out, the whole formation is going to get mucked up, so it's just as important as the next." Hazel describes the birds at the back as "back up." I subsequently link this to Wade's remark about "having his friends' back", and to the Māori idea of leading from the back. Cee emphasizes that "the cool thing is, when like a bird gets sick, two of the geese will fly down with the goose and look after it, 'til it's ready to go" (p. 45).

The thread of whānau runs through all stages of the graduate profile. There is the expectation that students move from being members of the whānau, to leaders, but whānau also describes all of the different elements and progressions. The graduate profile *is* whānau at its heart and in its expectations.

Having finally decided on progressions that we were all comfortable with we then made them highly visible throughout the school—as "word clouds," displayed on our school website, in newsletters, on classroom walls, in the school reception office. Traveling groups have had their graduate profile word cloud printed on their traveling uniform.

According to our graduate profile, Māori Warrior-Scholars, are young people with high academic skills, secure, empowered identity as Māori, as comfortable and competent on the traditional marae and in contemporary Māori settings as they are in the classroom, with all the tools they need to challenge and change inequity in their whānau, in their communities and in the wider world. Warrior-Scholars are self-determining and always transforming. They are informed advocates for social justice, critical thinkers, activists for social change and empowerment, and are competent in all three of the power lenses. The same applies to our Samoan and Tongan students, and to our small numbers of students from other ethnicities. Success and achievement are always described in these terms by Kia Aroha College.

What Did We Learn?

The solutions described through the practice of the schools in this story show that an intentional focus on developing a secure, conscientized, cultural identity *first*, drove and underpinned subsequent pedagogical and structural changes, which further supported achievement and success "as" Māori, as Samoan, as Tongan, and as Cook Islands Māori. This achievement is multi-faceted and holistic. One component of it is academic achievement. Other, equally important, achievements are the continuing development of cultural identity and competence, conscientization, and transformation—the "Warrior-Scholars" this chapter describes.

The work of the schools highlights their determination to give Māori and Pasifika parents authentic choices in the education of their children. For Clover Park Middle School, Te Whānau o Tupuranga and Kia Aroha College this meant asking different questions of our Māori and Pasifika communities about their aspirations for their children, then not allowing a prevalent Eurocentric, White-space agenda to influence the answers, or to reinterpret the answers to fit the preconceived ideas about what school looks like. The reason why this Otara community has managed to achieve three major changes to school structure over this prolonged period of time stems from the fact they were listened to the first time they asked for change. The schools did not see their request for change as opposition or an expression of dissatisfaction with the status quo. They saw it as a partnership and a journey to take together. The success of the first restructuring empowered the community to go on to seek further change.

The schools also focused on wider, holistic, definitions of success and achievement. They seriously challenged the narrow focus on literacy, numeracy and technical academic achievement as the primary measures of "success" and developed additional, culturally relevant assessment practice. Staff took into account the negligible impact of Whitestream approaches on equitable outcomes for indigenous and minoritized learners internationally, and from our national focus on these limited measures over decades of schooling "improvement" initiatives in New Zealand.

Our experience was that this is a systemic issue, therefore apportioning sectoral blame was counter-productive to finding meaningful solutions. We also realized that the systemic change we felt was necessary was unlikely to happen overnight, if at all. Our self-governing education system however, gives us an autonomy that gives us options and opportunities. The schools and the community, through the leadership of the board of trustees, have exercised this autonomy and flexibility. The greatest barrier to each one of us making this sort of change in our own school is our own thinking—which we *do* have the power to change. The schools in this study did think differently about learning and the outcome of this reflection was the critically conscious, culturally responsive approach this counter-story describes. This model addresses the issues of power and social justice, through a critical pedagogy based in whānau and Māori and Pasifika values and beliefs. The Coolangatta Statement on Indigenous Peoples' Rights in Education (World Indigenous Peoples' Conference on Education, 1999) concludes:

> We, the Indigenous peoples of the world, assert our inherent right to self-determination in all matters. Self-determination is about making informed choices and decisions and creating appropriate structures for the transmission of culture, knowledge and wisdom for the benefit of each of our respective cultures. Education for our communities and each individual is central to the preservation of our cultures and for the development of the skills and expertise we need in order to be a vital part of the twenty-first century.

The resources to challenge every school to empower non-White students to become self-determining learners exist in the community itself. The barriers that make this so difficult to achieve are inherent in the systemic, institutionally racist, White spaces this story identifies and names. However, Clover Park Middle School, Te Whānau o Tupuranga, and Kia Aroha College have proven that it is possible, in spite of significant odds, to give our children the educational sovereignty that should rightfully be theirs. There is no single, easy solution. The achievements of this community have been the result of long years of extremely hard work on the part of everyone involved. There is no miracle "recipe" that can be picked up and placed in another community or another school. Each community is different and each school needs to work to identify, then remove, their own barriers and to develop relationships of trust and reciprocity with their families and students.

There are however, lessons to be learned by schools and communities in the journey of these three schools to develop a counter-narrative to a dominant White system where most interventions and solutions have their origin in paradigms imbued with deficits, and which alienate Māori and Pasifika learners. These lessons are identified in the seven core principles common to the practice of these three schools and the three U.S.A. programs described in Chapter 8. These principles include making race, ethnicity and cultural identity central to curriculum and practice, and ensuring that the programs are strongly supported and driven by parents and community. The programs are based in authentic caring, aroha, and whanaungatanga, and in critical pedagogy, kaupapa Māori, critical race, and tribal critical race (Brayboy, 2005) theory. Students are involved in the identification of issues and the production of knowledge through participatory action research and learning draws heavily on other knowledges—traditional cultural knowledge and practices, youth knowledge and culture, and community knowledge. There is a high stakes "end result" that gives students a purpose for their learning. Finally, and most importantly, the programs are intentionally counter-hegemonic.

The collective, lived, experiences of everyone involved in the journey and achievements of the Kia Aroha College community serve to show indigenous and marginalized learners in Whitestream contexts everywhere, that there is a pathway forward to self-determination. Our education system's White spaces can be colored in by practice that gives a community voice, that listens, that responds, and that is underpinned by the cultural knowledge and beliefs of its people. This practice conscientizes whānau to resist the status quo, to demand more, and to transform the educational experiences of our children.

Ka rūia te kākano, kei ngā rangatahi, kia tipu ai ngā hua, whangāia ki ngā tupuranga.

Plant the seed in the young. It will grow and bear fruit to nourish future generations.

Notes

1. Excerpt from the poem, Te Whānau o Tupuranga: Tūturu ki te Kaupapa. Copyright © the Families Commission operating as the Social Policy Research and Evaluation Unit (Superu). Reprinted with permission of the author.
2. Be true to the philosophy, of the school.

References

Akom, A. (2007). Free spaces: Excavating race, class, and gender among urban schools and communities. *International Journal of Qualitative Studies in Education, 20*(6), 611–616. http://doi.org/10.1080/09518390701630700

Akom, A., Duncan-Andrade, J., & Ginwright, S. (2011). *Radical healing: Education for social transformation and community empowerment*. New Orleans, LA: Paper presented at the American Education Research Association Annual Meeting.

Beane, J. (1997). *Curriculum Integration: Designing the core of democratic education*. New York, NY: Teachers College Press.

Berryman, M., & Bateman, S. (2008). Claiming space and restoring harmony within Hui Whakatika. In *Claiming spaces: Proceedings of the 2007 national Māori and Pacific Psychologies Symposium* (p. 11). Hamilton: Māori and Psychology Research Unit.

Brayboy, B. M. J. (2005). Toward a tribal critical race theory in education. *The Urban Review, 37*(5), 425–446.

Dei, G. S. J. (2011). Indigenous knowledge and the question of development: Tensions of change, tradition and modernity. In G. S. J. Dei (Ed.), *Indigenous philosophies and critical education* (pp. 167–170). New York, NY: Peter Lang Publishing.

Driver, A. (2015). *Cultural leadership: The reciprocities of right relationship at Kia Aroha College*. Auckland: Auckland University.

Duncan-Andrade, J., & Morrell, E. (2008). *The art of critical pedagogy : possibilities for moving from theory to practice in urban schools*. New York: Peter Lang.

Duncan-Andrade, J. (2009). Note to educators: Hope required when growing roses in concrete. *Harvard Educational Review, 79*(2), 181–194.

Duncan-Andrade, J. (2010). *What a coach can teach a teacher: Lessons urban schools can learn from a successful sports program*. New York, NY: Peter Lang.

Duncan-Andrade, J., Tintiangco-Cubales, A., & Camangian, P. (2014). TEN (Teaching Excellence Network). Retrieved from https://www.10teaching.net

Durie, M. (2003). *Nga Kahui Pou: Launching Maori futures*. Wellington: Huia.

Durie, M. (2006). *Whānau, education, and Māori potential*. Paper presented at Hui Taumata Mātauranga V. Taupo, New Zealand.

Freire, P. (1972). *Pedagogy of the opressed*. Harmondsworth: Penguin.

Freire, P. (1998). *Pedagogy of freedom*. Lanham, MD: Rowman & Littlefield Publishers.

Ginwright, S. (2009). *Black youth rising: Race, activism, and radical healing in urban America* (192pp.). New York, NY: Teachers College Press.

Ginwright, S. (2010). Addressing root causes of health disparities: Promoting positive health & academic achievement among youth. In *Strengthening our practice: Refining our aim*. San Francisco, CA: Keynote address. National Professional Development (NPD) Conference.

Ginwright, S. (2015). *Hope and healing in urban education: How urban activists and teachers are reclaiming matters of the heart*. New York, NY: Routledge.

Kincheloe, J., & Hayes, K. (2007). *Teaching city kids*. New York, NY: Peter Lang.

Meyer, M. A. (2008). Indigenous and authentic: Hawaiian epistemology and the triangulation of meaning. In N. Denzin, Y. Lincoln, & L. T. Smith (Eds.), *Handbook of critical and Indigenous methodologies* (pp. 217–232). Los Angeles, CA: Sage.

O'Sullivan and Action Inquiry Contributors. (2011). *Thriving in practice: Connected—reflective—Effective*. Auckland. Retrieved from http://www.superu.govt.nz/sites/default/files/TPRACTICE_Resource_0.pdf

Scorza, D., Mirra, N., & Morrell, E. (2013, February 18). It should just be education: Critical pedagogy normalized as academic excellence. *The International Journal of Critical Pedagogy 4*(2) 15–34. Retrieved from http://libjournal.uncg.edu/ijcp/article/view/337

Shakur, T. (1999). *The rose that grew from concrete*. New York, NY: Pocket Books.

Smith, G. (2004). Mai i te māramatanga, ki te putanga mai o te tahuritanga: From conscientization to transformative praxis. *Educational Perspectives, 37*(1), 46–52.

Smith, G. (2003). *Kaupapa Māori Theory : Theorizing indigenous transformation of education & schooling*. Presentation to the Kaupapa Māori Symposium. NZARE/AARE Joint Conference, Auckland.

Wenger, E. (1998). *Communities of practice: Learning, meaning and identity.* Cambridge: Cambridge University Press.

World Indigenous Peoples' Conference on Education. (1999). *The Coolangatta Statement on Indigenous Peoples' Rights in Education.* Retrieved from http://ankn.uaf.edu/IKS/Cool.html

GLOSSARY

Notes on the Glossary

Where it is necessary to understand a concept or sentence at the time of reading, meanings of Māori words are provided in the text. Meanings of Māori words are provided in parentheses after their first use, unless they appear in a quotation. Other languages used in the text have had the meaning provided in parenthesis after the word or in an endnote.

The English meanings of Māori words in the following list are taken primarily from the *Te Aka Māori-English, English-Māori Dictionary and Index* (Moorfield, 2011, online version). Many words have a range of meanings. Those provided below are the meanings relevant to the context within which the word is used in this text. Māori titles of some of the literature, organisations, and/or programmes are also included in the glossary.

ako	to learn, to teach
ao Māori	the Māori world
Aotearoa	common Māori name for New Zealand often translated as "the land of the long white cloud"
ara	path

aroha	deep caring, love, compassion, empathy
aroha tētahi ki tētahi	look after each other
awhi, āwhina	to assist, help
hā	breath, essence
haka	war dance
hapū	kinship group, sub-tribe
haututū	mischievous, troublesome
He iwi kotahi tatou	We are one people
hikitia	to lift up, raise
Hui Taumata Matauranga	Māori Education Summit
hui whakatika	culturally responsive, self-determining interventions for restoring harmony
hurihanga	changing, turning
iwi	extended kinship group, tribe, nation, people
Ka Hikitia	The Māori Education Strategy
Ka whawhai tonu mātou mō ake tonu atu	We will keep fighting forever
kaha	ability, power, strength
kaiako	teacher
kaitiaki	custodian, guardian
kākano	seed
kapa haka	Māori cultural performing arts group
karakia	to recite ritual chants, say grace, pray
karanga	to call, a ceremonial call of welcome to visitors
kaumātua	male elder
kaupapa	philosophy, policy, plan, topic
Kaupapa Māori	Māori ideology—a philosophical doctrine, incorporating the knowledge, skills, attitudes and values of Māori society.
kia kaha	be strong
kia ora	be well, used as a greeting
Kōhanga Reo	"language nest"—Māori language preschool.
kōka	senior woman, aunty
kōrero	to speak, a speech, story

GLOSSARY

kotahitanga	unity
kuia	female elder
kura	school
Kura Kaupapa Māori	school operating under Māori custom and using Māori as the medium of instruction
mahi	to work, job, employment
mahi tahi	To work as one, work together
mana	prestige, authority, control, power, influence
manaaki	to support, take care of
manaakitanga	hospitality, kindness
manuhiri	visitor, guest
Māori	indigenous person of Aotearoa New Zealand.
marae	Courtyard—the open area in front of the wharenui, the complex of buildings around the marae
mārama	be clear, easy to understand
mātau	excel, knowledgeable
matua	father, parent, uncle
mihi	to greet, pay tribute, acknowledge, thank.
mōhio	to know, understand
mokopuna	grandchild
motuhake	be separate, special, distinct,
Ngai Tahu (Kai Tahu)	Māori tribal group of much of the South Island
oho	to wake up
ora	to be alive, well
oranga	welfare, health, living.
Pākehā	New Zealander of European descent, White person
papahueke	be relentless, be unyielding
Papatūānuku	The Earth Mother
poho	chest, bosom, seat of affections
poutama	the stepped pattern of tukutuku panels symbolizing genealogies and the various levels of learning and intellectual achievement
pōwhiri	to welcome, welcome ceremony on a marae.
rākau	tree

rangatahi	youth, younger generation
rangatira, rangatiratanga	sovereignty, chieftainship, right to exercise authority,
reo Māori	The Māori language
tāhuhu	ridge pole (of a house)
tamariki	children
taniwha	water spirit, powerful creature
tangata	man, human being
tangata whenua	local people, hosts, indigenous people of the land
tangi, tangihanga	funeral
taumata	summit, pinnacle, top of a hill, level, grade.
taurikura	to be at peace, undisturbed, free from distractions
tautoko	to support, agree
Te Hoe Nuku Roa	a longitudinal Māori household project with a focus on Māori cultural, social and economic development.
Te Whānau o Tupuranga	The name of the Māori bilingual program in Kia Aroha College – the family of future generations
teina	younger brother (of a male), younger sister (of a female), younger cousin (of the same gender). Used as the name for Years 7 students in Te Whānau o Tupuranga
tiaki	to guard, keep.
tikanga	correct procedure, custom
tīmata	to begin, beginning
tino rangatiratanga	self determination
tipuna/tupuna	ancestors, grandparents
tuakana	elder brother (of a male), elder sister (of a female), older cousin (of the same gender).
tuakiritanga	identity
tukutuku	traditional ornamental lattice-work
tupuna	ancestor
tupuranga	future generations, growth
Ukukura	ally school, schools in solidarity
waharoa	entrance to a pā, gateway, main entranceway
waiata	to sing. A song, chant
Wairua, wairuatanga	spirit, spirituality

wānanga	to meet and discuss. Seminar, conference, forum, a tertiary institution, school
whaea	mother, aunt, aunty, a respectful term of address to a woman
whakapapa	genealogy
whakatauākī, whakataukī	proverb, saying
whakawhanaungatanga	to build or maintain relationships
whānau	to be born, extended family group
whanaungatanga	relationship, kinship, sense of family connection
whāngaia	feed, nourish
whare	house, building
wharekai	dining hall
wharenui	meeting house, large house—main building of a marae

ABOUT THE AUTHOR

I am often asked who am I to tell this story? It is a legitimate question. Hotere-Barnes (2015) highlights, "the enduring challenges from Māori scholars and communities about the ethics of Pākehā educational researcher involvement in Māori communities." As a White woman working in a Māori/Pasifika community I believe I have a responsibility to regularly check that I never take this position for granted. I am very aware I am in this position by invitation, due to my three decades of involvement in this community, and as a member of the Kia Aroha College whānau, but I never assume I am involved as of right.

I grew up in a tiny, coastal, Māori community in New Zealand where my family was one of the very few White families in the community. With hindsight I realized that my Pākehā family had status in that community that we didn't understand. At Māori community celebrations and events we were treated as honored guests, but I never questioned this or thought about why. I absorbed the richness of a Māori community from a position of White privilege.

At the age of 16, I left the security of home and the beach, to be thrown into the world of study and teacher training in Auckland, and where again, no one ever challenged me to think about inequity or injustice. That conscientization did not happen for another two decades, when my own children, who identify as Māori through their father's heritage, began secondary school and their experiences of racism in our education system opened my eyes and forever changed my own teaching practice and the lens I looked through.

I am involved in the Kia Aroha College story on multiple levels. I am inextricably linked with the story as a teacher, from 1983, and between 1994 and 2016, as the principal of the three schools throughout the three major changes this story describes. My own learning as an educator and as a researcher, is woven into the fabric of the journey and has enabled me to have a deep understanding of what happened. I believe it would not have been possible for me to tell this story from the position of a neutral or disconnected viewpoint. My positioning is dependent upon mutual respect, trust and commitment to the philosophy of the school and the community involved.

Ladson-Billings (2000) powerfully explains that, "All of my 'selves' are invested in this work—the self that is a researcher, the self that is a parent, the self that is a community member, the self that is a Black woman" (p. 272). I acknowledge my position as one who continues to be involved intrinsically in the activities, practice and direction of Kia Aroha College. All of my "selves" have also been invested in this work —the professional self that is an educator, a researcher, a school principal, and member of the Kia Aroha College whānau, as well as the self that is a mother, grandmother, and great-grandmother of Māori children whose own school experiences have led to my personal stake in the education of indigenous and minoritized students (Milne, 2004). However, I am very aware that this is not my story, but the collective story of those who have been involved in these schools: students, parents, whānau, Boards of Trustees and community. I am privileged to be the story-teller.

References

Hotere-Barnes, A. (2015). Generating "non-stupid optimism": addressing Pākehā paralysis in Māori educational research. *New Zealand Journal of Educational Studies*, 50(1), 39–53. http://doi.org/10.1007/s40841-015-0007-y

Ladson-Billings G. (2000). Racialized discourses and ethnic epistemologies. In N K. Denzin, & Y. S. Lincoln (Eds.). *Handbook of Qualitative Research*. 2nd Edition. (pp. 257–274). Thousand Oaks, CA: Sage

Milne, A. (2004). "They didn't care about normal kids like me." Restructuring a school to fit the kids. (Unpublished Master's thesis). Massey University, Palmerston North,

INDEX

A

Aboriginal studies, 58
academic achievement, 18–19, 83, 89, 203
    as a goal of critical pedagogy, 88
    not enough, 18
    single focus on, 88, 106, 121
academic identity
    linked to cultural identity, 87
academic learning, 89, 95, 132, 172
    linked to cultural learning, 97, 152, 165
academic measurements
    linked to identity, 152
accountability, 10, 104
achievement,
    academic, *see* academic achievement
    as Māori, 19, 119
    gap, 5, 40
    individual, 81, 105, 147
    Māori constructs of, 146
    narrow technical definitions of, 19, 157, 183, 203
    tolerance of low levels, 157
action research, 21, 132
activism/activists, 90, 173, 185, 201
    normalized in everyday school activity, 172
    youth, 185
Adobe Youth Voices (AYV), 174
adolescence, adolescents, 50, 53
    developmental needs of emerging adolescents, 48
    identity development, 53–54
    Māori concepts of, 53
    peer influence, 89
ako (learning and teaching), 101, 146
Alaska Native Educators, 134
alienation, 20, 39–42, 197
    of Māori and Pasifika families from schooling, 89
    of Māori and Pasifika learners, 39, 73

American Education Research Association (AERA), 117, 188
aroha, 78–79, 104, 106, 109, 168, 181, 204
as Māori, 7, 14–16, 20, 39, 81, 152, 188
   achievement, 19, 119, 184, 202
   definition, 14–15
   Education Review Office question, 121
   education success, 14
   embedded in the school day, 81
   is political, 90
   live as Maori, 15, 59, 98, 162, 199
   Māori definitions, 120
   student research, 120–123
   See also live as Māori
   success as Māori, 138
   vs "of" Māori, 15
as Pākehā, 14, 19
achievement, 29
   as Māori, 19, 119
   as Pasifika, 21, 123
   as Samoan, 17–18, 89, 119, 202
   as Tongan, 17–18, 89, 101, 119, 132
assessment, 83, 129, 135, 147, 183
   as a White space, 131–133
   combining self and school lens results, 148–152
   decisions, 145
   Māori worldviews, 146, 183
   self–learning tool, 132
assimilation, 6–7, 10, 17, 22, 41, 51, 58, 116, 186
   schooling as a tool of, 8, 62, 122
at risk, 92, 191
audacious hope, 162, 185–188
authentic caring, 91, 104, 153, 168, 195, 204
authentic places, 158

B

backlash
   racist and negative attitudes, 75
   backlash pedagogies, 13

Banks' typology, 49, 144
Barrio studies, 169
be Māori, 5, 8, 81, 102, 120, 121
behavior, behavior management, 76, 83, 91, 102, 107–108, 142, 151, 185, 189–192
biculturalism, 49, 58, 190
bilingual learning, 75, 82, 103, 169
bilingualism, 75–76
Break Free program, 22, 187–193
   developing the database, 192
   evaluation of, 194
   referral process, 191

C

Camp César Chávez, 165–166
caring
   aesthetic, 104
   authentic, 91, 104, 153, 168, 195, 204
   critical, 104–106
   roles within whānau, 106
   womanist, 105
   cariño, 104, 168
challenged spaces, 167–168
charter schools, 11
citizenship, 111
   students' questions about, 111–112
Clover Park, 71–72
Clover Park Intermediate School, 72, 79
Clover Park Middle School, 72–75, 77, 147, 162, 180, 203
   ERO Report 2009, 131
collective, collectivist 8, 51, 91, 93, 98, 106, 130, 142, 168
   has priority over the individual, 8, 81
colonization, 22, 116, 122, 172, 180, 186
   British colonization in New Zealand, 10
   computer-mediated, 36–37
   schooling as a tool of, 8, 62
color-blind, 13
coloring book, 5
community, 5, 8–9, 41, 64, 71, 131, 134, 193
   as advocates, 72, 74–75, 136, 168

empowerment, 10, 61, 78, 84, 92, 164, 168, 203–204
community consciousness, 72, 181
community responsive pedagogy, 91, 104, 111–112, 124, 169
conscientization, 102, 153, 168, 179, 180, 203, 216
  cycle of, 99, 178
  of teachers, 97
Cook Islands Māori, 17, 20, 73, 151
  language, 82, 104, 116
Cook Islands Māori Indicators, 139
Coolangatta Statement on Indigenous Peoples' Rights in Education, 58, 204
counter-hegemonic, 153, 169, 181, 183, 205
counter-narrative/s, 33, 88, 118, 171, 204
counter-story/stories, 5, 12, 88, 110, 118, 120, 203
critical consciousness, 4, 8, 88, 110, 153, 173, 197, 200
  anti-racist, 64, 90, 136
Critical Hip Hop Pedagogy, 156
critical hope, 185–187
critical Indigenous theory, 54
critical literacy, 4, 34, *see also* literacy, critical
critical media literacy, 34, 185
critical multiculturalism, 55–56
critical pedagogy, 4, 88, 97, 157, 168, 204
  kapa haka as a platform for, 155
  normalized as academic excellence, 198
  three goals of, 88
  of indignation, 115
critical pedagogy of whānau, 21, 95, 101–102, 169, 171, 181, 187, 197
critical praxis, 168
critical race theory, 55, 168,173, *see also* Tribal critical race theory
critical theory, 168
cultural capital, 31, 33, 173
cultural differences, 200
cultural identity, 8, 29, 33, 39, 47–63, 77, 90
  "root shock", 62
  and schools, 63–64
  as resistance, 59, 177
  Banks' typology, 49
  biracial, bicultural, 49, 60, 190
  central to curriculum, 168, 204
  complex identities, 161
  critical dimensions, 54
  definitions, 47–48, 53
  development, 53, 153
  ecological models, 51–53
  embedded in every aspect of the school day, 81
  essentialist frameworks, 49–50
  impact of schooling on, 121
  linked to academic identity, 148, 151–152
  loss of, 36, 51, 58, 60, 63, 116, 180
  Māori and Pasifika research, 135, 183, 190
  measures of, 133
  multiple, hybrid, 51, 53
  of teachers, 97
  planning for learning, 153
  secure, 5, 8, 15, 88, 185, 202
  stage models, 49
cultural knowledge, 35, 38, 57, 88, 97, 134–136, 147, 169, 183–184, 200
cultural leadership, 88, 201
cultural neutrality, 13, 36, 51
cultural norms, 8, 13, 29, 89, 93, 182, 194
cultural reproduction, 13, 34
cultural skills and competencies, 131, 147, 200
cultural standards, 134–135
  Alaskan Native educators, 134
cultural superiority, 29
cultural understanding
  of Māori and Pasifika teachers, 133
cultural ways of knowing, 8, 29, 83, 184
culturally relevant teaching
  three goals of, 88
culturally responsive
  behavior interventions and support, 189–190
  See also behavior
culturally responsive pedagogy, 5, 96, 151, 171

critical questions, 8, 22, 177, 184
key domains (TEN), 195
marginalization of, 4
measures of success, 150–151
culturally responsive schools/schooling, 88
culture, 8, 29, 35–36, 49–50, 55, 100
   at the center of classroom practice, 95–96, 108
   definitions, 47–48
   exotic constructions of, 55
   Māori perspective, 47
   who defines this? 116–117
culture counts, 15, 96
curriculum, 9, 11, 40, 89
   as a mechanism for control of knowledge, 32
   as a White space, 31–34
   community, 168
   contexts for study, 81, 109–124
   covert, 31–32, 92
   critical curriculum of self-study, 197
   culturally responsive. See culturally responsive pedagogy
   integrated, 86, 108–109
   Māori and Pasifika performing arts, 154
   national, 95
   New Zealand, 146–147
   overt, 31–32
   school-learning, 95
   student-driven, 108–109
   whānau concept of, 102

D

deficit thinking, deficit views, 5, 13, 19, 33, 61, 91, 96–97, 118, 120, 204
Definite Dozen, 163, 178
designated-character, 4, 75–76, 123, 200
   revision of by officials, 77–78
   designated-character schools, 9, 76
digital media, 34
discipline, 102, 107, 190
   see also behavior
discourse analysis, 112–113

disengagement
   from learning, 39, 150–151
disparity
   of learning outcomes, 40
   See also educational disparities
diversity, 6, 29, 37, 41, 54, 57

E

East Oakland Community High School, 163–164, 169
ecosystems
   school classrooms as ecosystems, 62, 116
Education Review Office (New Zealand), 121, 123, 131
educational disparities, 14
   See also disparity
educational sovereignty, 5, 21, 78, 170, 185, 204
equity, 121, 162, 170
   See also Inequity
ethnic identity, 48, 54, 60, 63
   See also cultural identity
Ethnic Studies, 167
   opposition, 166–167
   See also Mexican–American studies
ethnicity, 47–49, 56, 63, 109, 168, 204
   See also culture, cultural identity
expectations, 22, 40, 83, 102, 104, 182, 185, 202
   high, 72, 90–91, 96, 121, 169, 184, 195
   low, self-fulfilling, 97, 105, 120
   See also graduate profile
experiences of school
   community, 57, 89
   family, 136, 205
   students, 48, 50, 89, 91, 95, 115, 120, 162, 198

F

fa'asamoa, 7, 138
Fale Pasifika, 86, 107

First Nations, 57–58, 110, 117–118
free spaces, 185–186
futures learning, 21st Century learning, 37, 185, 188

G

gentrification, 62, 116
gifted and talented, 92, 191
Global Education Reform Movement (GERM), 12
global-learning lens, 89, 161, 188
Graduate Profile, 4, 83, 123, 198–202
    as intentional goals, 153, 199–200
    process to develop, 199–200

H

Haahuupayak Independent School, 58
Hawaii, 57
Hawaiian epistemology, 78, 100, 129
hegemony, 7, 48, 53, 113–114, 122
    academic, 153
    hegemonic practices, 8, 18, 33, 58, 157
    hegemonic White spaces, 39, 92, 179, 181
    See also counter–hegemonic
High Tech Youth Network (HTYN), 22, 38–39
home-school relationships, 89, 91, 136
hope
    audacious, 162, 185–188
    critical, 185–187
    deferred, 186
    false, 186
    hokey, 186
    material, 186
    mythical, 186
    radical, 185, 187
    Socratic, 187
hopeful and healing spaces, 185
hui whakatika, 190
    restoration of harmony, 192

humanism, 105
humanization, 123, 168
hunger strike, 164–166
hybridity, 51
    weakness of, 52

I

identity
    "I" for Identity, 34–35
    adolescent identity development, 53–54
    as resistance, 20, 57, 59–60
    biracial, bicultural, 49, 60, 190
    collective, 52, 105, 142
    ecological models, 51–53
    essentialist frameworks, 49–50
    fluid, shifting, 51, 56, 161, 198
    found, 185–187
    impact on school engagement, 50
    lost, 61–63
    Māori, 33, 81, 137
    never a simple White/non-White binary, 41
    postmodern frameworks, 51–53
    racial. *See* cultural identity
    secure, 73, 136
    shape-shifting, 59
    stage models, 49
    See also cultural identity
Identity Indicators, 137–140
    Cook Islands Māori, 139
    Identity Indicators
    cultural, 144
    generic, 140
    Māori, 137
    Samoan, 138
    Tongan, 138
Idle No More, 110
immigration, 111, 116
In Lak'ech, 171, 201
inclusion, 40, 107
Indian Residential Schools, 57
Indicators
    peer relationships, 142

relationship with learning, 141
  using the indicators, 145–152
indigeneity, 35
Indigenous perspectives, 20, 53, 56–59
Indigenous consciousness, 36
individualism, 10, 122, 142, 147
inequality, 12–13, 28, 38–39, 116, 191
inequity, inequities, 31, 62, 107, 183, 187, 191, 202
  in health disparity in New Zealand, 62–63
information technology, 20, 35, 38, 185
  as a tool of colonization, 37
  as a two–edged sword, 35
  Māori control of, 36–37
  to revitalize language and cultural traditions, 35, 38, 185
  White spaces in, 37, 153

J

justice,
  marching for justice, 163
  running for justice, 166
  sitting–in for justice, 162
  starving for justice, 164
  See also social justice

K

Ka Hikitia, 14–16, 120, 162
  vision of, 14, 162
kapa haka, 137, 153–157, 172, 199
  as critical pedagogy, 155
  in self-lens learning, 155, 193
Kaupapa Māori in education, 99–100
  three key themes, 99
Kaupapa Māori theory, 52
key competencies (in the New Zealand Curriculum), 146–147
  alignment with a Māori worldview, 146–147

Kia Aroha
  marae, 16, 84, 86, 107, 137, 155–156
  meaning, 78–79
Kia Aroha College 71–78
  as a counter-story, 120
  behavior management, 108
  See also behavior
  bilingual programs, 75–76
  born out of struggle, 72
  designated-character. *See* designated-character
  enrollment, 75–76
  history, 41, 72–77
  information technology response, 38–39
  location, 71
  pedagogy and practice, 88–90, 102, 161
  philosophy, 72, 81
  philosophy definition, 88
  previous names, 72–75
  requirements for teachers, 96–97
  research by independent researchers, 63, 88, 122
  solidarity with international initiatives, 162–172
  student research, 18, 117, 120–121
knowledge
  co-construction of, 8, 157, 196
  conflict of knowledge systems, 134
  cultural. *See* cultural knowledge, cultural ways of knowing
  emancipatory, 136, 157
  indigenous, 8, 15, 100, 188
  performance of, 111
  politics of, 29, 31–34
  practical, 157
  preservation of, 36
  production of, 169, 204
  school knowledge, 6, 12
  technical, 157–158, 171
  traditional, 109
  whose knowledge counts?, 41, 113, 157–158
Kōhanga Reo, 99, 180
Kura Kaupapa Māori, 9–10, 75, 98, 122, 180

L

lessons to be learned, 204
literacy, 12–14, 41, 121, 130, 151–153, 157–158, 194
  as "back to basics", 34
  as a White space, 15, 33–34
  as dangerous, 33
  as the holy grail, 41
  critical, critical media, 4, 34
  role in cultural reproduction, 34
Little Village Lawndale High School Campus, 164–166
live as Māori, 7, 14–15, 59, 88–89, 98, 162, 199
  See also as Māori

M

mainstream, mainstreaming, 6, 15, 17, 51, 55, 58, 82, 88
majoritarian stories, 109–110
manutaki, 201
Māori
  as tangata whenua (indigenous people), 82, 137
Māori identity, 34, 81, 123, 137
  key markers, 135, 183
Māori education, 81
  Durie's three policy goals, 14, 18, 162
  marginalization of, 3, 113, 115
  radical changes, 180
  student investigation of, 112–116, 119
Māori language
  loss of, 33, 36, 60, 116, 147, 180
  revival, 38, 59, 72, 75, 99, 180
Māori performing arts. *See* kapa haka
Māori Principals' Association, 118
Māori responsive pedagogy, 12. *See* culturally responsive pedagogy
Māori values, 102, 153, 178, 181
Māori-centered healing, 190
marae. *See* Kia Aroha marae

marginalization, 3–4, 19, 28, 113–114, 187
Mexican-American Studies program, 110, 166
  opposition, 166
middle schooling, 73
Ministry of Education (New Zealand), 13, 15, 18–19, 29, 37, 72–73, 76, 86, 121, 123, 162
  "cleansing" of the Charter, 77
  opposition from, 73–74
minoritized learners, 6, 8, 31, 51, 96, 168, 187, 198, 203
multicultural education, 54
  five positions in, 55
multiculturalism, 6, 41, 51, 55
  benevolent, 55
  critical. *See* Critical multiculturalism

N

naming, 27–31
  as an exercise in power relations, 27
National Certificate of Academic Achievement (NCEA), 23
national norms, 13–14, 129, 157
National Standards, 10–11, 21, 123, 131, 158
neoliberal, neoliberalism, 9–10, 12, 20, 162
New Zealand
  education system, 5, 7, 9–10, 12, 14, 16, 30, 40, 76, 88, 130, 147, 203
New Zealand Association for Research in Education (NZARE), 119, 123
New Zealand Curriculum, 9, 146
  key competencies, 146
  See also curriculum
Nga Tamatoa, 110
Ngai Tahu, 59

O

Oakland, 163
Oakland Unified School District, 163–164, 169

Otara, 38, 71–72
　schools, 71
overall teacher judgments (OTJs), 11

P

Pacific epistemologies, 101
Pākehā (White) teachers, 30, 96
Pasifika
　definition, 17
　knowledges, 101, 152, 183
Pasifika Center. *See* Fale Pasifika
Pasifika community, 39, 86
Pasifika diaspora, 110
Pasifika education, 120
Pasifika Education Plan, 18, 99, 119
Pasifika identity
　recurring themes, 135
Pasifika performing arts, 153, 193
　in self-lens learning, 193
Pasifika spaces, 17–18
Paulo Freire, 114, 123, 168
pedagogy, pedagogies
　of love, resiliency, hope and healing, 172, 187
　community responsive, xviii, 170
　critically conscious, 55, 88, 97, 203
　See also critical pedagogy of whānau
　of poverty, 40
　of Whiteness, 96
peer relationships, 89–90
　collective, 91
　collectivist cultures, 141–142
　indicators, 142
　Western perspectives, 141
potential, 97, 154, 174, 194
　unrealised to unlimited, 92–93, 191
　potential approach, 92
poutama, multi-levelled steps, 130, 132
poverty, 12, 39–40, 122, 170, 172
　"head-in-the-sand" approach, 40
　education's "inconvenient truth", 41
　impact of, 41
　root causes of inequality, 39, 191

Power Lenses Learning Model, 89–93
　global-learning lens, 89, 161–72, 188
　key assumptions about learning, 92
　lenses interact and overlap, 188
　school-learning lens, 89, 95–108, 111
　self-learning lens, 129–153
　six relationships, 89, 135
power, power relations, 102, 116, 132, 140, 157, 167, 182, 185, 203
professional development
　teacher, 38, 82, 110, 147, 195–196
punishment gap, 40

R

race-bending, 60
racism, 16, 22, 27–29, 31, 38, 50, 56, 62, 88, 96, 136, 167, 186
　all Whites benefit equally, 28
　as a given. *See* critical race theory
　central feature of the education system, 31
　racist behavior, 29
radical healing, 22, 187–188
radical hope, 22, 185, 187
Raza Studies, 57, 169
reciprocal partnerships, 13, 90–91, 93, 96
reciprocity, 17, 91, 168, 181, 183, 204
red pedagogy, 52
relationship/s
　authentic partnership, 91, 136
　home-school, 89, 91, 136
　mutually beneficial, 90, 136
　positive, 5, 49, 96–97, 194–196
　reciprocal, 95–96
　student-teacher, 90–91, 97, 136
　with learning, 90
　with the world beyond school, 92–93, 161
Relationship with Learning Indicators, 140–141
residential schools, 57
　Vancouver Island, 57, 118
resilience, 152, 185

Studies in Criticality

General Editor
Shirley R. Steinberg

Counterpoints publishes the most compelling and imaginative books being written in education today. Grounded on the theoretical advances in criticalism, feminism, and postmodernism in the last two decades of the twentieth century, Counterpoints engages the meaning of these innovations in various forms of educational expression. Committed to the proposition that theoretical literature should be accessible to a variety of audiences, the series insists that its authors avoid esoteric and jargonistic languages that transform educational scholarship into an elite discourse for the initiated. Scholarly work matters only to the degree it affects consciousness and practice at multiple sites. Counterpoints' editorial policy is based on these principles and the ability of scholars to break new ground, to open new conversations, to go where educators have never gone before.

For additional information about this series or for the submission of manuscripts, please contact:

>Shirley R. Steinberg
>c/o Peter Lang Publishing, Inc.
>29 Broadway, 18th floor
>New York, New York 10006

To order other books in this series, please contact our Customer Service Department:
>(800) 770-LANG (within the U.S.)
>(212) 647-7706 (outside the U.S.)
>(212) 647-7707 FAX

Or browse online by series:
>www.peterlang.com

resistance, 8, 20, 29, 57–61, 78, 92, 99, 102, 120, 168–169, 177, 183–184
restorative justice, 190
　Māori perspective (hui whakatika), 190, 192
root shock, 62, 116
Roses in Concrete Community School, xviii, 164, 169–171

S

Samoan identity, 151
　Samoan Identity Indicators, 138
Samoan language, 138
San Francisco State University, 163
　Step to College, 163
school, schooling
　as a rigged game, 158
　school alienation, 20, 39–42
school design, 83–87
　classrooms, 85–86
　cultural spaces, 86
　external spaces, 87
　learning spaces, 74, 85
　Little Village Lawndale High School, 165–166
　whānau involvement in, 84–85
school organization, 82, 92, 182
　flexible timetabling, 103
　multilevelled, vertically grouped, 103
　team teaching, 103
school reform, 10–13, 32, 171
　accepts substantional inequality, 13
　deficit thinking, 118
　design, 12
　neoliberal, 20
school spaces
　as whānau spaces, 102–106
school-learning lens, 89, 95–98, 111, 182, 188
self-acceptance, 143
self-determination, 22, 56, 155
　See also tino rangatiratanga
self-determining spaces, 178–179

self-knowledge, 78, 131–133, 135, 152
　as legitimate high stakes learning, 132
　equal status with academic knowledge, 89, 132
self-learning, self-learning lens, 89, 129–153
　progress over time, 147–152
self-lens assessment tool, 147, 151
　and teacher perspectives, 151
　purpose of, 152–153
self-lens learning
　embedded in school policy and practice, 81
　high status learning, 89, 152, 183
　intentionally counter–hegemonic, 153, 169, 205
social justice, 41, 77, 88–89, 92, 97, 109, 153, 155, 157, 161–162, 172–173, 197, 202–203
Social Justice Education Project, 166
Social Justice High School, 165–166
social justice programs, 161
　commonalities, 168
　core components, 171
social toxins, 20, 61–63
　as a context for study, 116
social worker, 107, 192–193
socio-economic status, 39–41
　See also poverty
solidarity, 64, 90, 97, 104, 107, 162–166, 195
　schools in solidarity, 170, 172
　with students' communities, 187, 195
solutions
　lessons learned, 82, 100, 185
South Auckland, 4, 11–12, 71
stereotypes, 5, 49, 30, 55, 96, 106, 172
student leadership, 88, 201
Studio, 274, 38–39, 173–174
success and achievement, 39, 92, 130, 200–203
　as Māori. See as Māori
　different Māori and Pākehā attitudes, 130
　redefining, 198–201
　whose knowledge is of most worth?, 41, 157
　See also, achievement

Advance praise for Coloring in the White Spaces

"*Coloring in the White Spaces: Reclaiming Cultural Identity in Whitestream Schools* is a major achievement. It is the story of a collective journey of three schools that eventually merged into one school over a three-decade period. It tells of the struggles and the victories of the administrators, teachers, students, families, community, and school board members in their journey to fulfill the dream of responsive schooling. The realization of that dream is tied to the collective belief that it is possible to make education fit our children's needs in spite of the presence of fierce opposition at every step. This book tells the story of a New Zealand school. But the story has global implications. It addresses the most fundamental issues of our times: issues of power, social justice, identity development, and school change through a critical pedagogy based in whānau and Māori and Pasifika values and beliefs. This book tells the story of the power of a community's determination to create a school where historically marginalized students could realize their full potential and develop into informed advocates for social justice, critical thinkers, and activists for social change. In this book these issues are treated with the depth and the detail they deserve.

This is a 25 year counter-story of a New Zealand school and the determination of its community to resist and reject alienating school environments in favor of a relevant culturally-located, bilingual learning model based in a secure cultural identity, stable positive relationships, authentic caring, and love. This counter-story describes the power of a critically conscious, culturally responsive approach to education and chronicles the efforts of a school that steps outside education's deficit spaces to create new spaces, to reclaim educational sovereignty and the absolute right to allow students to 'be Māori,' 'be Pasifika,' or to 'be who they are' in school. These stories are brought together to illuminate conditions of schooling for minoritized students in New Zealand and around the globe and to present an alternative view of what schooling can be—confirming that change is possible, if we don't give up. Most important, this book provides evidence that we can change our educational landscape for the better.

While it tackles some of the most fundamental problems of our times, it leaves the reader with a critical hope and a more optimistic vision for facing the many challenges that lie ahead—challenges that we must face if we are serious about promoting justice and equity through education. This very informative book is sure to be a great help to the education community.

Every teacher, school administrator, parent, [and] community and board member should read it. It can serve as an accessible, practical, and essential tool for those who are interested in creating students who are self-determining learners; who have the tools they need to challenge and change inequity in their lives, in their communities, and in the wider world; who are critical thinkers and informed advocates for social justice."

—*Professor Arnetha F. Ball, Stanford University Graduate School of Education*